D0782300

DISCARD

Chicago Public Library

Form 178 rev. 1-94

R & TAYLOR

GRENDON

CLARENDON STUDIES IN CRIMINOLOGY

Published under the auspices of the Institute of Criminology, University of Cambridge, the Mannheim Centre, London School of Economics, and the Centre for Criminological Research, University of Oxford

GENERAL EDITOR: ROGER HOOD

EDITORS: TREVOR BENNET, ANTHONY BOTTOMS,
DAVID DOWNES, NICOLA LACEY, PAUL ROCK,
ANDREW SANDERS

Other titles in this series:

GRENDON

A Study of a Therapeutic Prison

Elaine Genders and Elaine Player

CLARENDON PRESS · OXFORD
1995

Oxford University Press, Walton Street, Oxford OX2 6DP

Oxford New York

Athens Auckland Bangkok Bombay
Calcutta Cape Town Dar es Salaam Delhi
Florence Hong Kong Istanbul Karachi
Kuala Lumpur Madras Madrid Melbourne
Mexico City Nairobi Paris Singapore
Taipei Tokyo Toronto
and associated companies in
Berlin Ibadan

Oxford is a trade mark of Oxford University Press

Published in the United States
by Oxford University Press Inc., New York

British Library Cataloguing in Publication Data

Data available

Library of Congress Cataloging in Publication Data
Genders, Elaine.
Grendon: a study of a therapeutic prison / Elaine Genders and
Elaine Player.
(Clarendon studies in criminology)
Includes bibliographical references (p.   ) and index.
1. HM Prison Grendon.
2. Prisoners—Mental health services—England—Buckinghamshire.
3. Insane, Criminal and dangerous—Rehabilitation—England–Buckinghamshire.
4. Therapeutic communities—England—Buckinghamshire—Case studies.
I. Player, Elaine. II. Title. III. Series.
RC451.4.P68G46 1994 365'.66—dc20 94-28887
ISBN 0-19-825677-9

Set by Hope Services (Abingdon) Ltd.
Printed in Great Britain
on acid-free paper by
Biddles Ltd.
Guildford & King's Lynn

General Editor's Introduction

It is not often that a new criminological series emerges. It is now over fifty years since Leon Radzinowicz and J.C.W. Turner began *English Studies in Criminal Science* under the Macmillan imprint, which, after ten volumes, became the internationally renowned *Cambridge Studies in Criminology*. Forty-one further volumes were published under the editorship of Sir Leon by Heinemann Educational Books, led by the distinguished publisher, the late Alan Hill. Ten more volumes, published by Gower and Avebury books, appeared under the general editorship of Anthony Bottoms before the prestigious Cambridge Series was unexpectedly and sadly wound-up.

The Cambridge Institute of Criminology then approached Oxford University Press in the hope that the series could be continued in another form at a time when, co-incidentally, the Press had begun to discuss the prospects for a criminological series with the Mannheim Centre for Criminology and Criminal Justice at the London School of Economics. With the energetic support of Richard Hart, these two institutions decided on a joint venture with the Oxford Centre for Criminological Research in which each would provide the members of the Editorial Board for a new series to be called *Clarendon Studies in Criminology*. I was honoured to have been asked by my colleagues (whose names are listed next to the title page) to be the General Editor for the first three years.

Clarendon Studies in Criminology aims to provide a forum for outstanding work in all aspects of criminology, criminal justice, penology, and the wider field of deviant behaviour. It will welcome works of theory and synthesis as well as reports of empirical enquiries and will be international in its scope. The first titles, Philip Schlesinger and Howard Tumber's *Reporting Crime: The Media, Politics of Criminal Justice*, John Vagg's *Prison Systems: A Comparative Study of Accountability in England, France, Germany, and the Netherlands*, and now Elaine Genders and Elaine Player's *Grendon: A Study of A Therapeutic Prison*, already indicate the potential range of the Series.

Grendon psychiatric prison has long been regarded as the jewel of the English Penal System, providing a constructive and humane regime for prisoners convicted of grave crimes who have in the past shown a resistance to change. While several attempts have been made to evaluate its impact on the mental health of the inmates (most notably the study by Professor John Gunn and his colleagues *Psychiatric Aspects of Imprisonment* (1978)), there had been no broader sociological analysis of the tension between Grendon as a prison and as a therapeutic community. Indeed, a vital question for the penal system as a whole is whether it is possible to provide effective therapy within the confines of a penal institution where control and security are also important objectives. This is the key to Elaine Genders and Elaine Player's fascinating book. By describing the way in which Grendon operates, from selection of inmates to their eventual discharge and re-integration into other prison regimes, they are able to describe therapy as a process and to chart and analyse the stages through which inmates must pass if they are to be counted as successes. By combining techniques of observation with those of in-depth interviewing, they shed light on the factors which shape the structure and culture of the institution and its staff. And they examine perceptively Grendon's impact on the self-concepts, values and behaviour of the prisoners subject to its unremitting therapeutic regime. The dilemmas inherent in carrying out research of this kind are analysed with frankness and insight. The findings are, most unusually in these days of penal pessimism, remarkably positive. Yet they are set within a perceptive critique of the proper role of therapy within the modern post-Woolf prison system. The editors welcome this stimulating and important addition to the series.

Roger Hood
Oxford, August 1994

Contents

List of Figures

List of Tables

Acknowledgements

It is rare for researchers who are limping to the finishing line of their project to declare that the experience has been enjoyable. Adjectives such as 'interesting', 'stimulating', and 'worthwhile' litter the pages of acknowledgements, but the concept of pleasure is notable for its absence. For us, the unprecedented degree of help and support we received from the staff and inmates at Grendon ensured that the fieldwork was a congenial as well as an intellectually demanding and satisfying period in our careers. We would like to thank everyone at Grendon, and especially the wing communities, who gave us every assistance in carrying out the research and who went out of their way to welcome us and to make us feel at home.

Given that so many people facilitated the fieldwork it is perhaps invidious to pick out certain individuals for special thanks. However, some people played such an important role that it would be inconceivable not to acknowledge their special contributions. Mr Michael Selby, who was then the Governor of Grendon, gave us a free rein throughout the establishment, kept us well informed and demonstrated a continued interest in our endeavours. Dr Jack Wright, then Deputy Head and subsequently Head of Medical Services, helped us in ways too numerous to mention and, under the Fresh Start Action Plan, was afforded the dubious title of Oxford Research Co-ordinator. The lengthy discussions we had with him served to inspire and encourage us, and he undoubtedly played an important role in the development of the study. Our thanks are also extended to Senior Officer Alan Jackson who painstakingly collated the data on inmate referrals to Grendon, and whose precision and diligence earned him the much coveted Research Assistant of the Year Award. A debt of gratitude is also owed to the Psychology Department and, in particular, Edgar Darling who guided us in the record work and advised us on the interpretation of the psychological test scores. We would also like to thank all the doctors and psychologists for allowing us to attend their weekly meetings and for being so patient when, for impeccable research reasons, we routinely disrupted them. We are, of course, especially grateful to our groups on the three wings for their hospitality and to all the staff and inmates who generously gave of their time and candidly expressed their thoughts and feelings during long and sometimes difficult interviews.

A note of thanks should also be sent to all the referring medical officers, many of whom endured the taxing experience of a telephone interview. Thanks are also due to the governors and staff who facilitated our visits to their institutions in order to follow up inmates who had been transferred from Grendon.

The study was carried out while we were employed as research fellows at the Oxford Centre from Criminological Research and was commissioned and funded by the Home Office Research and Planning Unit on behalf of the Prison Medical Service. We are grateful to Mrs Mary Tuck and Mr Roy Walmsley from the RPU for their continued support, and to Dr John Kilgour, the former Director of the Prison Medical Service, and Dr Rosemary Wool, his successor, for their interest and practical help during the course of the study. John Ditchfield acted as our liaison officer in the Home Office Research and Planning Unit, and has guided the study through the bureaucratic processes with his usual efficiency and good humour. We have also benefited from the advice and guidance of a distinguished consultative committee which was chaired by Roy Walmsley and included John Ditchfield, Mr Peter Done, Professor John Gunn, Dr Roger Hood and Professor Rod Morgan.

A special word of thanks must go to Dr Roger Hood, Director of the Centre for Criminological Research, for his support throughout the study and for his help and advice in preparing the manuscript for publication. He has carefully and rigorously commented upon each draft and his constructive criticism has been invaluable in helping us to shape our arguments and refine their expression. Later drafts have also benefited from the comments received from Professor Andrew Ashworth and Dr Jack Wright. Lynn Stewart saved us valuable time by taking on some of the coding and statistical analysis and Sylvia Littlejohns and Jackie Neate painstakingly typed our original report to the Home Office. The final manuscript was typed with patience and good humour by Laura Masters.

Finally, we thank our families and friends for their encouragement and support.

E.G./E.P.
London, March 1994

1

The Study of a Therapeutic Prison

Back to Basics

At the Conservative Party conference in October 1993 the Home Secretary announced that the success of the government's criminal justice policy would not be judged by a reduction of the prison population. Indeed, he anticipated that measures contained in the 1993 Criminal Justice Bill, which were designed to 'tilt the balance' in favour of the police detecting more offenders and the courts convicting more of the guilty, would inevitably swell the numbers received into custody. To rapturous applause he denounced the pessimism which had dogged penal debates for the past two decades and declared that 'prison works'. Despite a notable absence of any reference to empirical evidence which supported this assertion, and a blatant disregard of that which directly refuted it, he observed that prison 'works' by keeping persistent offenders out of circulation and by acting as a deterrent at both an individual and general level. He did not, however, stake a claim for the rehabilitative potential of imprisonment.

After the demise of the rehabilitative ideal in the early 1970s, prisons functioned in a climate of despair and on intellectual territory that perpetuated a doctrine which conceived of them as a social evil which, at best, should be diminished to an irreducible minimum. In consequence, the task of prison staff came to be defined as an exercise in damage limitation and, throughout this period, the Prison Service was ravaged by successive waves of industrial action. Further strain was placed upon the management of the system by the inexorable growth of the prison population and the deteriorating state of prison buildings. When the Prison Department's attention was turned to questions of penal purpose and regimes, it was largely due to the mutinous activities of prisoners and was consequently preoccupied by issues of security and control.[1] During the 1970s, prisoner unrest was concentrated in the high-security, dispersal system and was responded to with military methods of riot management and by the introduction of control units which were to provide harsh and punitive regimes for the hard core of serious troublemakers.[2] After the riots of the 1980s, the rotten-apple theory became more difficult to sustain because disorder had spread across a wide range of institutions and had involved prisoners in low-security categories. Explanations about the causes of these riots shifted to consider questions about the adequacy of prison regimes and the nature of relations between inmates and staff.

This spate of disorder arguably reached its peak when, over a period of twenty-five days, prisoners at HM Prison Strangeways engaged in the longest and most devastating riot in British penal history, and a sequence of disturbances broke out in more than thirty other establishments. On the fifth day of the uprising, the Home Secretary announced that an independent public inquiry would be carried out under the direction of Lord Justice Woolf (as he then was). This marked a significant departure from previous Home Office responses to prisoner unrest, which had either entrusted the Prison Department to mount its own internal investigation or delegated the task to the prison inspectorate.[3] The Home

[1] See Bottomley, A. K. (1994), 'Long-Term Prisoners', in E. Player and M. Jenkins (eds.), *Prisons After Woolf: Reform Through Riot*, London: Routledge; Bottomley, A. K. and Hay, W. (eds.) (1991), *Special Units for Difficult Prisoners*, Hull: Centre for Criminology and Criminal Justice, University of Hull; King, R. D. (1994), 'Order, Disorder and Regimes in the Prison Services of Scotland and England and Wales', in E. Player and M. Jenkins (eds.), *Prisons After Woolf*; Adams, R. (1992), *Prison Riots in Britain and the USA*, London: Macmillan.

[2] See Home Office (1984), *Managing the Long-Term Prison System: The Report of the Control Review Committee*, London: HMSO.

[3] In 1986 Sir James Hennessey, Her Majesty's Chief Inspector of Prisons, published a report following his inquiry into disturbances which had occurred in more than twenty establishments: Home Office (1987), *Report of an Inquiry by Her Majesty's Chief Inspector of Prisons for England and Wales into the Disturbances in Prison Service Establishments in England between 29 April and 2 May 1986*, London: HMSO. In 1988, after riots at Haverigg and Lindholme prisons, an in-house inquiry was undertaken by Mr Gordon Lakes, then Deputy Director General of the Prison Service. His report was never made public. Less than a year later, a disturbance occurred at Risley Remand Centre and this was investigated by Mr Ian Dunbar, then a Regional Director of the Prison Service. A summary of his report was produced: Dunbar, I. (1989), *Report to the Secretary of State on the Inquiries into a Major Disturbance at HM Remand Centre Risley 30 April to 3 May 1989 and the Circumstances Surrounding the Disturbance—Summary*, London: Prison Department.

Secretary invited Lord Justice Woolf to interpret his terms of reference as he saw fit. Woolf decided to adopt what he called 'a broad
canvas approach', addressing issues which were concerned not only
with events surrounding the course of the riots but with their
underlying causes and how they might be prevented in the future.

The Woolf Report, published only nine months after the riots,
has been widely acclaimed as the most important and wide ranging
examination of the prison system in England and Wales since the
Gladstone Report of 1895.[4] At the root of Woolf's thesis is an elab-
oration of the contribution which the prison system itself has made
to the occurrence of riots, most notably by the fomenting influence
of impoverished regimes and strained relationships between inmates
and staff. The report concluded that, within prison establishments,
a balance has to be struck between the requirements of security and
control, on the one hand, and the need for prisoners to be treated
with humanity and justice, on the other. Woolf maintained that too
little emphasis had been given to the latter and that the resulting
disequilibrium had created a fertile environment for the collective
protest of prisoners. His proposals and recommendations stressed
the importance of reducing the barriers to communication which
have traditionally existed between inmates and prison staff; of fostering an ethos of co-operation in the achievement of common
goals; and of developing relationships which enable security and
control to be maintained with a minimum resort to overtly coercive
mechanisms.

Although Woolf refrained from engaging in a theoretical review
of the competing justifications and purposes of imprisonment, pre-
ferring instead to accept as his starting point the Prison
Department's own Statement of Purpose, he none the less provided
a critical perspective from which to reconceptualize these tasks. He
recorded that the Statement of Purpose imposes three key duties
upon the Prison Service:

(a) to keep secure those whom the courts put in its custody; (b) to treat
those who are in its custody with humanity; and (c) to look after those in
its custody in such a way as to help them to 'lead law-abiding and useful
lives' (i) while they are in custody and (ii) after release.[5]

---

[4] Departmental Committee (1895), *Report from the Departmental Committee*
(Gladstone Report), C 7702, Parliamentary Papers, vol. 56.
[5] Woolf, Lord Justice H., and Tumim, Judge S. (1991a), *Prison Disturbances*

The final task clearly signals the continued adherence of the Prison Service to a rehabilitative ambition. Although this had typically been interpreted as a requirement to minimize the negative effects of incarceration, Woolf injected a new vitality into the concept by insisting that, as an integral component of the criminal justice system, the Prison Service had an obligation to protect the public by discouraging criminal behaviour and reducing the likelihood of prisoners reoffending. But Woolf distinguished between the old discredited model of rehabilitative treatment, whereby offenders were sentenced to imprisonment *for* reformative treatment, and the new rehabilitative approach. This is based upon providing opportunities for prisoners to address their offending behaviour and to prepare themselves for release within an environment which promotes individual responsibility and prevents 'a creeping and all-pervading dependency by prisoners on the prison authority'.[6]

The Government broadly accepted the central propositions of the Woolf Report in its White Paper, *Custody, Care and Justice*, which aimed to chart 'a course for the Prison Service . . . for the rest of this century and beyond'.[7] Arguably the White Paper placed a greater emphasis upon the provision of more effective measures of security and control than upon improvements to the quality of justice and the humanity of regimes. But throughout the document there is a repeated commitment to a broadly rehabilitative purpose:

Programmes must give sentenced prisoners every opportunity to acquire the skills and resolve necessary not to commit further crimes.[8]

Prison programmes should . . . improve prisoners' educational levels and technical skills; give them opportunities for self-advancement and self-fulfilment; challenge sentenced prisoners about their criminal behaviour—so that they leave prison better adjusted, less likely to be bitter about their experiences, and more likely to lead constructive and law-abiding lives.[9]

The Prison Service is likely in future to be holding a larger proportion of prisoners who have committed particularly serious offences involving violence and sexual deviance . . . Some of these prisoners might be able to avoid reoffending if they could be helped to understand what they have

---

April 1990: Report of an Inquiry by the Rt. Hon. Lord Justice Woolf (Parts I and II) and His Honour Judge Stephen Tumim (Part II), London: HMSO, para. 10.11.

[6] Ibid., para. 14.13.

[7] Home Office (1991), *Custody, Care and Justice: The Way Ahead for the Prison Service in England and Wales*, London: HMSO, Cm 1647, 3.

[8] Ibid., para. 7.1.   [9] Ibid., para. 7.2.

done, what its consequences have been and how to avoid repeating such behaviour in future.[10]

Prisons which provide for prisoners in these ways are . . . more likely . . . to reduce the chance of sentenced prisoners offending again . . . The Prison Service has an opportunity to play a greater part in helping to reduce crime. It must take it.[11]

A new statement of rehabilitative intent has thus risen out of the embers of the 1990 riots and a renewed interest and significance have been accorded to regimes and programmes which reflect these ambitions.

During the course of his inquiry Lord Justice Woolf visited Grendon prison and commented favourably in his report upon its regime, proposing that a similar establishment should be set up in another part of the country. Indeed many of the strategies proposed by Woolf to improve the quality of life for both staff and inmates, and to increase the prospect of prisoners being treated decently and with humanity, were already established working practices in this institution. Yet for most of its thirty years of operation Grendon has inhabited an ideological wilderness, out of step with the prevailing ethos and marginal to mainstream penal practice. Post-Woolf, however, the tide has turned, and Grendon now finds itself embraced by contemporary penal politics and fêted as a prodigal son made good. But important differences remain between Grendon and the rest of the system, in that Grendon aspires to be more than just a decent and humane training prison: it aims to be a *therapeutic prison*.

A Therapeutic Prison

The Development of Grendon

Grendon prison was opened in 1962, under the direction of a medical superintendent, as a unique experiment in the psychological treatment of offenders whose mental disorder did not qualify them for transfer to a hospital under Section 72 of the Mental Health Act 1959. The stimulus for its inception may be traced back twenty-three years to the publication in 1939 of a report by Dr W. Norwood East and Dr W. H. de B. Hubert, which concluded that:

---

[10] Ibid., para. 7.38.   [11] Ibid., Introduction, para. 5.

'the most satisfactory method of dealing with abnormal and unusual types of criminal would be the creation of a penal institution of a special kind'.[12] The purpose which Grendon was originally intended to serve was 'to investigate and treat mental disorders generally recognised as responsive to treatment, to investigate offenders whose offences in themselves suggest mental morbidity, and to explore the problems of dealing with the psychopath'.[13]

In the thirty years of its history Grendon has undergone a number of changes, the most significant and fundamental of which have taken place in the last decade. Originally, Grendon operated outside the traditional management structure of the Prison Service. But in March 1984, the Home Secretary announced his intention of setting up an advisory committee to review the therapeutic regime at Grendon (ACTRAG) and 'to consider its future orientation, with the aim of broadening the roles it can play in the humane containment and treatment of inmates who require psychiatric facilities in the prison system'.[14]

The report of the committee, published in July 1985, recommended that Grendon's role within the Prison Service should be developed in four principal and overlapping areas. The first was in the treatment of 'sociopaths', a diverse group whose common feature is a lack of social awareness, and with whom, it was argued, Grendon had a proven track record of success. The second area was the treatment of sex offenders, another group which Grendon was already receiving into therapy in substantial numbers and which was able to exist there without the usual protection of segregation under Rule 43. Thirdly, the committee suggested that Grendon could play a greater role in the management of the long-term prison population, especially those serving life imprisonment, by providing detailed assessments of individual prisoners to contribute to the process of sentence planning, and by assisting the Parole Board by preparing pre-release reports on particularly difficult cases. The final recommendation was that a rescue unit should be set up, separate from the psychotherapeutic wings, where short-

---

[12] East, W. N. and Hubert, W. H. de B. (1939), *The Psychological Treatment of Crime*, London: HMSO, para. 172.

[13] Commissioners of Prisons (1963), *Report for 1962*, London: HMSO.

[14] Home Office (1985), *First Report of the Advisory Committee on the Therapeutic Regime at Grendon*, London: Prison Department.

term treatment could be given to prisoners suffering from an acute breakdown or a severe prison crisis.

Virtually all of the ACTRAG report's recommendations were implemented. In addition the post of medical superintendent was replaced by a senior governor grade and the organization and management of the establishment began to edge towards those of the traditional prison model. During this period there was a dual system of managerial accountability. The first was to the Prison Department Regional Director, by way of the governor and his managerial team, who were responsible for the day-to-day running of the prison. The second was to the Director of the Prison Medical Service, via the senior medical officer, who retained full reponsibility for the therapeutic programme. In 1987, however, the Prison Department radically transformed the management of prison establishments by the introduction of Fresh Start.[15] This fundamentally relocated the medical establishment in Grendon's command structure, harnessing it within a line management that positioned the governor at the apex of the organization, with the senior medical officer, while still responsible for therapeutic activities, reporting to the governor.

Grendon is now classified as a category B training prison and may be described as a multi-functional establishment, accommodating three adult therapy wings which operate as therapeutic communities, an assessment and induction unit, an acute psychiatric unit (now destined for closure) and, most recently, a treatment wing designed specifically for sex offenders.

Therapeutic Initiatives in Prisons

Grendon is not the only establishment within the British prison system to offer psychological or psychotherapeutic treatment to convicted offenders. Both group and individual psychotherapy and counselling can be found in other institutions, provided by a wide range of professional staff including teachers, probation officers, psychologists, and psychiatrists. Since the demise of the rehabilitative ideal in the 1970s the development of these facilities has tended to be *ad hoc*, emanating from individual initiatives in particular establishments rather than from any centralized planning or policy development at Prison Service headquarters. As recently as 1989

---

[15] On 3 April 1987 the Prison Service issued Bulletin No. 8 which set out the details of Fresh Start.

the Prison Department Working Group, set up to enquire into the problems generated by the increasing numbers of prisoners held in segregation for their own safety, recommended the establishment of a system of vulnerable prisoner units. Yet, no mention was made in its report of the provision of treatment facilities in these new units.[16] This omission met with considerable criticism at establishment level and led staff at Bristol and Maidstone prisons to express their determination to provide regimes specifically tailored to the needs of a predominantly sex-offender population with a view to changing its behaviour through therapeutic intervention.[17] In an effort to catch up with grass-roots enterprise the Prison Department conducted a survey in 1989 which revealed that sixty-three prisons in England and Wales had made some specialist provision for sex offenders. The unco-ordinated growth of these schemes, however, ensured that the nature and scale of the programmes varied considerably from institution to institution.[18]

In the light of this accumulated evidence and in the face of a growing population of sex offenders in prison, the Prison Service published its plans to rationalise the provision of treatment facilities for sex offenders. On 7 June 1991 the Home Secretary announced that a co-ordinated core programme would be introduced into twenty prisons by the end of the year. This would be designed to tackle offenders' distorted beliefs about relationships, enhance their awareness of the effect of sexual offences on victims and help develop strategies of prevention. Extended programmes were also to be organized at a small number of establishments for those deemed to represent the greatest risk to society, and six prisons were designated as centres for the assessment and allocation of offenders to the various programmes.

Another group for which the Prison Department has centrally co-ordinated special provision is the highly disruptive segment within the population of long-term prisoners. Following the report of the Control Review Committee[19] in 1984, four special units have

---

[16] Home Office (1989), *Report of the Prison Department Working Group on the Management of Vulnerable Prisoners*, London: Prison Department Internal Document.

[17] Prison Reform Trust (1990), *Sex Offenders in Prison*, London: Prison Reform Trust, 18.

[18] Ibid. 28.

[19] Home Office (1984), *Managing the Long-Term Prison System: The Report of the Control Review Committee*, London: HMSO.

been established, at Parkhurst in 1985, Lincoln in 1987, Hull in 1988 and Woodhill in 1993. The primary orientation of these units is to contain and manage prisoners who have represented a serious control problem in the dispersal system. These units do, however, offer therapeutic intervention. C-Wing at Parkhurst, for example, accommodates up to eighteen prisoners and provides individual and some group psychotherapy under the supervision of a visiting consultant psychiatrist. It is, however, regarded as a non-health-care setting and is primarily staffed by prison officers under the management of a prison governor.

Prisoners other than sex offenders and the disruptive minority of long-termers have fared less well in respect of treatment provision. Within the adult male prison system only four treatment units have been established at the initiative and under the explicit direction of the Home Office to cater for a more general population.[20] Of these, H wing at Pentonville and the unit in Albany on the Isle of Wight have reverted from their auspicious beginnings to conventional regimes. The two remaining facilities are the hospital annexe at Wormwood Scrubs and Grendon itself.

The annexe was opened in 1972, having been specifically designed to provide a therapeutic milieu for the treatment of a wide variety of prisoner addicts, from drug dependents and alcoholics to compulsive gamblers and over-eaters. Since then, the annexe has also opened its doors to sex offenders. Currently it offers accommodation for up to forty prisoners and functions as a therapeutic community, providing group psychotherapy as well as individual sessions, and life and social skills training. As at Grendon there is a prohibition on the prescription of psychotropic medication and the treatment process involves a wide range of staff groups. Unlike Grendon, however, the community is stratified, in that addicts and sex offenders are generally treated separately from each other and in different group sessions.[21]

Other treatment-oriented prisons exist outside England. The special unit at Barlinnie Prison in Scotland was opened in 1973 with accommodation for only ten men. It was designed with a narrower

[20] Facilities for women prisoners exist at Holloway, and for young offenders at Feltham and Glen Parva.

[21] Glatt, M. M. (1985), 'Reflections on the Working and Functioning of an Addicts' Therapeutic Community within a Prison: The Wormwood Scrubs Annexe', in Prison Reform Trust (ed.), *Prison Medicine: Ideas on Health Care in Penal Establishments*, London: Prison Reform Trust, 83–98.

field of objectives than either Grendon or the annexe at Wormwood Scrubs and more closely resembles the special units in England. The development of Barlinnie was generated by the need to reduce serious violence and tension within the Scottish prison system. In consequence, the major aim of the unit has been to manage and control disruptive and violent long-term prisoners. Its tiny population largely consists of men who have demonstrated considerable reluctance or inability to conform to conventional prison life and upon whom harsh sanctions have had little deterrent effect. Typically, these men have lost all prospects of early release and have little to lose by persevering in their anti-authority behaviour. But the Barlinnie unit also has another function. It serves as a pre-release facility for those inmates in the latter stages of very long sentences who require detailed assessment and intensive help to prepare them for eventual re-entry to outside society.[22]

In Denmark, the Herstedvester special institution, with accommodation for 131 prisoners, serves several functions within the penal system. It offers intensive psychiatric therapy for prisoners diagnosed as suffering from severe personality disorders, and has established a strong tradition in the treatment of 'sexually deviant' offenders. It also provides an acute psychiatric unit, receiving from other prisons inmates displaying symptoms of psychiatric disorder, and it has a special ward for offenders from Greenland who are deemed to be too 'dangerous' to serve their sentences within the country's open prison system.[23] In sharp contrast to Grendon, however, psychotropic drugs are used in combination with psychotherapy to provide a treatment regime which may, in extreme circumstances, be administered on an involuntary basis.

In Geneva, La Paquerette sociotherapeutic centre at Champ-Dollon Prison has been explicitly modelled upon Grendon, providing a treatment regime derived from pedagogy and social education for prisoners diagnosed as suffering from severe personality disorders with sociopathic traits. It is, however, considerably smaller

---

[22] Whatmore, P. (1990), 'The Special Unit at Barlinnie Prison, Glasgow', in Bluglass, R. and Bowden, P. (eds.), *Principles and Practice of Forensic Psychiatry*, London: Churchill Livingstone, 1361–2.

[23] Kramp, P. (1990), 'Danish Forensic Psychiatry' in Bluglass, R. and Bowden, P. (eds.), *Principles and Practice*, 1336–70.

than Grendon, offering accommodation for only twelve inmates within a single therapeutic community.[24]

Across the Atlantic, the Clinton Diagnostic and Treatment Centre in New York appears to be the nearest worldwide equivalent to Grendon. Opened in 1966 for fifty inmates, it now houses 100 prisoners who remain within the institution for between six and eighteen months. It offers a pre-release, pre-parole programme and operates according to the method of the therapeutic community. The setting is one of maximum perimeter security within which inmates are permitted the greatest possible freedom of physical movement and personal expression. Many of those accommodated within the Centre are persistent offenders who return to prison because they are unable to adjust to life in outside society. Typically, they fail to hold down a job and drift in and out of criminal activity. In consequence they have been described not so much as habitual criminals but as habitual prisoners.[25] The treatment programme at Clinton is thus specifically geared towards the re-education and re-socialization of these men to enable them to lead more law-abiding lives on release.

Medical Control

There is good reason to be sceptical about the concept of a therapeutic prison, particularly at a time when government policy espouses the need to rehabilitate offenders while simultaneously reproducing inequality and increasing the gap between the 'us' who 'have' and the 'them' who 'have not'.

The rich have become richer and the poor have become relatively poorer during the 1980s and early 1990s . . . Indeed social polarisation in the 1980s has been greater than in any comparable decade since income statistics were first published. But the Government . . . has so far refused to concede that the poor have grown poorer in absolute terms since 1979.[26]

[24] Bernheim, J. and Montmollin, M. J. de (1990), 'A Special Unit in Geneva' in Bluglass, R. and Bowden, P. (eds.), *Principles and Practice*, 1355–7.

[25] Angliker, C. C. J., Cormier, B. M., Boulanger, P. and Malamud, B. (1973), 'A Therapeutic Community for Persistent Offenders: An Evaluation and Follow-Up Study on the First Fifty Cases', *Canadian Psychiatric Association Journal*, vol. 18, no. 4, 289–95. See also Cormier, B. (1975), *The Watcher and the Watched*, Montreal: Tundra Books.

[26] Townsend, P. (1993), 'The Repressive Nature and Extent of Poverty in the UK: Predisposing Causes of Crime', extracts from a speech given at the Howard League Conference on 8 September 1993: *Criminal Justice*, vol. 11, no. 4 (October), 4–6 at 4.

The epistemology of Grendon's therapeutic programme does not deny the structural causes of criminality, nor does it insist that crime is primarily a function of personal pathology. It is, in fact, agnostic on this subject, largely because therapy at Grendon is not *primarily* directed to the prevention of crime. It may put this forward as a legitimate ambition, or as a justification for its existence, but the principal undertaking of therapy is to facilitate and promote the welfare of each individual inmate. By so doing, it may succeed in enabling some inmates to avoid reoffending after their release, but this is a secondary or consequent effect which derives from the improved well-being of the individual.

To make such a statement is itself verging on the heretical. There are, as every penal lobbyist knows, 'no votes' in being 'soft' on criminals. Grendon's managers have always been aware of the powerful role which public opinion can play in promoting or inhibiting the regime's survival. Currently the risk of being portrayed as a 'soft option', as a cosy retreat where violent criminals are helped to feel less angst, has to be guarded against at all costs. The strategy for survival in today's penological arena demands that the discomforting rigours of therapy for offenders, and the ultimate reduction of harm to victims, is at the forefront of Grendon's publicity. But to conceive of Grendon primarily as an apparatus of crime control is to misconstrue its purpose and to produce a myopic and distorted depiction of the institution.

All the men received into Grendon have a history of personal failure, not least in relation to their criminal activities which have caused serious harm to their victims as well as to themselves. Their inability to break this cycle of ineffectiveness and disappointment has led to their shared and abiding sense of discomfort and dissatisfaction with themselves and with their situations. Therapy at Grendon is thus geared to providing the men with an opportunity to re-evaluate their circumstances and to develop alternative ways of responding to them. The legacy of medical power, however, continues to promote an image of Grendon as a psychiatric prison. Yet, the regime does not operate according to the principles of a pure medical model. Foucault defined the medical model according to a particular set of practices and power relations, which may be summarised as having three specific features.[27] First the doctor

---

[27] Foucault, M. (1973), *The Birth of the Clinic*, London: Tavistock.

assumes the right to choose what shall be in the best interests of the patient and largely dispossesses the individual of any control over his treatment. This is typically encapsulated in the well-worn phrase, 'the doctor knows best'. Secondly, the concepts of 'dysfunction' and 'treatment' are emptied of moral significance and perceived solely in rational and deterministic terms. Finally, it assumes that the 'sickness' resides inside the individual and that, although the cause may not be a physiological process, the malfunctioning can be treated separately from any environmental factors that may have contributed to its cause.

The organization of therapy at Grendon contradicts the orthodoxy of a medical model in a number of important respects. The programmes on each of the wings reflect a multi-disciplinary approach and are negotiated with all categories of staff. Central to the Grendon ethos, too, is the notion that each individual has a central role to play in determining his own treatment, and that active engagement in therapy is the responsibility of each member of the community. Accordingly, considerable emphasis is placed upon inmate self-governance and democracy. In the words of one of the medical officers: 'Therapy is done by the prisoners aided and abetted by a few lonely staff.' None the less, this does not negate the significance of the medical input on the three therapy wings. Each is allocated a psychiatrist, who participates as a member of the community and staff team, and who is expected to play an important role in monitoring the mental health of men on their wing, thereby preventing serious psychological damage arising from the rigours of the therapeutic process. Psychiatrists also have a duty to maintain the physical health of the inmates and to link this with their psychological condition in ways which further the therapeutic enterprise. This holistic approach was somewhat eroded, however, during the course of the fieldwork, when the daily sick-call was relocated from the wings to the hospital out-patients' department, where the doctors would daily take it in turn to run a surgery for the entire establishment.

Although deviating from Foucault's ideal typical medical model, Grendon could nonetheless still be criticized for pathologizing and individualizing the men's problems, at the expense of recognizing their political and sociological significance. However, the structural impotence of the men is not explicitly denied by the therapeutic process. It is just that it is not deemed to be wholly determinative.

What Grendon attempts to do is to empower individuals to take control over that which is within their power: namely, their ability to make choices which alleviate their own and others' victimization, and to anticipate, and take responsibility for, the consequences of their actions. To this extent, Grendon undoubtedly serves a conservative purpose, in that it encourages lawful, non-violent, conciliatory and, above all, *individual* resolutions which do not address or challenge the root causes of the men's *collective* problems. In this way it sustains and preserves the existing social order, locating the problem within the individual rather than within the structural organization of society. Yet to portray Grendon purely as a mechanism of repressive state power, shrouded by a restrained medical imperialism, is to overlook an important humanitarian factor in the equation. The men who go to Grendon are typically in a state of distress: Grendon seeks to relieve their pain. That is the essence of its rehabilitative task.

Research

Our research began in 1987 and constitutes one of a number of projects carried out at Grendon. In the late 1960s Tony Parker was given permission by the Home Office to tape-record conversations with prisoners and staff within the institution. Over a period of three months he interviewed approximately two-thirds of the prisoners and half of the staff. He published the transcripts of these conversations in his book, *The Frying-Pan*, in which he presents a graphic portrayal of the lives of the inmates, inside and outside the prison, and the experiences and attitudes of the staff.[28] By such means Parker provides a unique insight into Grendon through the eyes of those individuals who live and work within the institution.

Two other studies which have taken a more strictly scientific approach have been conducted by Margaret Newton and by John Gunn, Graham Robertson, Suzanne Dell, and Cynthia Way. Newton, a Prison Department psychologist, compared the reconviction rates of prisoners who had spent time at Grendon with a matched sample from Oxford Prison.[29] Her results were not

---

[28] Parker, T. (1970), *The Frying-Pan: A Prison and its Prisoners*, London: Hutchinson.

[29] Newton, M. (1971), 'Reconviction After Treatment At Grendon' in *Chief Psychologist's Report, Series B*, No. 1, London: Office of the Chief Psychologist, Prison Department, Home Office.

encouraging for those who seek to promote and justify the purpose of the therapeutic regime as the reduction of recidivism.

The study by John Gunn and his colleagues at the Institute of Psychiatry compared the population, regime and treatment offered at Grendon with that of the annexe at Wormwood Scrubs.[30] A sample of prisoners received into each establishment was drawn and these men were interviewed and tested for changes in their psychological functioning during their period of treatment. In addition, a postal questionnaire was administered to the men after they had left prison in an attempt to examine their social circumstances and post-release behaviour. A controlled reconviction study was also carried out on the Grendon sample after these men had been at liberty for at least a year, and then again ten years later.[31] The authors concluded that, while there were significant and positive changes in the psychological test scores of men during their time in Grendon, their experience in therapy appeared to have had no impact upon their subsequent pattern of offending, when they were compared with prisoners with similar probabilities of reconviction who had been held at other prisons.

Important structural changes in the organization of Grendon have clearly taken place since this work was carried out. But there has also been a marked shift in the nature of the population received into the establishment. The demographic characteristics and criminal histories of a sample of seventy-one prisoners received into Grendon between June 1987 and October 1988 were compared with the cohort of 107 men drawn by John Gunn and his colleagues, who were received between 1 June 1971 and 31 May 1972. This revealed that the average age of inmates had increased by four years: from twenty-seven to thirty-one. But, most importantly, it demonstrated a marked shift in the criminal profile of Grendon's population towards the 'heavy end of the market'.

Among the 1971–1972 sample, fewer than half (41 per cent) were serving sentences of more than three years, in comparison with virtually all (99 per cent) of the 1987–1988 receptions. As Table 1.1 demonstrates, more than half (57 per cent) of the earlier sample were property offenders and only a third (32 per cent) were serving

[30] Gunn, J., Robertson, G., Dell, S. and Way, C. (1978), *Psychiatric Aspects of Imprisonment*, London: Academic Press.

[31] Gunn, J. and Robertson, G. (1987), 'A Ten Year Follow-Up of Men Discharged from Grendon Prison', *British Journal of Psychiatry*, 151, 674–8.

their sentences for offences against the person. In contrast, 81 per cent of the later sample had been convicted of offences against the person. Furthermore, at the end of the 1980s, the men shared between them an average of only ten previous convictions in comparison with as many as twenty-one fifteen years earlier. In essence, Grendon's population has become increasingly weighted away from shorter-term recidivist property offenders in favour of long-term prisoners serving sentences for offences of sex and violence (see Table 1.1).

Table 1.1. *Receptions into Grendon, by offence* (%)

Offence	1971–1972		1987–1988	
Violence against the person	17		15	
Sexual	7	32	41	81
Robbery	8		25	
Burglary/theft/fraud	57		13	
Other	11		6	

Our study was intended to build upon the earlier research and upon the observations and recommendations made by ACTRAG. The 1985 report of the advisory committee made clear the value which it placed upon research in the development of Grendon's role within the prison sytem, and unambiguously stated:

We lack basic data about the way prisoners flow from the rest of the system through Grendon and then either back into the system or on to release. Gunn's study provides a valuable starting point, and the base maintained at the establishment also contains useful material. But further research is needed to answer such basic questions as: who goes to Grendon? How are they selected? What sort of prisoner is considered but refused—and why? Which types of prisoner are allocated where and how? How long do prisoners stay and how is a decision reached that a prisoner should move on? Is there some sort of progressive programme governing a prisoner's stay? What sort of prisoners have to be transferred out prematurely, and why? How does the period at Grendon fit in with a prisoner's sentence as a whole?

The empirical study was, therefore, designed to meet the following aims:

  (i) to describe the population and regime at Grendon Prison;
 (ii) to examine the processes by which inmates are selected for and transferred from Grendon;
(iii) to describe the nature of social relations at Grendon, both among inmates and between inmates and staff;
 (iv) to explore the extent to which patterns of behaviour at Grendon are consistent with the system of beliefs held by Grendon's staff and inmates, and the referring medical officers, about the Grendon experience;
  (v) to examine the nature of the progression or career of inmates as they pass through Grendon;
 (vi) to explore whether the Grendon experience has any consequences for the management of inmates who are transferred to normal location within the prison system.

In addition, we intended to reflect upon Grendon's role, and the functions it serves, within the wider Prison Service. We did not embark upon this task, however, with an open mind. We began with the view that a therapeutic prison was not a feasible proposition: that the demands of custody and treatment were antithetical. We denounced as heresy the positivist suppositions implied in a 'treatment model' and anticipated that our task would be to reveal Grendon's 'hidden agenda' of penal control. Our mission was, however, confounded. Although many of our original assumptions were valid, they were to become largely irrelevant. The issue was not whether custody and treatment were antithetical, but how these unconsenting bedfellows were being accommodated within a single institution. It was not that crime causation could only be understood by reference to the structural constraints of a society divided by gender, race and class, but how individuals attempted to adjust to their sociological fate. And it was not that therapy could be used to exert control, but how such control differed from that enforced in other prisons and what purposes it served. Our conclusions could not have been envisaged or imagined by us at the outset of this research. We have been persuaded that a therapeutic prison is not only possible but that it is desirable.

2
Methods of Research

The Value of Methodological Explanation

Describing the methods by which a piece of research has been carried out can be a tedious task which, for the general reader, engenders as much interest and entertainment as a car repair manual for the average motorist. It is for this reason that methodological details are frequently relegated to the backwaters of an appendix, to be unearthed by the enthusiast while discreetly closeted from the rank and file. This tradition tends to be broken when researchers have undertaken fieldwork with a strong participant observation component. In such cases it is not uncommon for there to be a lengthy discussion in the heart of the text about how the fieldwork was set up and accommodated, how the researchers performed their fieldwork roles, and how difficulties were managed and triumphs achieved.[1] Such examples rarely take the form of a technical treatise, which tests the resolve of all but the most dedicated or obsessive reader. Instead they are often engaging stories which breathe life into the process of data collection, and which justify their liberation from an appendix by the claim that the subtleties of the evolving fieldwork situation have shaped the nature of the information collected, and may even have influenced its presentation.

There is, however, a somewhat less academic justification for the high profile given to participant methodologies, which is rarely made explicit but which, in our view, is likely to be a powerful motivating force. At its most basic level the reality is that researchers involve themselves in a human situation, in which demands are made upon their personal resources, to such an extent that it is their own social skills which are in large part central to the success of the whole venture. Their ability to engender confi-

---

[1] See Whyte, W. F. (1955), *Street Corner Society* (2nd ed.), Chicago: University of Chicago Press; Polsky, N. (1971), *Hustlers, Beats & Others*, Harmondsworth: Penguin.

dence in the subjects; to establish a balance between respondents' demands for reciprocity and their own professional need for rapport, so that sufficient distance is maintained to fulfil the requirements of objectivity and sustain a stance of non-alignment; and to discriminate between various causes of action and sensitively decode and disentangle conflicting pieces of information, are all 'make or break' factors in ensuring the viability and continuity of the fieldwork. It is not, in other words, a style of research which can neatly be designed in advance, and then carried out according to a pre-ordained plan which depends solely upon technical competence for its achievement. As a consequence, the personal investment which researchers make as participant observers may, in some circumstances, require a process of withdrawal and reflection before the study can be conceived as complete. Writing about the social construction and dynamics of the fieldwork situation can thus serve not only to mark the importance of the endeavour, both in relation to the individuals concerned and to the collection and interpretation of the data, but also to enable a cathartic process of disengagement to take place on the part of the authors. Although varied methods of research were used in our study of Grendon, we would readily admit that it was interest in the social processes of interaction which most significantly shaped and influenced the overall methodology.

It is perhaps trite and unnecessary to point out that the choice of any methodology should be based upon the research problems which need to be addressed. Too frequently, however, and particularly in policy-orientated research, there is a hierarchy of credibility which discriminates between the two broad categories of qualitative and quantitative techniques. The latter is considered to yield 'hard' data which are reliable and valid; the former is perceived as anecdotal, non-scientific, non-representative and, in consequence, not a proper basis from which general conclusions should be drawn. Such a critical appraisal was not made in designing and carrying out this study. While it can be argued that some degree of representativeness should be pursued in terms of the numbers and types of persons from whom particular views or experiences are sought, a rigid application of this approach may well leave concealed some of the more subtle nuances of the social processes which are in operation and may reveal little about the significant representations of particular processes or events.

The multifarious aims of this research required an approach which would enable us to calculate the prevalence of certain activities or beliefs, but which would also uncover the organization and pattern of social processes which operate both within the institution and outside it. For these reasons a varied methodology was developed which included the analysis of official records; semi-structured interviews with inmates and staff of all grades; questionnaires for self-completion by the civilian staff, namely the governors, doctors, psychologists and teachers; and lengthy periods of obervational work throughout the prison.[2] The eclecticism of this approach was clearly called for by the diversity of the information being sought. But during the course of the fieldwork it became apparent to us that it would be a mistake to conceive of each element of the methodology as constituting a discrete area of research, to be undertaken and completed in isolation. Rather, they were overlapping and complementary components which needed to be pursued and understood in relation to each other, in order to produce a coherent picture of the life of the institution. Collectively they enabled the cross-checking of information and made it possible to identify the internal consistency of particular findings which, it is hoped, will act to strengthen the validity of the final conclusions.

One of the complicating factors in this study was that it attempted to capture certain fundamental truths about an institution which was in a constant state of change. This, of course, is an inevitable feature of any research concerned with the study of social processes. However, in this case, the difficulties were exacerbated by the fact that, during the two years of fieldwork, the establishment was subjected to radical organizational change emanating from outside the institution. The major effects were felt as a result of the introduction of Fresh Start, a programme imposed throughout the prison service to reorganize and rationalize the management of prisons and to restructure the deployment of staff, their pay and conditions of service. A direct and immediate consequence of this reorganization was the introduction of regular contracted hours of employment and the abolition of unrestricted overtime by prison officers. It was agreed throughout the Prison Service that the consequent short-fall of staff on duty at any one time would be

---

[2] Appendix 1 provides a summary of all the data sets used in the research.

offset by the recruitment of new officers. At Grendon concern was expressed that, even if the promised cavalry did arrive, they would be too few in number to compensate for the loss of overtime hours, and that inevitably the therapeutic regime would be damaged. As anticipated, the influx of new officers and the changed pattern of working resulted in a reduction of continuity of staff attendance on the wings. This was said to impede seriously the proper functioning of the communities and to inhibit the achievement of therapeutic goals. In consequence, staff at all levels voiced considerable cynicism about the changes. They believed that the restructuring of working conditions had served only to bolster the interests of a streamlined prison bureaucracy, and they raised questions about the commitment of senior management within head and regional offices to the continuance of Grendon's therapeutic programme. It was feared that the unique identity of the establishment was at risk of being lost for lack of interest.

The perception of being in a state of siege was not, however, an entirely new perspective within the institution, particularly among some of the longer-serving members of staff. A widely shared view was that, ever since the post of Medical Superintendent had been abolished five years previously, and replaced by the appointment of a prison governor, the special status which Grendon had enjoyed as a unique part of the Prison Medical Service had been seriously eroded and its distinction from other institutions progressively blurred. Frequent references were made to a 'Golden Age' in Grendon's history when the powerful support of the Medical Directorate had ensured that resources were made available, that the value of therapy was clearly understood, and that the uniqueness of the establishment and its independence from the concerns of the mainstream Prison Service were never seriously threatened. The lack of such protection, it was argued, had resulted in Grendon becoming more like a conventional prison and thus increasingly subject to the rules and regulations governing life in other category B training establishments.

During the period of the fieldwork the validity of this argument was perceived to be demonstrated when, as a result of a ministerial commitment to empty police cells at a time of acute prison overcrowding, the governor and his staff were informed that they were required to receive an additional sixty inmates. It was agreed that these men would be prisoners currently serving their sentences under Rule 43, and that the only way of introducing such an influx of new inmates, without seriously disrupting the social ecology of the therapeutic communities, would be to house them in a separate unit. Apart from the fact that the concept of a segregated unit for Rule 43 prisoners was an anathema to the Grendon ethos, the practical consequences resulted in a considerable upheaval which affected the whole institution. In order to make available suitable accommodation, one of the four adult wings was forced to close and its members either dispersed to the other communities or transferred to other establishments; the young offender unit was relocated on two occasions; and the assessment unit was rehoused and its functioning temporarily suspended in order to accommodate men who had vacated places on the therapy wings while awaiting transfer to other establishments.

Although assurances were given by the Prison Department that these arrangements were not intended to become 'permanent', an atmosphere of uncertainty and a high degree of cynicism prevailed amongst inmates and staff concerning the Prison Department's commitment to the therapeutic regime at Grendon. Formal protests were registered with the Department by the doctors and psychologists; the prison governor expressed his concern about Grendon's future in interviews with the press; and Lord Donaldson intitiated a debate on the issue in the House of Lords.[3]

The changes brought about by the introduction of Fresh Start and the disruption caused by the opening of a separate, non-therapeutic wing for Rule 43 prisoners had consequences for the pace at which the research could progress. The prevailing sense of crisis distracted staff and inmates from their usual business and, in some respects, distorted the processes which the research was designed to study. The air of despondency led to the expression of jaundiced views during the interviews, which marked a notable break with the earlier responses, and largely reflected a transient and ephemeral reaction to the issues of the moment. In consequence, interviews had to be halted until the institution regained a sense of equilibrium, while the observational work had to take account of the effects which the structural changes had upon the processes to be observed without becoming distracted from its purpose.

There are, of course, two sides to every story and, regardless of

[3] *Guardian*, 13 November 1987; *Hansard*, 11 January 1988, vol. 491, no. 56, col. 1042–56.

the disruption caused to the study, it is possible to recognize, in retrospect, that certain benefits also undoubtedly accrued. In many ways we were presented with a golden opportunity to study the institution during a period of considerable change and to observe processes of decision-making, and methods of resolving conflict, which might never have become so accessible to us without the catalyst of these external events.

In the following sections we will describe how we embarked upon the research and explain the methodological approaches we adopted in our efforts to achieve the various aims of the study. In particular we will discuss why these methods were selected, how they were applied, and what consequences they had for the formulation and interpretation of the data.

Getting Started

For a number of years prior to our submitting a formal research proposal, the study of Grendon had featured as a prospective project in the annual Home Office Research Programmes. Thus, there was a pre-existing level of interest and a clear prospect of commitment on the part of the Prison Department and, in particular, the Directorate of Prison Medical Sevices, to see a project of this kind carried out. The proximity to Grendon of the Oxford Centre for Criminological Research had led to the development of some professional links between the two institutions, in that prison visits for students and visiting academics were periodically arranged, and Grendon staff occasionally attended seminars in Oxford.[4] This pre-established connection required and enabled us to make contact with the governor in order to discuss the possibility and feasibility of undertaking a study of the establishment. Well in advance of any formal proposal being sent to the Home Office we had a series of meetings with the governor, psychologists, and doctors at Grendon, during which we debated some of the issues which might be included in the research, and some of the implications which these would have for the institution in accommodating the fieldwork. Throughout these preliminary negotiations, however, the message we received from the professional staff at Grendon was that research of the kind we were proposing was long overdue;

[4] At the time of the research Elaine Genders and Elaine Player were Research Fellows at the Oxford Centre for Criminological Research.

that it was in line with the ACTRAG recommendations; and that it would receive their full support and co-operation in encouraging Home Office approval and facilitating the study on the ground.

Prior to the fieldwork beginning, the governor was very keen for us to inform all members of staff and all inmate members of the wing communities about the purpose of the study and how, in broad terms, the research would affect them. The thinking behind this strategy was that, if everyone was made aware of the project and had an opportunity to hear at first hand what the work was about and what it hoped to achieve, any anxieties or concerns could be voiced and allayed. In trying to fulfil this ambition we spent a day in the establishment, moving from one group of people to another, during which time we outlined our plans on thirteen separate occasions. As a result of this, together with the publicity spread by the governor, it is probably fair to say that virtually everyone in the establishment knew who we were and was aware that we were there to do some research. Beyond this, it was apparent that individuals' powers of attention and recollection varied enormously.

An additional and unanticipated consequence of this public relations exercise, however, was that, by generating advance knowledge, one was also generating certain presumptions and expectations. The fact that we were identified as researchers from the University of *Oxford* apparently led some members of the uniformed staff to surmise that a weighty piece of academic work was to be undertaken and that the Prison Department must have a serious reason for commissioning such research. Needless to say, the extreme suspicion with which those in head office were viewed led to the speculation that an elaborate plan had been laid to justify the closure of Grendon. It was presumed that the Department had foreseen the resistance it would meet from Grendon's allies in Parliament, in the press and in penal reform groups, and that an effective means of disarming their counter-attack would be to select research evidence which identified and proved the case for radical change. That we clearly did not, as one member of staff put it, fulfil a 'donnish' image, and that we also appeared open and interested in their views only served to confirm the suspicion that they were being lulled into a false sense of security.

We sailed through our first few weeks of fieldwork in blissful ignorance of this. Indeed, it was only after some of the staff had decided that we were not conscious conspirators in the plot that these anxieties were revealed to us. Our immediate response was one of amusement and amazement that such a complicated and incriminating story had arisen. It was only later, however, that we realized that what had initially appeared to be an absurd misreading of events did, in fact, raise issues of much broader significance. It became apparent that, across all staff groups, there was a real concern about how our research would eventually be presented and how the findings would be interpreted and construed. What this graphically demonstrated was how the staff, virtually in unison, perceived the purposes of the research, and how this perception had emerged less from what we had explicitly said about the study and more from the historical relationship which existed between Grendon and Prison Department headquarters. In essence, apart from anything else it was designed to do, the research was primarily defined as an evaluation of Grendon's performance, and as such it would be used to shape future policy for the establishment. Thus, while the research was manifestly welcomed as a potential means of good publicity, and every effort was made to co-operate with the day-to-day demands of the fieldwork, there were undercurrents of anxiety about the potential risks attendant upon the exercise.

Record Analysis

The study was intended to incorporate a description of the population at Grendon and to examine the processes by which inmates are selected for treatment and the means and mechanisms by which they are eventually transferred from the establishment. Achieving these goals clearly required the collection of some basic quantitative data about the men who had been referred to Grendon, those who had been accepted into therapy, and those who had been transferred from the establishment after varying lengths of stay.

Access to the relevant sources of information was never problematic for us, since the members of staff who were responsible for compiling the various records were not only helpful in a non-obstructive sense, but also willing to co-operate actively with the task at hand. Difficulties of accessibility arose, however, in relation to the ways in which the data we required could be retrieved or extracted from the official records. Prisons, like all organizations, maintain records in ways which enable them to be functionally useful to the institution; unfortunately, these may not always be convenient or expedient for the researcher, who has a different working purpose. Some of the information we sought was simply not available, since it had not been necessary for the institution to record it. Other data had to be literally dug out from their usual locations and reorganized in new and unfamiliar formats. Needless to say, the process of collecting and analysing the appropriate information was often time-consuming and laborious. The frustrated groan of, 'If only they'd done it this way' was a not unfamiliar lament during some of the more cumbersome excavations.

The first major area of research which required access to official records was the task of describing the *population* at Grendon. Fortunately, the psychology department had maintained a detailed index of every inmate who had ever been received. Drawing from the information held on these index cards, a census of the Grendon population was taken at the beginning of the study, on 2 February 1987, revealing a total of 138 inmates in treatment, and again two years later, on 2 February 1989, when, as a result of the institutional changes, the population in therapy had dropped to eighty-eight. A wide range of factors in three major areas was coded for each inmate: personal information, such as his age and marital status; criminal background, including his current offence and his age when first convicted; and, finally, his prison career, the length of his current and previous sentences, and whether or not he had spent time on Rule 43. The analysis of these data yielded some interesting findings, which not only provided a relatively detailed profile of the population in treatment but, when compared with certain features of the national prison population, dispelled the myth that Grendon took only the 'boy scouts' of the system.

In attempting to discover how men are *selected* for Grendon, we collected data on the population which had been referred over an eighteen-month period, from 1 June 1987 to 31 December 1988. This yielded a total of 332 inmates from forty-six prison establishments. Only limited information was available on each of these cases, since the data were drawn from an analysis of the '1080' forms, which are brief official documents that doctors throughout the service complete about prospective candidates and send to Grendon for their consideration. A great deal of demographic information which would have been of interest to us—such as the man's age, ethnicity, details of his criminal career—was simply absent from these records since it was not administratively required for this part of the organization's operation. None the less, it was possible to chart the pattern of referrals made from different establishments and to provide some basic information about the men who were accepted or rejected.

Discovering the circumstances under which inmates left Grendon was, of course, as important for this research as uncovering the processes by which they were referred and selected. The length of time prisoners spend at Grendon and the method and reasons for their departure shed light upon the social processes which structure the day-to-day life in the institution. For example, the duration of a man's stay may reveal something about his personal suitability for the regime, or it may say something about the ability of Grendon to tolerate certain kinds of individuals, with certain kinds of behaviour problems, or, indeed, it may raise issues for both. In order to gain some fundamental quantitative information about the population leaving Grendon, we again compiled a census from the prisoner index held by the psychology department. This consisted of eighty-two men who had been transferred from the establishment over a period of twelve months, between 1 March 1988 and 28 February 1989. This period was chosen because it enabled the inclusion of the maximum number of men who had been selected for interview during the course of the fieldwork. In line with the two population censuses, demographic data and information about their criminal backgrounds and prison careers were recorded but, in addition, we coded the psychological test scores which had been collated for each inmate shortly after his arrival at Grendon.[5] The purpose of this exercise was to examine whether the length of time men spent at Grendon was associated with any particular personal characteristics, prior criminal record, or previous patterns of behaviour in other prisons.

The difficulty of approaching this question in this way is that an

[5] The following psychological tests were administered to all men within two months of their reception into Grendon: Raven's Standard Progressive Matrices, which is used as a general guide to intelligence; Eysenck's Personality Questionnaire, which assesses the degree of psychoticism, extroversion/introversion, and neuroticism; Fould's Hostility and the Direction of Hostility Questionnaire, which measures the degree of self-criticism, sense of guilt, and actual and paranoid hostility; Rotter's Internal/External locus of control, which indicates the degree to which behaviour is controlled by internal or external factors.

annual census of inmates leaving the establishment will inevitably produce an over-representation of those who have stayed for shorter periods of time. An alternative, or additional, method would have been to compile an annual census of men received into the establishment and to chart the length of time they spent at Grendon. This would have made it possible to examine more accurately the average length of stay for particular categories of offender, rather than to identify the characteristics of those who stayed for particular periods of time. Thus we extracted a census of inmates received between 1 April 1985 and 31 March 1986. The year 1985 was chosen because it was necessary to go back at least three years to ensure that all receptions would have completed their period of therapy and left the establishment. We found, however, that the rate of turnover and average length of stay of inmates had substantially changed between the 1985–6 reception census and the 1988–9 transfer census. In consequence, the reception census had to be abandoned as a source of information because it did not represent current practice at Grendon.

Official records were also used in that part of the study which was designed to explore whether the Grendon experience had any consequences for the management of inmates who had been transferred back to other prisons. The personal dossiers of a sample of forty prisoners were consulted in an attempt to assess whether their institutional behaviour had demonstrated any notable changes after being at Grendon. An evaluation was made of each prisoner's disciplinary record together with that section of the dossier entitled 'information of special importance', which details any evidence or suspicion of behaviour which is considered to pose a threat either to the inmate himself or to others. These measures were extremely rough and ready, and inevitably reflected levels of institutional tolerance as well as prisoners' actual behaviour, but they nevertheless provided a rare opportunity to estimate quantifiable changes in those areas of inmate behaviour which are considered problematic for prison management.

Interviews

A major focus of the fieldwork was an examination of how far and in what ways the so-called therapeutic objectives of Grendon were being achieved and accommodated within the custodial environment. Two areas of enquiry were central to the attainment of these goals, and both could only be realized by recourse to direct and systematic questioning of the participants concerned. The first required us to uncover the various attitudes and beliefs, held by inmates and by the different staff groups, about the purposes and activities which constitute the therapeutic business of Grendon, while the second called for an examination of the subjective experiences of those who, from varying perspectives, encounter and participate in the social dynamics of the institution.

A central research task in attempting to understand the inmate experience at Grendon was the examination of the concept of a therapeutic process and, in particular, the notion that inmates progress through a treatment career. In order to do this it would have been methodologically preferable to have followed a cohort of men from their arrival to their departure, so that their individual progression through the various institutional processes could have been carefully monitored. This was not feasible since it could not have been completed within the permitted time-scale of the field-work. Instead, we sought to compensate for this by carrying out interviews with three overlapping samples of men who were at different points in their Grendon 'career'. However, in adopting this approach we had to make the assumption that, if these populations shared certain features in common and were subjected to the same therapeutic programmes and penal regime, their responses might be expected to reflect broadly similar patterns at each stage of the process.

First, interviews were conducted with a random sample of seventy-one inmates who were within the first two months of their reception into Grendon. Most of these interviews were undertaken while the men were accommodated on the assessment unit, but included in the sample was a small number who had been received directly on to one of the treatment wings.

Secondly, we interviewed a total of 102 men who were in therapy on the three treatment wings. These constituted all of the inmates who were in therapy during the time that we were based on their particular wing. In practice, we worked together on one wing at a time, completing all the interviews and observational work before moving on to the next. As a consequence of this system, some of the men we interviewed on the assessment unit were later interviewed again, because they had been received on to one of the treatment wings by the time we arrived there to carry out the fieldwork.

Finally, we interviewed a sample of sixty-nine inmates shortly before their departure from Grendon, pending either their release or their retransfer to other prisons. These men were drawn from each of the three treatment wings and, again, might have been included in one, or indeed both, of the earlier interview samples.

The demographic profiles and criminal histories of the men in each of these samples were broadly in line with the characteristics of the populations held on the treatment wings over the period of the two censuses. Inmates across the three samples also expressed similar types of reasons for coming to Grendon, and held similar views about the sort of help they expected from the therapeutic regime. The only major difference between the samples was the lower proportion of life sentenced prisoners amongst the reception group. Fewer than one in twenty of the receptions were lifers in comparison to approximately one in five of the men who were interviewed during their period of therapy or immediately prior to their transfer.[6]

All the interviews conformed to a structured format, in that within each of the samples all of the respondents were asked the same series of specific questions. This did not, however, destine the interviews to be rigid and narrowly circumscribed. Virtually all the questions were open-ended and designed to encourage the men to disclose their own views and experiences, determine their own priorities and largely govern the pace at which the interviews proceeded. As a consequence, the duration of the interviews varied enormously, from just under one hour to eight hours spread over four separate occasions. In every case the interviews were conducted by us in a 'one-to-one' situation and in a private setting. We guaranteed to treat all information given to us in the strictest confidence and to ensure anonymity in any future publication. None of the interviews was tape recorded, because we felt that, for some of the men, it could severely inhibit the openness of their responses. In addition, however, we felt that the process of transcribing the tapes would be too time-consuming, given the amount

---

[6] There was a tendency for lifers to remain at Grendon for longer periods than determinate-sentenced men. This resulted in their greater propensity for appearing in the daily population in therapy, than appearing in the populations received into the establishment over a given period of time.

of fieldwork which had to be completed and the resources we had available. Instead we wrote down the inmates' responses to the questions during the interviews. In the event, this method proved to have two advantages. First, it gave the interviewees some time to think: frequently while we were recording one response the man would add to, and clarify, earlier remarks. Secondly, we found that some prisoners were encouraged by the fact that we were writing down what they had said because it enabled them to feel that their contributions were worthwhile and significant.

Remarkably, none of the inmates we approached refused to be interviewed. This was largely owing to two factors. First, we spent considerable time on the wings, chatting informally with the men and participating in the activities of the community. This undoubtedly helped to allay confusion and anxiety about what the research was about and enabled us to establish a more informal identity in the eyes of the prisoners as well as in those of the staff. Secondly, we were very careful in selecting the first candidates to be interviewed on each of the wings. Although it was sometimes a nerve-racking experience, we targeted the men who appeared to be at the top of the inmate pecking order. The assumption was that, if we could gain their co-operation and approval, other inmates would be reassured that it was a relatively 'safe' exercise, and that those who were inhibited for one reason or another might be persuaded by the encouragement of the most respected members of the community.

The purpose of the interviews with inmates was to acquire some insight into the factors which led to their arrival at Grendon; the ways in which they defined the problems they were seeking to address; their experience and evaluation of the therapeutic process; the circumstances of their transfer; and their assessment of how their time at Grendon might influence their future behaviour.

In addition to the interviews we conducted with inmates at Grendon, forty men were followed up after they had been transferred to other prisons. In selecting these prisoners, an attempt was made to cover a range of different types of establishment with differing institutional reputations, and to include inmates who had spent varying periods in therapy, and who had been back in the system for different lengths of time. Efforts were made to concentrate this work upon inmates whom we had already interviewed at Grendon. However, locating such men proved to be an arduous task, owing to their movement within the system and the fact that many of them gained release on parole within a relatively short time of leaving Grendon. In order to increase the number of interviews with men who had been back in the conventional system for more than a year, it was necessary to include prisoners who had not previously participated in the study and to incorporate a substantial proportion (43 per cent) of men sentenced to life imprisonment. The follow-up interview could thus be seen to constitute a fourth overlapping sample, but the scale of the exercise was relatively small and the task largely exploratory. The primary purpose was to pilot whether it was possible to identify any enduring and measurable changes in the attitudes and behaviour of men returned to the mainstream system.

Interviews were also conducted with a total of thirty-nine prison officers, including thirty-one of the basic grade, four senior officers and four principal officers. This represented virtually all the uniformed staff attached to the three therapy wings and the assessment unit. The purpose of the interviews with the officers was to discover their views and beliefs about the regime at Grendon and, from a detailed examination of their experiences within the establishment, to identify some of the dilemmas they faced in performing their dual roles of custodian and therapist and adapting their working practices to accommodate two potentially competing sets of demands. Specifically, the staff were asked how they came to be posted to Grendon; how they believed that Grendon differed from a conventional prison; and how they would describe their relationships with inmates. Their responses were recorded in writing at the time of the interview. Again, all these interviews were on a 'one-to-one' basis and conducted under conditions of privacy and confidentiality. In general, they tended to last for about two hours, although some of the longer-serving officers took more time, since they would discuss at length the changes which they felt the establishment had undergone during their years of service. Only one basic grade officer refused to be interviewed.

Officers and civilian staff on the treatment wings also took part in a paper exercise. This required each of them, individually, to rate the therapeutic success of all men transferred from their unit over a twelve-month period, and to explain the reasons for the men's departure. The purpose of this was twofold: first, to elicit staff views about the level of success they felt they achieved with the inmates they received and, secondly, to examine and assess the degree of concordance among members of staff about individual cases.

The civilian staff at Grendon were not subjected to a systematic interview. Instead, the governors, doctors, psychologists, probation officers, and teachers each completed a written questionnaire. We spent a considerable amount of time with the civilian staff in informal discussion and, therefore, questionnaires were preferred over interviews because they represented the most efficient means of assessing the responses of all civilian members of the wing staff. Broadly, the purpose of the research with the civilian staff was to enable some examination of how the various professional groups perceived their roles and identified the stresses and rewards associated with them; and the extent to which they had a common understanding of the purpose of Grendon and a shared perception of the inter-relationship between their professional responsibilities in the therapeutic process.

Finally, as a contribution to that part of the study concerned with examining how certain inmates are selected for Grendon over others, we interviewed thirty medical officers and visiting NHS consultants who were in a position to refer inmates to Grendon. The selection of the sample sought to include doctors working within all types of establishment and with different rates of referral to Grendon.[7]

The Participant Role

As two women entering the social world of a men's prison, our ability to undertake a participant observer role was obviously circumscribed, and clearly could not incorporate an undercover 'fly on the wall' approach. During the period of the research there were a small number of female civilian staff who were attached to the wing communities, but there were no women prison officers. In consequence, those women who were present were highly conspicuous. Given that 'going native' was not an option for us, our role could be described as participant, in the sense that we were present

[7] This did not include doctors working in open prisons because Grendon's security classification, together with the requirement that inmates have a minimum of eighteen months to serve at the time of referral, meant that hardly anyone was referred from open conditions.

and took part in many of the formal and informal activities of inmates and staff which took place within the institution.

In an effort to understand how the establishment as a whole managed to incorporate the potentially competing demands of a prison and a therapeutic community, we observed the proceedings of a wide range of institutional committees. These, of course, convened only periodically and thus represented a relatively small part of our fieldwork. The vast majority of our observational work took place within the therapeutic communities. We worked together on one wing at a time, for between six and nine months, during which time we each regularly attended one small group and the community meetings. This permitted a considerable degree of continuity, enabling us to observe the ways in which the groups, and the community as a whole, accommodated new members and said farewell to their graduates and rejects; how they managed particular areas of therapeutic concern; and how they defined and coped with deviant members. We were also present for the staff meetings on the three treatment wings, and for the weekly assessment meetings on the assessment unit. These gave us the opportunity to witness how the uniformed staff dealt with the incongruities of their dual role as prison officers and community therapists; how power and authority were exercised by the various staff members; and how therapeutic issues within the community were identified and individuals' progress evaluated.

In all these forums we made contemporaneous notes which detailed the content of the proceedings and any immediate thoughts we had on what we were observing. Subsequently, we would review the notes and highlight issues which had arisen, which could then be examined in relation to information gained elsewhere. At first, our copious note-taking was a distracting influence, as inmates and staff explained anxieties about what we were writing and who would read it. As with other concerns, however, this was relatively quickly dispelled, as the communities acclimatized to our presence and realized that we were willing to allow them to read the notes if they wished to do so.

In addition to the formally timetabled activities within the communities, we also spent a considerable amount of time on each of the wings performing the classic 'hanging out' role, in which we would talk informally to both staff and inmates and generally attempt to penetrate beneath the surface of the day-to-day events in the communities. These sessions proved to be particularly fruit-ful in helping us to unearth information about the range of illicit inmate activities within the communities, and the extent and nature of self-policing which they undertook to define and control deviant conduct. The informality of these interactions was the essential key to their success. The details were therefore not recorded at the time but were noted after the conversations had taken place.

A criticism which is frequently levelled against studies which have relied upon methods of participant observation is that there is little guarantee that what has been observed and reported is truly representative of what normally occurs. This is seen to be espe-cially problematic when the observers are known to be particularly visible and likely to influence the proceedings they are there to record. One way researchers have attempted to overcome this problem has been to adopt an approach in which the number of times a particular event occurs is recorded and its typicality is established in relation to its relative frequency. Such an approach is most appropriate when research is focused upon discrete occur-rences, which can be identified and isolated from other phenomena within the social situation. It is considerably less relevant when the unit of study is conceived as a sequence of interrelated social processes. In the course of this research, a sociometric approach to the observational work had only limited value, since most of the research questions we sought to address fell into the latter, rather than the former, category. None the less, it was a method which was effectively employed in formulating some of our observations of the assessment process on the assessment unit. Here, for exam-ple, it was useful to quantify the number of occasions when indi-viduals were assessed as either suitable or unsuitable for treatment, and to evaluate the frequency with which certain reasons were used to structure the decision.

In our view, however, the validity of most of the observational work we carried out within the communities could not be judged in relation to the regularity with which specific events or patterns of activities recurred. For example, our interest in understanding how inmates at Grendon adjusted to the obligation placed upon them to breach the conventional concept of prisoner solidarity, and feed back confidential information about fellow inmates to the whole community, was not greatly advanced by simply counting the number of occasions on which inmates explicitly conformed to the rules of the therapeutic community. A more profitable approach, in our view, was to use observational materials to identify key issues from which it might be possible to construct ideal types of social organization. As Thomas Mathiesen has pointed out, this method does not necessarily depend upon a process of quantification, but implies some kind of comparison between empirical cases and the ideal-type, which is a deliberate and conscious exaggeration of reality.[8] Thus, in our example, the questions we posed were designed to provide some insight into whether, and how, inmates were able to differentiate between the concept of 'grassing' and the principle of therapeutic feedback; whether and how a traditional inmate hierarchy could be seen to influence the identities of those who provided the feedback, and those about whom feedback was provided; and whether and how certain kinds of information were selected as relevant feedback topics, while others were excluded.

All empirical research, however, is to some extent shaped by the interests, attitudes, and physical presence of the researchers. Max Weber, in his classic discussion of research methods in the social sciences, denied that such effects invalidated the objectivity of the data and also disputed that such issues were exclusive to social science methodologies.[9] He argued that the process of collecting information is inevitably interactive, even within the natural sciences, and that understanding this process of interaction, and the impact it is having upon the data being gathered, is an intrinsic part of the method and a fundamental means whereby the findings can be interpreted as objective truths. In our study of Grendon it was manifestly apparent that our presence within the institution affected the nature of the social environments that we wanted to observe. At an immediate and relatively simplistic level, the fact that the staff perceived the research, at least in part, as an evaluation of their professional performance tended to bring about an initial flurry of 'best' behaviour. This was not necessarily contrived to hoodwink us, but was largely born out of a conscious attempt by staff to think carefully about what they were doing so that they could explain, clarify and justify events and procedures to us. As

[8] Mathiesen, T. (1965), *The Defences of the Weak: A Sociological Study of a Norwegian Correctional Institution*, London: Tavistock.
[9] Weber, M. (1949), *The Methodology of the Social Sciences*, New York: Free Press.

the months passed, the novelty of the situation inevitably wore off, and the overt attentiveness dissipated as we became a more routine presence. However, in order to counteract the risk of imposing our own unsubstantiated interpretations upon the observational material, it was necessary to seek clarification by asking direct questions about certain activities we had witnessed. We attempted to minimize the disruption this caused by, for example, trying to restrict questions to the ends of staff meetings rather than constantly interrupting the flow of business. Nevertheless, there were occasions when, by our asking staff to explain why they had behaved in a particular way, individual members came to recognize and articulate motives which they had previously ignored, and, as a direct consequence of this, modified their behaviour.

An example of this occurred on one of the wings, when a decision was made during a staff meeting that a particular inmate should be expelled from the community and transferred to another prison. The decision was interesting in that it was carried by a majority vote, in which all the uniformed staff voted for the man to leave and all the civilian staff voted for him to stay. In discussing the case after the meeting with the wing doctor, we questioned how he saw his role, and whether he saw any contradictions between the functioning of a democratic approach to decision-making and a formal structure of accountability, in which he was ultimately responsible for the operation of therapy within the community. As a result of these discussions, the doctor reviewed the decision and reconvened the staff meeting to inform the staff that he would not sanction the transfer. He explained his reason to the staff and suggested ways in which the inmate concerned could be given 'one last chance'. In the event, the staff, while somewhat disappointed at the prospect of having to soldier on with what they regarded as an eminently unrewarding case, accepted the right of the doctor to veto their decision.

In this instance it was obvious to us that the process of seeking clarification had led to an outcome which would have been fundamentally different if we had not been there. Such a conclusion, however, need not necessarily have negative repercussions on the objectivity of the method if the research is dedicated to discovering how the dynamics of social processes are structured, rather than simply gathering information about the incidence of discrete events. So, although in this case the original decision was varied as a consequence of the researcher-effect, we gained valuable insights into the ways in which power and authority operated among the various staff groups and how individuals perceived the limits of their own jurisdictions.

Another consequence of our efforts to gain clarification emerged when we were seeking to understand certain staff practices which were used, not to rationalize and justify the working principles of the therapeutic community, but to resolve some of the conflicts inherent in the duality of the officers' institutional role. On one occasion a decision was taken by the uniformed staff, in the absence of the wing doctor and psychologist, to expel a man from the community. The meeting at which this took place lasted for only five minutes and was unusual, in that there was a tacit acceptance of the necessity and inevitability of their decision and very little discussion about the reasons for the man's expulsion. When we attempted more clearly to discern the factors which had informed this decision, the responses we received served only to mystify us still further, since they constituted a series of pretexts which could have been applied equally to other men on the wing. As we proceeded with our questions we were aware that the officers were finding our incursions increasingly uncomfortable: the more they searched for justification and proffered different explanations, the less convinced we became. As we pieced together the different versions, it became clear that the inmate concerned was an irritant to staff, in that he used his highly developed intellectual skills to devalue and de-skill the officers when they attempted to perform their therapeutic roles. Their inability to counteract his disruptive behaviour led them to welcome any excuse to be rid of him. This is not to suggest that the staff deliberately and consciously conspired to expel this troublesome member of the community. Rather, they grasped an opportunity and, in their relief, failed to examine their underlying motives. However, our relentless pursuit of the issue succeeded in irritating several of the officers, one of whom left us in no doubt of his feelings when he said that we reminded him of a dog with a bone and that we really got 'right up his nose sometimes'. Needless to say, the effect of this was to create considerable feelings of anxiety and tension which, at the time, seemed intolerable. Few people enjoy being the subject of others' annoyance and our immediate feeling was to let sleeping dogs lie and run for cover. The significance of this brief event, however, in pointing to variations in the degrees of tolerance the uniformed staff were able to extend to members of the therapeutic community, and in identifying one of the informal mechanisms by which staff seek to resolve the incongruities of their job, led us to conclude that, despite the discomfort, it had been a valuable and necessary experience.

The risks we ran of permanently damaging important fieldwork relationships were never very great, in that we had, by this time, built up a good rapport with the various staff groups and, in the main, individual members of the staff teams were willing to listen to the reasons we gave for pursuing our questions. With the benefit of hindsight, it is possible to think of ways in which we might have been less direct and hound-like. However, the lesson we learned from this was that, despite the congeniality of being welcomed into the bosom of the institution, we were not there to win a popularity contest but to find out how the establishment functioned. On occasions this meant that we had to run the gauntlet of displeasing some people by bringing to the surface issues which they might otherwise prefer to have left unaddressed.

In addition to what could be described as the unanticipated or unintended effects which we, as researchers, had upon the fieldwork situation, there were effects which we deliberately orchestrated. These were occasions when we directly intervened to structure a situation so that we could observe the events which followed. Examples of this took place when we generated focused discussions between the doctors and psychologists. These were usually directed towards gaining some insight into their different interests and perspectives regarding the management and distribution of professional responsibilities within the therapeutic communities, and were invariably controversial issues which were otherwise typically avoided.

It would be misleading, however, to suggest that our participatory role in the fieldwork situation was entirely of our own making. The reality was that the staff and inmates at Grendon made it impossible for us passively to observe what was going on. Within a short period of our arrival staff and inmates directly sought out our opinions or advice. The ethos within the therapeutic communities, which defines all activities as contributing to therapy, pulled us within its orbit, so that we, too, became potential resources which could be utilized in the therapeutic process. Increasingly we were drawn into playing the role of therapist, which, despite its inherent problems for the objectivity and independence of the research, was extremely seductive. It was, for example, flattering to be asked for an opinion and to be showered with gratitude for the smallest of offerings. But over time it was also the case that, as we became more familiar with individual inmates and members of staff, a sense of loyalty developed which induced in us a desire to help. The fact that there were two of us undoubtedly helped to inhibit the impetus to act as a therapeutic Mother Theresa. Together, we spent a great deal of time discussing how to handle particular cases, and we were ruthless in pointing out to each other occasions when we were overstepping the line. In the main we developed a strategy whereby we were open to approaches made to us within the communities, but responded by listening and asking questions, rather than proffering advice or personal opinions. It was a method which earned us a reputation for being interested in the views, experiences and problems of individuals, but also defined us as independent of the formal processes of therapy and of the bureaucratic structure of the establishment. To some extent, we took on the role of confidant, so that a number of staff, as well as inmates, sought us out to discuss certain issues which they did not wish to disclose in a more public setting. Sometimes there were matters which had been raised during an interview and which, after further consideration, they wanted to talk about in more detail.

The nature of our fieldwork inevitably raised questions, not only about the technical validity of the method, but also about the ethics of the approach. A major condition for the success of the research clearly hinged around the prospect that the staff and inmates would be willing openly to discuss their attitudes and experiences, to the point almost of indiscretion. A nightmare consequence of this, however, may be that one is told more than one wants to hear. On several occasions during this study the words of a popular song reverberated in our ears: 'I wish I didn't know now what I didn't know then'. Invariably the difficulty was that we were given knowledge which implied a serious responsibility. We were told about misconduct on the part of an officer which constituted a criminal offence; on more than one occasion inmates admitted to serious offences for which they had not been prosecuted; and one inmate confided crucial information about his past life, which he felt helped to explain much of his subsequent behaviour but which he felt he could not reveal to the community.

Our status within the institution was predicated upon the guarantee of confidentiality which we extended to everyone who took part in the study. But the question we had to ask ourselves was whether there were not other higher moral issues at stake which would justify the breach of this undertaking, and the consequent disruption to the fieldwork setting. Despite the obvious academic advantages of the purist approach adopted in most methodology textbooks, our view is that it is extremely problematic to advocate an absolute solution. At the end of the day researchers rely upon their own judgement. In some of the more problematic cases we examined the motives which had triggered the revelations, and these considerations undoubtedly informed our decision-making about what should be done. It was evident, for example, that in some instances we were confided in as a form of preparation or rehearsal prior to a more public performance before members of the community. We asked those concerned whether they wanted to be able to reveal their information to their groups and all of the men who said that they did managed shortly afterwards to do so. In these cases our strategy was to play a waiting game. The inmate who made allegations against a member of staff, on the other hand, said that he did not want to divulge the story to all members of the wing for fear of retaliation from other inmates. When we asked him whether he wanted or expected us to keep the information secret, or to communicate it to the relevant authorities, he said that he hoped we would pass on the information so that the officer would be brought to justice. Under the circumstances we decided to inform a member of staff, telling him exactly what we had been told, but without revealing the identity of the inmate. Finally, there were those cases in which we decided that the motives for disclosure were less reputable and had been triggered by a desire to manipulate us in some way. On the two occasions on which this happened we decided to take no action at all but to keep a generous and cautious distance from those individuals in the future.

On no occasion did we breach the confidentiality we had promised, but it has to be said that this probably had more to do with luck than judgement. Obviously the most expedient tactics for coping with these ethical dilemmas are those which have an in-built early warning device, enabling the researcher to avoid the discomforting confessions being made in the first place. None the less, in our experience, the unpredictable nature of fieldwork ensures that unwelcome and unsolicited materials can be generated as instantaneously and as inexplicably as a rabbit from a magician's hat.

In any participant observation study the personal characteristics of the researchers will affect the ways in which they are received by their hosts, and will structure the opportunities they have to carry out their chosen roles. Immediately visible factors, such as age and sex, are typically identified as being influential in this respect, but other examples might include a shared interest between the researcher and the subjects, or a common life experience. In our case there is little doubt that the most influential features which shaped our reception at Grendon were our age and gender. Being perceived as relatively young women, we generated a whole series of expectations and assumptions which, in some respects, made our work easier and, in others, more difficult. It was clear, for example, that among the staff we constituted an additional security risk, in so far as we were perceived as being vulnerable to physical or sexual assault, or to being taken hostage. Also in the history of the establishment there had been a small number of 'notorious incidents' in which female members of staff or visitors had established intimate relationships with inmates which had resulted in considerable controversy. At the beginning of our fieldwork a warning had been unambiguously and paternalistically issued to us by a senior member of staff, leaving us speechless with astonishment and outrage, but in absolutely no doubt that our age and gender represented not only a potential predicament for the good order of the institution, but also a risk to our personal integrity. We accepted that these sensitivities were not without foundation and that it was necessary, both for the smooth running of the research, and for our own safety, to demonstrate some recognition of these concerns. There was a formal requirement that all women should remain on the ground floor of each of the wings, where the communal rooms and offices were located, and not venture on to the upper floors which were entirely devoted to the cellular living accommodation. In addition, during the course of the study, a new set of regulations was issued after a female visitor had been sexually assaulted, which required women, when seeing inmates alone, to do so only in a room possessing an alarm bell and a door fitted with a glass viewing panel. We rigidly adhered to these rules but also developed some rather more ostentatious routines in an effort to convince officers on the wing of our desire to co-operate. We would always inform staff of our arrival on the wing and tell them briefly what we would be doing, and who we wanted to see. Also, when we were hanging around and chatting informally to inmates, we routinely attempted to do this in places which enabled us to be highly visible to the officers and which negated the need for them to come looking for us.

Although we made considerable efforts to acknowledge the security implications of our presence within the communities, we did not acquiesce to all of the paternalistic demands made upon us. An illustration of this took place on one occasion in the summer, when one of the governors asked to see us to explain that some of the uniformed staff had expressed concern that we were at risk of sexual assault because of the brevity of our skirts. We had given careful consideration to the nature of our dress throughout the study and had consistently avoided clothing which we felt could be construed as 'overtly provocative'. Conscious that such judgements are endlessly subjective, however, we attempted to develop a slightly more objective yardstick of suitability by deciding whether or not a particular outfit would be appropriate to wear if one were working in a branch office of a building society. The clothes which passed the test were deemed to be acceptable to wear to Grendon. The controversial skirts in this case were, in fact, knee-length and by no stretch of the imagination could be described as 'mini'. Their shortness was perhaps exaggerated by the transition from the all-embracing long winter skirts and boots to generally less-consuming summer clothes. However, we felt that we did not have an obligation to go into purdah; that there was an inherent confusion between women's appearance being construed as 'attractive' and as 'provocative'; and that, instead of seeking to deal with the issue by controlling our freedom of expression, it was incumbent upon all those operating within the therapeutic environment to encourage male members of the community to recognize their indubitable sexism and to impose control by revising their own definitions of 'the problem'.

Our gender was clearly an influential factor in shaping the nature of the rapport we were able to develop with staff and inmates. Some inmates, for example, found it relatively easy to discuss difficult personal problems with us because they generally felt less need to construct and maintain their defences when talking to women rather than men. Others, however, were considerably more inhibited, particularly when their problems focused upon a deviant sexuality. This was notable in some of our observations of the group work. There were occasions when certain men, usually new recruits to the group, were seriously inhibited in revealing details about their offences where these concerned the sexual abuse of either women or children. When this occurred it did not go unnoticed, but was directly addressed by other members of the group. In those instances the man was forced to explain his hesitancy and was encouraged to overcome his inhibitions. Clearly our presence during these sessions structured both the conduct and content of the group. However, in so doing, it also facilitated valuable insights into the techniques which the groups used to encourage the participation of their more solitary and unforthcoming members.

Inevitably there were numerous inducements to maximize the time we spent with inmates we found more personally agreeable than others, and who provided us with the most valuable information. However, this was fraught with difficulties and it was necessary to tread a very fine line between exploiting the fieldwork opportunities and creating a cadre of 'favourites'. We were well aware that we were as much observed as observing, and that any demonstration of partiality on our part could be seriously misconstrued and result in the realization of some of the staff's worst fears. The delicacy of the balance we were wrestling to achieve was graphically brought home to us when one of the inmates, who had previously been friendly and co-operative, burst into the television room where we were talking with two other members of the community, and hurled a tirade of abuse at us because he believed that one of us had given him a 'dirty look'. Thus, we came to realize that the build-up of jealousies and resentments was, to some extent, inevitable and beyond our control: the best we could hope for in the situation was to employ an effective strategy of damage limitation.

For us, the most uncomfortable way in which our gender structured the fieldwork related to the ways in which we were used by a small number of inmates as objects of sexual fantasies. These were made known to us either by being told to us personally by the man concerned, or by the subject being openly addressed in the groups or community meetings. The most notable example occurred when one inmate revealed to his group, in the presence of one of us, details of a sadistic fantasy in which he envisaged sexually assaulting us both. The most disturbing aspect of this event was that he confessed to having laid detailed plans to carry out his fantasy, and specified several occasions on which he had intended to do so, but had been disabled either by circumstance or by loss of nerve. Again, this example can be seen to demonstrate the ways in which the content of group discussions were altered by the effects of our presence. However, set against this, the incident provided us with invaluable opportunities to witness the ways in which relationships and attitudes towards women were expressed and dealt with by a predominately male community.

The effects which we, as researchers, had upon the fieldwork must, however, be understood as part of an interactive process, in which we were both shaping and being shaped by the social environment of the study. It was, for example, an inevitable and integral part of our work to listen to a catalogue of appalling crimes in which precise and intimate details of the offences were made known. In the realm of most people's experience there is a moral consensus which trenchantly condemns serious violent and sexual abuse, particularly where vulnerable victims are involved. In order to conduct the research, it was necessary for us to repress inherent feelings of shock and disgust and to focus upon issues of intellectual, rather than emotional, concern. Within a short period of time, which could be measured in days rather than weeks, we had adjusted to a state of numbness in which the retracing of exceptional and aberrant acts was being routinely and inscrutably analysed. Such adaptations were clearly in line with the behaviour of the staff at Grendon, whose experience in this matter was probably indirectly influential in shaping our response. But although such desensitization was necessary for the accomplishment of the fieldwork, it raised for us personal anxieties that we might become immune to 'normal' human feelings. This is not to suggest that there were no occasions when fundamental feelings of disgust, pity or shock were triggered by what was revealed to us, but it was as if these sentiments had shifted several points along a notional scale of tolerance.

Another way in which we were affected by the research environment stemmed from a pattern of learned behaviour on our part, in which we consciously and unconsciously developed strategies of interaction which were specifically geared to encourage others to divulge detailed personal information to us. Although initially we were aware of the tactical nature of our behaviour, it later became automatic and intuitive, spilling over into our personal and professional relationships outside Grendon. One of the consequences of this was that a whole series of people, some of whom we hardly knew, began to discuss with us their personal problems. The cumulative effects of this were slow in dawning, but eventually we realized that we felt weary and burdened by what seemed to be an incessant flow of distress. We had learned a new way of relating to people, which was described to us by our victims in various ways, from intensely perceptive to downright interrogative. We became most aware of our inquisitorial approach to social life, however, after we had completed the fieldwork and left the establishment. Participant observers often write about the difficulties of leaving their research environment, emphasizing, for example, the sense of affection and loyalty they felt towards their subjects, and the ambivalence and guilt they felt in 'abandoning' interest in them once they had served their own research needs. In our cases we experienced an uneasy sense of dislocation, recognizing that our adaptation to the therapeutic communities would have to be readjusted for everyday living in the outside world. In many respects, after leaving Grendon we continued to learn about the institution and the interactive effects of our participation upon the objects of our study. As we reflected upon our personal process of disengagement and rehabilitation, we were able to see clear parallels between our own re-establishment and the difficulties of re-integration which have to be faced by prisoners upon their release or transfer to another prison. In addition, the concern expressed by prison staff throughout the fieldwork about the need for organized 'breaks' from therapy to 'recharge the batteries' was given fresh insight and understanding.

3

Getting into Grendon

In describing how men are referred to and selected for treatment at Grendon this chapter examines the formal criteria for admission and the various routes which lead to an inmate's arrival at the establishment. It considers the views of the referring medical officers on the role which they believe Grendon plays and describes the criteria they claim to use when making referrals. It provides a statistical profile of all referrals made over an eighteen-month period, and it details the functioning of the assessment unit and reports on the views of staff about the selection of inmates for Grendon. The chapter also affords some insight into the inmates' own knowledge, and experiences, of the referral and reception processes. And finally, it presents a description of the resulting population at Grendon, drawn from two censuses conducted at the beginning and end of the fieldwork period.

Formal Criteria for Admission

The types of prisoner which the Prison Department considers suitable for the therapeutic regime at Grendon are described in the 1987 Circular Instruction.[1] According to this, inmates must be motivated to participate in the group therapy process and have the ability 'to learn to communicate openly within a group without recourse to physical violence' (paragraph 4). Those who are identified as 'best suited' to the programme which Grendon has to offer are men with personality disorders, especially those who have demonstrated persistent anti-social behaviour. Inmates suffering from acute psychiatric illness and those who are 'highly disturbed' are defined as unsuitable, since a tenet of the psychotherapeutic approach is that all individuals must be able to accept responsibility for their own actions.

[1] Home Office (1987), Prison Department Circular Instruction 21/1987.

Following the recommendations of the Advisory Committee on the Treatment Regime at Grendon (ACTRAG),[2] the Department published a list of criteria for admission to the therapeutic communities at Grendon.[3] *Sentence length* is deemed relevant in so far as an inmate should normally have at least twelve months left to serve in order to have enough time to participate in the treatment programme. Apart from this, determinate-sentenced prisoners are eligible for referral at any time during their sentence. There are no restrictions placed on *type of offence* or *behavioural characteristics*, although certain categories of offender may be considered to represent particularly relevant candidates, since it is claimed that Grendon has developed some expertise in treating 'explosive, aggressive individuals, arsonists, sex offenders, unusual murderers, those who deliberately self-mutilate and the isolated and hostile individuals who prove difficult in other prisons' (paragraph 3). Some limitations do, however, pertain to *security risk*, in that, as a category B training prison, Grendon is not equipped to accommodate category A prisoners or those who are regarded as serious escape risks.

There are also two categories of offenders which, while not statutorily excluded, are presented as questionable subjects. *Drug abusers* are identified as generally unsuitable for referral, because it is believed that they can undermine the treatment of others. And inmates *over the age of 40* are considered unlikely to benefit from Grendon. But the most important criterion for selection is defined as a genuine *motivation* to change, and this may override all other features which could normally weigh against a prisoner's admission. In general, the likely medical diagnosis of the candidates is that of *personality disorder*, as outlined in the Ninth Review of the International Classification of Diseases, and possibly some neurotic disorders such as anxiety states and depression.

Routes into Grendon

All inmates who are admitted to Grendon have chosen to be there and are sentenced men who have been referred by doctors working

---

[2] Home Office (1985), *First Report of the Advisory Committee on the Treatment Regime at Grendon.*
[3] Home Office (1987), Prison Department Circular Instruction 21/1987, Appendix.

in other prisons: no one comes direct from the court. Although workers in a number of criminal justice agencies may be responsible for first suggesting to a prisoner that he should spend time at Grendon, or, in some cases, the prisoner himself may initiate enquiries, the process of referral is via the prison medical officer or visiting psychiatrist.

It should be pointed out, however, that, although all inmates are free to choose to come to Grendon, the exercise of this choice is inevitably influenced by the fact of their imprisonment, and may be associated with considerable costs. It is questionable, for example, how far a man who is serving an indeterminate sentence, and whose eventual release is contingent upon written reports by prison staff, is able to make an independent and autonomous decision when faced with a recommendation that he should go to Grendon. Furthermore, inmates who are approaching a parole review may also be faced with a dilemma. In order for them to have enough time in therapy, they may need to postpone, or even forgo, consideration for parole.

During the period of our fieldwork, prison medical officers referred their patients by completing a '1080' form, which was sent to the Directorate of Prison Medical Services, now re-named the Directorate of Health Care, and from there on to Grendon, where the man would be placed on the waiting list if he had enough time left to serve. The list operated not on a first come, first served basis, because this would obviously have discriminated against prisoners serving the shorter sentences, but according to the amount of time a candidate had left to serve before his earliest date of release (EDR), not taking into account the possibility of an inmate's early release at the discretion of the Parole Board. The important point to be made about the 1080 process, however, is that referral to Grendon did not automatically guarantee that an inmate would be accepted into treatment, only that he would be considered for a period of assessment in order to evaluate his suitability. Hence, all referrals were essentially recommendations, and access to treatment in the therapeutic communities was determined by Grendon staff.

Although the standard 1080 procedure accounted for the vast majority of receptions into Grendon, access could also be gained through three other routes (although a 1080 form had to be completed, at some point, in every case). First, a man could be admitted following a 'recruitment drive' whereby a medical officer from Grendon would visit particular establishments to interview prisoners, some of whom would already be formally processed under the 1080 scheme, while others would be presented for consideration on the day.

The second route into Grendon would be used when the establishment was specifically requested by other prisons, or Prison Department divisions, to relieve them of particularly difficult and disruptive prisoners. These constituted what may be called the 'rescue cases', in that Grendon effectively rescued either the system from particular individuals, or particular individuals from the system—or indeed both. For example, one man was transferred from Wandsworth within the first few months of an eight-year sentence after concern had been expressed about his extreme vulnerability to the pressures of a conventional prison regime. He had withdrawn from routine social activities and had made a serious suicide attempt, thus representing a risk to himself and a management problem for the establishment.

The third avenue into Grendon was reserved for the lifer population. Men serving life sentences could be admitted to Grendon by any of the previously discussed routes, but, in addition, the Prison Department division responsible for adult male life-sentenced prisoners could ask Grendon to admit a prisoner in order to undertake a detailed assessment of him. These men generally fell into two categories. First, there were those who were referred to enable Grendon to consider their life sentence career plans. The aim was to evaluate whether an individual could benefit from the therapeutic regime and, if not, to recommend alternative courses of action for him. Secondly, there were those for whom an assessment was required in order to judge the degree of risk they would pose to the public in the event of their release. Typically these were cases which were troublesome to the Department because of the serious and sometimes bizarre nature of their crimes, and because the men had remained 'unknown quantities' throughout their period of imprisonment.

One man, for example, was referred after he had served twelve years of a life sentence for rape. He was received into Grendon after he had spent two months on a pre-release employment scheme which had culminated in his being transferred back into closed conditions after his behaviour had 'caused concern' to hostel staff. It was reported that he had isolated himself from other residents and had engaged in what was perceived as 'anti-social behaviour'. He was accused of damaging property, walking around naked at weekends and having a short temper 'when criticized or faced with adversity'. His work record was said to have been satisfactory, but his home probation officer claimed that he had 'symptoms of sexual problems', although she did admit that she could not 'support her feelings with any concrete evidence'. Grendon was asked to admit this man with a view to assessing his potential risk to society, and with a particular request to examine his sexuality for evidence of associations between sex and violence.

Medical officers within the prison service were the primary gatekeepers to the therapeutic communities at Grendon. They played a pivotal role in composing the Grendon population and, for this reason, it was important to discover how they viewed Grendon and how, in practice, they made their decisions to refer certain prisoners rather than others. A sample of thirty doctors was interviewed, drawn from all Prison Department regions and from a wide range of prisons, although most were based in either local (47 per cent) or category B (33 per cent) establishments. About a third of the sample were senior medical officers, just over a quarter were medical officers, and a further third of the sample consisted of visiting consultant psychiatrists who were normally based within the National Health Service.[4] Not all the doctors had psychiatric training but, as a group, they were highly experienced in prison work: the mean length of their prison service was just under ten years, and they had spent an average of eight years in their current establishment.

Among these physicians there proved to be a high level of agreement about the purposes which Grendon served within the prison system. Regardless of their status within the system, or the type of establishment in which they worked, three-quarters thought that Grendon's primary function was to provide a rehabilitative treatment resource. Six of them (one in five) also thought that it acted as a departmental showpiece, serving as a public relations exercise by demonstrating that, at least somewhere in the system, some efforts were being devoted to the rehabilitation of prisoners. Only two doctors in the entire sample thought that its purpose was to provide a means of controlling inmates who represented a problem

[4] One principal medical officer and two part-time medical officers completed the total sample.

for prison discipline, and only five (one in six) thought that its function was to relieve other prisons of men who, for whatever reasons, strained the abilities of prison managements. In short, the majority view was that Grendon is primarily a therapeutic facility, principally functioning to offer treatment to a selected population of prisoners.

There also appeared to be relatively broad agreement amongst the doctors about the sorts of inmates which they thought Grendon was best suited to help. These men did not fall within particular offence categories, nor could they be identified by virtue of specific personal characteristics, such as their level of intelligence or their age. Instead, their typification was based upon individuals possessing certain kinds of problems, which were thought to be amenable to group psychotherapy, but which did not indicate mental illness. In the main these were behavioural problems associated with social interaction and the ability to communicate with other people, and were collectively diagnosed as symptomatic of a personality disorder. The manifestation of these problems was, however, variously described:

I think Grendon is designed to help those who, for want of a better word, are social inadequates. They crack on in life making error after error but without any real insight into how their behaviour is affecting other people. (Visiting Consultant Psychiatrist—category B prison.)

In my view it's designed particularly for those men who find it difficult to express their feelings in ways which the rest of society generally regard as socially acceptable. I'm thinking particularly here of men who have difficulties in controlling aggressive impulses and violent outbursts. (Senior Medical Officer—local prison.)

It's really, I think, to help people who are trapped in a cycle of behaviour which they're unhappy with but which they can't see any way out of. (Medical Officer—local prison.)

A third of the medical officers, however, also held the view that Grendon was only really designed to help those who were appropriately equipped to cope with the therapeutic process. These were men who were thought to be sufficiently robust to undertake group work and capable of withstanding and utilizing direct personal criticism.

Despite this relatively high degree of concordance, half the doctors stated that they lacked sufficient information about Grendon.

In the main, they wanted to know whether those responsible for therapy at Grendon had particular preferences for referrals of specific types of inmates. Virtually all these doctors felt that they were referring prisoners from within a vacuum, in which they were simply guessing which cases were appropriate. But a quarter of them also said that they needed more information about the treatment which was offered at Grendon. In particular, they wanted to know more about the nature of the psychotherapy which took place and the ways in which group work was related to the functioning of the therapeutic community. A similar proportion also wanted information about the effects of treatment upon the individual, both in terms of general reconviction rates and, more specifically, in relation to the progress of their own referrals.

Only one in three of the doctors had ever visited Grendon and, for some, this had been many years ago. Over half (57 per cent) said that most of their information had come from talking with medical officers who worked at Grendon and who had either visited their establishment, or had been introduced to them at conferences. Home Office circulars were mentioned by four out of ten physicians as useful sources of information about Grendon, but it seemed that these failed to reach those medical officers working in the system part-time and completely by-passed the visiting NHS consultants.

The task of referring prisoners to Grendon was not an everyday occurrence for these physicians: more than three-quarters (77 per cent) of the doctors estimated that, over the last year, they had referred fewer than one man every two months, and two of them had referred no-one at all during this period. Despite their wish for more information about referral criteria, the types of prisoners they were recommending were broadly in line with the specifications in the Circular Instruction and also mirrored their own view about the sort of inmate that Grendon was designed to help. Three-quarters said that they tended to refer men who were suffering from relatively mild personality disorders, which were manifested in their inability to relate to other people without recourse to interpersonal conflict or other kinds of social difficulties. Seven out of ten also argued that an important factor in their decision was whether they thought the man would be responsive to therapy. In this respect they made two fundamental assessments: first, whether the man was motivated to change; and secondly, whether he could reasonably be expected to contend with the stringency and rigours of group therapy. However, despite their general view that Grendon was not designed to help men who had committed particular types of offences, almost half (43 per cent) of the sample said that, in practice, they tended to refer certain categories of offender, notably men convicted of sex offences (33 per cent) and those convicted of violence (22 per cent).

In line with the Circular Instruction, the majority (77 per cent) of the doctors thought that age was an important factor when considering referral to Grendon. But this was a criterion which was variously interpreted and employed. Some felt that men should ideally be in their late 'teens or early twenties, because at this stage they were thought to be unlikely to have become 'set in their ways'. Others argued that the most promising age-group consisted of men in their thirties, who had reached a watershed in their lives and who were sufficiently experienced to recognize the fallibility of their previous behaviour. There was general agreement that it became increasingly difficult for individuals over the age of forty to effect changes in patterns of thought and conduct which had been established over many years. However, only one-third of the doctors said that they would rule out a referral on grounds of age alone.

The stage a man had reached in his sentence was also regarded as an influential factor. But whereas the Circular Instruction suggests that determinate-sentenced prisoners may be referred at any time during their sentence, as long as they have at least twelve months left in which to participate in the treatment programme, referring medical officers generally preferred to refer a man to Grendon towards the end of his sentence, so that he could anticipate release either directly from Grendon or shortly after transfer back into the system. A third of the sample, however, felt that the timing of a referral should not be linked at all to the stage of a man's sentence, but should be based solely on his needs.

Referring medical officers were asked why they thought there were so few ethnic minority inmates at Grendon. Virtually all of them admitted that they rarely referred prisoners of Afro-Caribbean (black) or Indo-Asian (Asian) origin. They claimed that in the course of their work they infrequently came across ethnic minorities, largely because these men were rarely referred to prison doctors for psychological problems. About a quarter of them thought that this was because black and Asian prisoners tended to be stereotyped by prison staff in ways which made any consideration of psychiatric intervention wholly irrelevant. Asian prisoners were thought to be typified as having inadequate skills in English to cope with 'talking therapies', whereas black prisoners were thought to be stereotyped as intrinsically volatile and unamenable to any kind of social control:

I just don't see them. And I think there may be a number of reasons for that, but I think that probably the main one is that the management of the prison define the Afro-Caribbean prisoners as culturally alien to the kind of treatment offered at Grendon, or come to that, anything else that they might see as a 'soft' option. (Medical Officer—local prison.)

I think this is the same in psychiatry in general. People have difficulty in understanding them and distinguishing their problems or their illnesses from cultural norms. (Visiting Consultant Psychiatrist—category B prison.)

However, over half (56 per cent) the doctors interviewed thought that the reason they saw very few ethnic minority prisoners was that black and Asian inmates selected themselves out of the picture and failed to seek help from prison staff of any description. The explanations offered for this were varied:

The point is that it's often the prisoner who initiates the referral and I think that possibly a lot of ethnic minorities don't even know about it. So they don't put themselves forward. (Part-time Medical Officer—local prison.)

I think that ethnic minorities are suspicious of psychiatric facilities. In a way it's a fear of the unknown. It's very much rooted in their culture, especially first and second generation Asians. (Senior Medical Officer—dispersal prison.)

Many blacks feel alienated from this society and particularly from the prison. So anything on offer just isn't taken up. I've never had an ethnic minority prisoner come to me saying he wanted help. (Senior Medical Officer—local prison.)

Among a small minority of doctors, however, a less systemic view was adopted which may be summarized in this extreme example of racial prejudice, which was directed at both Asian and Afro-Caribbean prisoners:

Perhaps I shouldn't say this but if you want my honest opinion, they're dim, feckless and don't take life seriously. They're not motivated one iota. A lot of them don't speak very good English and in general they set up a huge barrier to any kind of communication. (Visiting Consultant Psychiatrist—local prison.)

Although prison doctors were the primary gate-keepers to Grendon, the process of referral frequently involved a wide range of other groups. Three-quarters of the physicians interviewed said that other prison staff would refer inmates to them specifically for consideration for Grendon. Typically, it was the prison probation officers who were thought to be most active in this respect, although, in some prisons, psychologists were also said to exert a significant influence. Fewer than a third of the doctors thought that the uniformed staff ever played a part in promoting a referral to Grendon. But it was the inmate population which, along with the doctors themselves, was thought to provide the major driving force. Half the sample said it was fairly evenly divided as to whether the suggestion to go to Grendon was initiated by the candidate or by themselves, and a further one in five thought that the idea usually originated with the inmate. But despite the highly active part played by prisoners in launching the referral process, it was a role which was inevitably limited by their relative lack of power. Virtually all (93 per cent) the doctors said that they did not refer everyone who asked to go to Grendon, but that they used their discretion to sift out those they considered to be unsuitable candidates. Only two of the doctors thought that the man's offence was a relevant criterion for such a decision, and only six said that they would rule someone out solely on the basis that his problems were too severe, or too mild, to warrant referral to Grendon. Instead, the decision tended to be based upon an assessment of personal qualities and a projected view as to how the individual might be expected to respond to therapy. Most notably, the question they asked themselves was whether the man before them would run a serious risk of being damaged by undergoing group therapy.

Hence, there appeared to be a considerable degree of agreement among prison doctors about how the process of referral *actually* operated, and about how it *should* be operated. The criteria which underlay their decision-making were also broadly consistent, although they were given different weights when addressing different questions. So, for example, when they were considering what kind of prisoner Grendon was designed to help, what kind of prisoner they typically referred, and what kind of prisoner they tended to sift out, the same factors came into play but were given different levels of importance according to the decision which had to be made.

The Referrals

Over an eighteen-month period from 1 June 1987 to 31 December 1988, Grendon received 332 referrals to the adult treatment wings.

Prisons

The referrals came from a total of forty-six establishments in all four regions. Some prisons, however, referred significantly more inmates than others (see Table 3.1). Almost half (45 per cent) of all

Table 3.1. *Number and proportion of total referrals, by prison*

Establishment	Number of referrals	% Total referrals
Wandsworth	76	23
Wakefield	23	7
Liverpool	19	6
Long Lartin	18	5
Dartmoor	15	4

referrals came from five establishments, with Wandsworth accounting for almost one-quarter (23 per cent) of the total number. The high number of referrals from Wandsworth might be accounted for by the location at this prison of a large Rule 43 unit, housing vulnerable prisoners who might be deemed particularly likely to benefit from therapeutic intervention.

Most referrals were received from local prisons (54 per cent, see Table 3.2), but this largely reflected the high proportion of referrals from Wandsworth. If Wandsworth is excluded the total number of

Table 3.2. *Number and proportion of total referrals, by type of prison*

Type of prison	Number of referrals	% Total referrals
Local	180	54.2
Dispersal	56	16.9
Category B	30	9.0
Category C	36	10.8
Category D (Open)	30	9.0
TOTAL	332	100

referrals from the remaining local establishments stands at just under one-third (31 per cent) of the total. The dispersal system was next in line in terms of its contribution to the total number of referrals received (17 per cent). Fewer men were referred from each of the remaining categories of establishment.

There were approximately twenty-five adult male establishments which had not referred anyone to Grendon over the eighteen months studied. These were evenly distributed across all regions and tended to be category C or open prisons. However, they also included five local prisons which had not referred anyone during this period, although in some cases this may have been due to the fact that these establishments primarily contain remand prisoners (see Appendix 1).

Types of Referrals

Two-thirds (66 per cent) of referrals were made on behalf of men serving relatively long sentences of five years or more and 15 per cent of all referrals were for lifers (see Table 3.3). Those serving less than three years were rarely referred, accounting for only twenty-two men, or 7 per cent, over the eighteen-month period studied.

Table 3.3. *Number and proportion of total referrals, by sentence length*

Sentence length	Number of referrals	% Total referrals
Less than 3 years	22	6.6
3 years up to 5 years	92	27.7
5 years up to 10 years	134	40.4
10 years plus	35	10.5
Life	49	14.8
TOTAL	332	100

Note: Mean sentence length for determinate sentence prisoners = 70.6 months, s.d. = 33.75.

At the time of referral to Grendon approximately three-quarters (72 per cent) of the prisoners had more than two years to run to their EDR, the mean length being twenty-nine months (see Table 3.4). Only 3 per cent were referred with less than a year left to serve.

Table 3.4. *Number and proportion of total referrals, by time left to EDR*

Time left to EDR at time of referral	Number of referrals	% Total referrals
Less than 12 months	10	3.0
1 year up to 2 years	83	25.2
2 years up to 3 years	92	27.9
3 years up to 5 years	74	22.4
5 years plus	23	7.0
Life	48	14.5
TOTAL	330*	100

Notes: Mean sentence length for determinate sentence prisoners = 29.25 months, s.d. = 13.15.

   * 2 cases missing data.

Outcome of Referrals

Of the 332 cases which had been referred over the eighteen months studied, 111 (33 per cent) had been received into Grendon; 128 (39 per cent) were on the waiting list; and ninety-three (28 per cent) had been either been rejected or had withdrawn their applications (see Table 3.5).

Table 3.5. *Number and proportion of total referrals, by outcome*

Outcome of referral	Number of referrals	% Total referrals
Received in Grendon	111	33.4
Rejected	54	16.2
Withdrawn application	39	11.7
Pending on waiting list	128	38.6
TOTAL	332	100

The outcome of a referral was related both to the length of sentence and the length of time an individual had left before his EDR. The shorter the sentence, and the shorter the time before his EDR, the less likely the individual was to succeed in getting to Grendon. Those serving less than five years accounted for two-thirds of all those who failed to get to Grendon (see Table 3.6). Almost nine out of ten referrals who were serving less than three years, and almost half of those sentenced to between three and five years, were refused or opted out, in comparison with fewer than one in five of those with sentences of more than five years.

Table 3.6. Number and proportion of referrals refused or opted out, by sentence length

Sentence length	Numbers refused or opted out	% Each length band refused or opted out	% Total refused or opted out
Less than 3 years	19	86	20
3 years–less than 5 years	43	47	46
5 years–less than 10 years	21	16	23
10 years plus	3	8	3
Life	7	14	8
TOTAL	93		100

Notes: Mean: 49.6; s.d. = 23.4.
  $\chi^2 = 105.79$; df = 6; P < 0.01.

The outcome of a referral was not related to the type of prison from which it had come, nor was it related to whether the referral came from a specific prison. When the top five referring prisons were compared, there were no significant differences in the proportions of their referrals which were received into Grendon, nor in the proportions which were refused or opted out.

Of the referrals which were not admitted into Grendon, half were rejected because the man had too short a time to his EDR. Very few (7 per cent) were rejected because they had been deemed unsuitable for therapy after being interviewed by a Grendon doctor on a recruitment drive. But a relatively high proportion of those who were not admitted had chosen to withdraw their applications (42 per cent). Their reasons for opting out were not known. They might have felt that they had overcome the problems which initially stimulated the referral; they might have been transferred to what they regarded as a comfortable location and wanted to stay there; they might have been deterred by what they had subsequently heard about Grendon; or they might have received help for their difficulties elsewhere in the system.

Consistent with Grendon's policy of attempting to take prisoners towards the end of their sentences, three-quarters of those who were received into the establishment over this period had less than three years to run before their EDR, although only a quarter had less than two years to serve (see Table 3.7).

Most (71 per cent) of those who were received into Grendon over the eighteen-month period had been on the waiting list for

Table 3.7. *Number and proportion of referrals received into Grendon, by time left to EDR*

Time left to EDR	Numbers received	% Received
Less than 12 months	2	1.8
1 year up to 2 years	26	23.4
2 years up to 3 years	55	49.5
3 years up to 5 years	15	13.5
5 years plus	1	0.9
Life	12	10.8
TOTAL	111	100

Notes: Mean = 28.04; s.d. = 9.78.
χ^2 = 185.96; df = 10; P < 0.01.

less than six months. On average, inmates waited just over four months for their place.[5]

These findings stand in striking contrast to those of John Gunn and his colleagues, which were based upon a sample of new receptions to Grendon drawn between June 1971 and May 1972. At that time the inmates admitted were serving shorter sentences, averaging three and a half years, as opposed to almost six years today. In consequence, they were sent to Grendon earlier in their prison careers: three-quarters were received within the first year of their imprisonment, in comparison with 14 per cent today. More than half (55 per cent) of the receptions who were interviewed during the course of our research had arrived at some point within the second year, although a substantial minority (31 per cent), usually men serving very long terms, or life sentences, had already spent over two years in the system. The time the prisoner had left to serve was also shorter in the earlier work: an average of just under sixteen months, in contrast to twenty-eight months in this study.

The Assessment Unit

When inmates first arrived at Grendon they were accommodated in the assessment unit where their suitability for treatment was evaluated. This unit was originally set up in 1986 in response to a recommendation by ACTRAG that the pre-existing and somewhat

---

[5] In practice inmates tend to wait about twice as long as this, since they measure the period from the time the referring medical officer says he will make the referral, and not from the time Grendon actually receives the 1080 referral.

limited arrangements for assessing new referrals should be replaced by a discrete induction unit.[6] Prior to the opening of this unit all receptions spent a short period of assessment in the hospital, where they were accommodated alongside men who were awaiting transfer back to other prisons, either because they had completed therapy or because they were considered unsuitable for Grendon.

The assessment unit was established for the express purpose of 'enabling the process of assessment to be in greater depth, providing a more specific treatment programme for those selected, and making possible a more prompt return to the originating establishment for those assessed as not likely to benefit from the treatment offered' (paragraph 7). It was also suggested that the new induction process should provide an introduction to group work prior to the inmate being exposed to the 'more intense atmosphere' on the therapy wings.

In 1987 a meeting was held at Grendon, to which all the psychiatrists, psychologists and wing principal officers were invited, in order to discuss the role of the assessment unit and the service it should provide for the therapy wings. These staff arrived at four proposals, which were largely consistent with the ACTRAG recommendations. The first was that the unit should act as an information-gathering agency, collating and summarizing relevant details about each prisoner; the second was that it should filter out those unsuitable for treatment; thirdly, it should prepare prisoners for therapy by slowly weaning them off 'nick culture' and exposing them to alternative ways of relating to staff and other prisoners; and, finally, they argued that it should co-ordinate all receptions and transfers, and allocate prisoners to wings on a random basis as vacancies occurred. Unlike ACTRAG, however, they did not consider it appropriate for staff on the assessment unit to develop a detailed treatment programme for each prisoner. This was a task which, they believed, should fall to the separate wing communities.

Each prisoner usually remained in the assessment unit for approximately eight weeks. During this period a dossier on him was compiled consisting of a report from his personal officer, reports and test data from education and psychology staff, and, subject to availability, any previous psychiatric or probation reports prepared for the court. In addition, there was a General

---

[6] Home Office (1957), *First Report of the Advisory Committee on the Treatment Regime at Grendon*, para. 7.

Health Questionnaire (which was typically used by the personal officer as a means of 'breaking the ice' with the prisoner to get him to talk about himself), the inmate's prison disciplinary record, and a variety of other documents from his prison record, such as the original letter of referral from the prison doctor, which may or may not be available in individual cases.

Assessment meetings were held once a week and were typically attended, wherever possible, by the psychiatrist responsible for the unit, the probation officer, the education tutor, the psychologist who conducted the battery of tests, and any of the uniformed officers who happened to be on duty. When the unit was first set up, all constituent staff were consulted and all had a vote regarding each prisoner's suitability for treatment. This led, however, to a number of decisions to reject from Grendon individuals whom the psychiatrist felt should stay. In these situations the doctor was faced with either accepting the outcome, or overruling the staff group. In the event he chose to resolve these difficulties by redefining and clarifying the process by which decisions should be taken. He took the view that all medical, psychiatric, and psychotherapeutic treatment was ultimately the responsibility of the doctor and that the final decision regarding access to therapy should therefore rest with him. Thus, the process of assessment which was in operation at the time of our fieldwork was one in which all staff members were consulted and served as advisors to the psychiatrist. Inmates on the unit played no part at all in deciding who was, and who was not, suitable for treatment.

The process by which prisoners were assessed became more standardized as the unit became better established. The evaluation of a prisoner's suitability for transfer to the therapeutic communities entailed a close scrutiny of the extent to which he had met certain criteria. At the bottom line, the man had to be perceived by the staff as having problems, and these tended to be defined and assessed in the context of his offending and his behaviour on the unit. But, in addition, these problems had to be seen to fall within the realm of Grendon's expertise. In essence these were defined as problems which stemmed from an individual's difficulties in interpersonal relationships, and, on this basis, virtually everyone was deemed to qualify. The candidate also had to be defined as willing to participate in the therapeutic programme and as motivated to modify his attitudes and behaviour. In other words, staff had to believe that the man wanted to change. Again, the overwhelming majority were presumed to qualify and would only be disqualified as unmotivated if their behaviour in the unit indicated a demonstrable lack of concern to participate in the treatment process. Finally, a man had to be deemed capable of withstanding the rigours of the therapeutic process. What was required here was an ability to participate and understand what was going on in therapy. This criterion related to the intellectual capacity and 'psychological fibre' of the individual and stood apart from the others in that it was relevant to the assessment process only in so far as it *disqualified* the individual from the treatment programme.

During an eight-month period a total of sixty-seven assessment cases were observed and, of these, thirteen (19 per cent) were defined as unsuitable for therapy and transferred back to their referring establishment.[7] Of these thirteen, ten were rejected because it was felt that, although they had problems, and might be motivated to do something about them, they lacked the necessary capacity to cope with the rigours and demands of group therapy. Typically, these were men of low intelligence, having been graded within the lowest two categories (D or E) on the Ravens Matrices, and were described as being 'generally inadequate'.[8] It was feared that for most of these men, exposure to the intensive programmes in the communities would be intellectually perplexing and potentially emotionally damaging. The view was that a group psychotherapy approach would do them more harm than good and that what was required was either one-to-one therapy or, more commonly, educational/training programmes which would provide basic skills and an opportunity for these men to experience a sense of achievement.

It is worth noting that the factors which staff on the assessment unit took into account when evaluating an inmate's suitability for treatment were broadly in line with the criteria which shaped the referral practices of doctors in other establishments. Yet, although intellectual capacity and 'psychological fibre' were the most important variables in determining whether an inmate was assessed as

---

[7] A higher proportion of receptions on to the assessment unit were returned to the system because some men decided for themselves that they did not want to stay at Grendon and they were therefore not formally assessed.

[8] Ravens Standard Progressive Matrices. This test measures non-verbal intelligence and is used as a guide to general intelligence. The scores are classified from A (well above average) to E (well below average).

unsuitable for membership of the therapeutic communities, the 1987 Circular Instruction, which details specific criteria for selection, contains no reference to these qualities.

Staff Views on Inmate Suitability and the Process of Selection

About half of the officers interviewed felt that they had no understanding of the basis upon which inmates were selected for Grendon. Most of these men, however, were officers on the treatment wings who felt distanced from the process of selection. All the regular officers on the assessment unit claimed to know how the selection process worked and were able to cite specific criteria which they thought shaped the procedure. In the main, these matched the criteria detailed in the 1987 Circular Instruction, but also included the need for a sufficient IQ to benefit from therapy. However, the majority of staff who identified criteria for selection, including those on the assessment unit, maintained that factors which related to the management and organization of the prison system were also taken into account when reaching a decision. What they were alluding to here were the so-called 'rescue cases', which they claimed represented political favour-giving and reflected the 'old pals' network of senior management. Such practices, they argued, raised questions about the purposes which Grendon was intended to serve: whether it was meant to be a sophisticated control unit, a sanctuary for vulnerable prisoners, a treatment facility, or a combination of all three.

Despite the fact that relatively few officers expressed familiarity with the selection process three-quarters of them believed that it was possible to identify certain types of inmate who were particularly suited to the Grendon regime. Most typically staff thought that they had the greatest success with violent and aggressive prisoners, who were said to change visibly as they learnt alternative ways of dealing with feelings of anger, frustration and antipathy towards authority. Virtually all officers (92 per cent), however, felt that the vast majority of prisoners in the prison system could benefit from some exposure to the therapeutic communities at Grendon. And although an inmate's motivation to change was believed to be an important consideration in the selection process, the view expressed was that this was not necessarily crucial since, in some cases, the experience of being in Grendon could induce in a man the recognition of his potential for change, and thus awaken his desire to participate in therapy.

Sex offenders constituted one category of prisoner which, it was claimed, Grendon had developed notable expertise in treating.[9] Yet the uniformed staff were divided in their views regarding the suitability of these men. One in seven officers identified sex offenders as particularly suitable for Grendon, but an equal number defined them as eminently unsuitable. Other types of prisoners they designated as unlikely candidates included drug addicts, serious professional criminals motivated by financial gain, and those loosely described as 'inadequate'.

Doctors and psychologists expressed varying degrees of knowledge and understanding of the prevailing selection procedures. However, their general views about the criteria which informed the process were largely in line with those of the uniformed staff. Similarly, their appraisals of the types of prisoners most and least suited to Grendon reflected those outlined by the officers. But where the depictions drawn by the uniformed staff were portrayed with broad brush strokes, those constructed by the doctors and psychologists represented more detailed characterizations which combined specific psychological and behavioural features, producing notional profiles of ideal typical candidates:

My best bet is a bright aggressive recidivist who is trapped in an adolescent pattern of impetuosity.

Ideally, someone who is relatively intelligent, anxious, introverted and motivated to change their offensive/offending behaviours.

Profiles of those considered to be most unsuitable were similarly detailed:

I'm unhappy about acquisitive offenders and drug offenders for whom short-term satisfactions appear to outweigh long-term benefits.

Clearly those suffering from psychoses, organic brain damage and the clinically depressed. But also those who are grossly socially inadequate, compulsive liars, drug addicts and some paedophiles, especially if they are middle-aged or elderly.

Despite a number of humorously cynical comments about the existing process of selecting prisoners for Grendon, two-thirds of

[9] Home Office (1987), Prison Department Circular Instruction 21/1987, Appendix.

the uniformed staff, and all the doctors and psychologists, felt that, on the whole, the right inmates were reaching the therapy wings. One doctor, however, did mirror the concerns of the officers that extraneous, systemic factors were entering into the equation:

Broadly, yes, the right inmates are getting through. Although there has been some distortion of late due to such factors as the shortage of Rule 43 and category B security places.

The work of the assessment unit was generally valued within the institution. Three-quarters of the uniformed staff approved its introduction, favouring a separate unit of this kind rather than a system of direct entry on to the treatment wings.[10] The virtue of the assessment unit was said to lie in its performance of three specific functions. First, eight out of ten officers placed value upon the role it played as a coarse sieve, sifting out those inmates who were palpably unsuitable for treatment. Secondly, seven out of ten staff believed it served a useful purpose in providing a period of induction into Grendon. This was typically described as a process of acclimatization, or being 'Grendonized', in which traditional values associated with 'nick culture' would begin to be dismantled. Finally, a small number of officers (29 per cent), in the main comprising those who were working in the assessment unit, emphasized the importance of the information-gathering service which was intended to assist staff on the treatment wings to get to know their new recruits.

Most (71 per cent) of the officers, all the psychologists, and all but one of the doctors, agreed with the assessment unit's policy of admitting inmates towards the end of their sentences so that they might be released straight into the community from Grendon. But, despite the fact that the majority of the civilian and uniformed staff endorsed the guidelines for referral set out in the Circular Instruction, three-quarters of the officers, and all the psychiatrists and psychologists, identified improvements they would like to see made to the selection process. For the most part, their concerns

[10] The few who expressed a preference for direct entry were mainly located on the one wing which, at the time the officers were interviewed, received inmates directly from the sending establishments. In the main, these officers felt that the admission of prisoners to the treatment wings should be under the control of the wing management. They felt that the intimate knowledge which wing staff had of the inter-personal dynamics of their community enabled selection procedures to take account of the social balance of the population.

related to the need to develop a clearer definition of the bases of selection and a more rigorous and effective application of standards. One suggestion put forward by both psychologists and the uniformed staff was that Grendon should develop more specific criteria in accordance with its defined objectives and realm of expertise.

The selection process could be vastly improved by defining what Grendon does, identifying who benefits most and least from Grendon and thus being able to provide positive criteria for admission.

Another recommendation, which largely underlined the referring doctors' perceptions of the therapeutic purpose of Grendon, was that the establishment should desist from providing favours to the prison system; in other words, the process of selection should operate solely on a prisoner-based system of needs and not on an organization-based system of needs. It was also thought that a more stringent and effective application of standards could be achieved by an increase in the level of personal contact and exchange of information between Grendon and the referring establishments. One proposition was that Grendon doctors, and possibly members of the uniformed staff, should visit other prisons more frequently in order to weed out unsuitable candidates before they reached the assessment unit.

Inmates' Experience at Referral and Reception

In order fully to understand the process by which men travel to, and eventually arrive at, the gates of the establishment, it is necessary to take into account the inmates' experience of the journey and, in particular, to consider the reasons they gave for coming to Grendon and the role they felt they had played in achieving their transfer.

Referral to Grendon

The descriptions which inmates gave of the events leading up to their reception into Grendon were not incompatible with the doctors' portrayal of their referral practices. Half the seventy-one men who were interviewed within the first two months of their reception into the assessment unit said that they had known of Grendon's existence prior to any consideration of their referral.

Usually, men had heard about Grendon on what they called the 'prison grapevine', from other inmates they had met either on their current sentence or on previous sentences. The initial proposition that they themselves might consider going to Grendon appeared to emanate from a number of different sources, both inside the prison and outside, including doctors, family and friends, solicitors and judges. Only one-third of the men said that the original suggestion had come from a prison medical officer or visiting psychiatrist. A quarter of them maintained that they themselves had initiated the idea of coming to Grendon without prompting from anyone else.

Since all referrals to Grendon must be made by a doctor, it came as no revelation that all the interviewees had discussed the prospect of coming to the institution with either a prison medical officer or a visiting psychiatrist. But virtually all of them (90 per cent) had also talked over the idea with other people. In the main it was other inmates who were consulted, in fact two-thirds of the receptions said that they had spoken about it to fellow prisoners, many of whom had themselves spent time at Grendon. Four out of every ten had also discussed the matter with probation officers in the prison, and a third had spoken of it with their home probation officers. Fewer than one in five had talked over the idea with prison officers.

There was wide variation in the level of detail and the accuracy of the information which the men had received about Grendon at their referring establishments. A quarter had been given no information at all about the therapeutic regime, but most (78 per cent) had been told that Grendon was a therapeutic community, or that it ran group therapy. None the less, despite their having been told about the regime, it is questionable whether many of the inmates understood, or had a clear conception of, what it all meant. What they did know, however, was that Grendon was a place where they could get help, and was thus a unique resource within the prison system.

In general, the newly received men had heard very little adverse or distorted comment about the prison and, where they had, it tended to come from inmates who had either been rejected by Grendon or who had never been there. One in five had been told that Grendon was a 'nonce prison', full of sex offenders; and one in ten had heard that it was a 'nut-house' or 'lunatic asylum'.

Most (78 per cent) of the receptions interviewed had come to

Grendon directly from their referring establishment and, from the time of their interview with the doctor, had waited on average between eight and nine months for their place, even though, as noted earlier, the average time on the waiting list was just over four months. About half the men reported that they had encountered difficulties in getting to Grendon; most commonly, the complaint related to the time they had been kept waiting and the lack of communication about their referral during this period.

I spoke to Doctor X and he said it would all be arranged. But then nothing happened. No-one came back to me and when I tried to find out what was going on the P.O. [principal officer] just told me I'd got to wait and be patient. But I was worried in case they'd lost my papers or changed their minds. Then after about six months I was asked if I was still interested in going to Grendon and when I said 'Yes', they said, 'OK, pack your bags, you're off tomorrow'.

However, one in ten of the receptions said that the major obstacle they had faced had been in persuading the medical officer that they were suitable candidates for Grendon.

I got turned down by the doctor at X prison, who said that I wouldn't get into Grendon. So I petitioned the Home Office, but before anything came of that I was moved to Y Prison and put down to see Dr. Y and she said I could see the Grendon doctor when he came up.

Five other men felt that their paths to Grendon had been hindered by other prison staff, most notably prison officers.

When I applied to see the doctor at X prison I was told that I couldn't. So I smashed all the windows in my cell and refused to plead at my adjudication, so they'd think I was insane and put me down for the psychiatrist. But instead they just shipped me out to Y Prison, and when I asked about Grendon there the officers just laughed and said 'no chance.' So I barricaded myself in my cell because I thought they were playing head-games with me. Then I saw Dr. Y and he must have sorted it out.

Reasons for Coming to Grendon

The Circular Instruction of 1987 emphasizes the voluntary nature of treatment at Grendon.[11] The effect of this was reflected in the fact that almost every one (96 per cent) of the men who were interviewed said that it had been wholly their own choice to come to

[11] Home Office (1987), Prison Department Circular Instruction 21/1987, para. 4.

Grendon, and that they had not felt pushed or pressurized into the decision. Despite their status as prisoners and the structural constraints upon their decision-making, it is important to note that there were only three men, all of whom were serving determinate sentences, who felt that they had been obliged to comply with what they considered to be the forceful recommendation of the medical officer. Even so, none of these men had been unwilling to give the place a try.

A number of reasons appeared to underlie inmates' decisions to come to Grendon. Almost a quarter said that they had suffered a personal crisis in the prison system and had felt a desperate need to seek help. One man, for example, had suffered what he described as a 'breakdown' after his wife had initiated divorce proceedings and refused to allow him any contact with his children. Another had attempted suicide shortly after receiving a life sentence for the murder of his baby daughter. One in ten of the sample stated that they had come to Grendon, at least in part, because they had been unable to cope within a conventional prison regime. Typically this latter group consisted of men who had reacted to their imprisonment by becoming emotionally withdrawn and socially isolated.

Inmates were specifically asked whether the decision to come to Grendon had been influenced by the desire for an amelioration of their prison lifestyles. Although two-thirds of the inmates had spent some part of their sentence in segregation under Rule 43, and for half of these the period spent in these conditions was in excess of twelve months, fewer than one in five of them admitted that the opportunity to avoid these restrictive conditions had entered into the equation. One in ten had thought that doing time in Grendon would be an easy option; and four inmates confessed that at least part of the reason for coming was that they had been bored and wanted a change. The possibility of scoring points with the Parole Board and securing an early release had also been influential for 14 per cent of the sample.

But for nine out of ten new receptions the main impetus to come to Grendon had stemmed from a need to resolve specific problems and to relieve their sense of personal unease and discontent. For the great majority (84 per cent) of the men interviewed, concern focused upon their criminality and the risk of their re-offending, but half of the men also recognized that their problems related to other personal and social difficulties. Indeed, two-thirds of the sample hoped to gain personal and social as well as criminal rehabilitation from their therapy at Grendon. For example, one 29-year-old, serving four years for indecently assaulting a teenage boy, said:

I wanted to discover myself and know what I want out of life. I know that seducing young boys isn't really me—it's the same with drugs. I want to learn to socialize in situations and not feel insecure or inferior.

Another man in his late twenties, who was serving six years for robbery and possession of amphetamines, commented:

I've got to learn to handle problems rationally without running to violence or drugs. And my personal relationships—I've got a lot to sort out there. Because I'm frightened, I can't get by without lying or conning people, literally every day. All I want really is to be myself without making out I'm something better. I want to show them that I do care and love them without it making me look weak or soft.

There were, however, important differences in this respect between men of different ages. Younger inmates in their twenties were significantly more likely than those over 30 to adopt this broader and more holistic view of their problems.[12] Men in the older age groups were much more likely to define their problems solely in terms of their criminality.[13]

A 49-year-old serving five years for indecent assault expressed a degree of curiosity:

I want to know what's happened to me, why I've changed. For years I was a burglar—and that's all. But now this. I've got to know why and stop. I can't keep coming back to these places, I'm too old. It will be a long time the next time.

And another man aged 39, imprisoned for five years for rape and incest, claimed:

I've got to sort out the last five years of my life. I can't let it happen again. I have to try to understand why I did it, why my offence.

As these examples show, the problems which the men define are not always homogeneous or one-dimensional. Indeed, at this early

[12] 66% of the 21–30 age group, compared with 36% of those aged over 30. $\chi^2 = 5.01$, df = 1, P < 0.05.

[13] 21% of those in their twenties; 40% of those in their thirties; and 66% of those aged over forty. $\chi^2 = 6.20$, df = 1, P < 0.05.

stage of their career in Grendon, half the sample were able clearly to articulate specific difficulties in ways which indicated some understanding of their inter-connected nature:

It was appalling of me to abuse my daughters' bodies, as well as their trust in me as their father. But I don't believe I'm sick. I think I'm emotionally immature, vulnerable. I know it's got something to do with my failure to cope with success. I was a successful . . . at the time, a local hero, and it just went straight to my head. I had affairs with other women. And my parents split up after more than thirty years together. But I just tucked away my feelings and refused to think about it. It was the power that went to my head. I wanted power over my children, but it came out as sexual, when what it was that I wanted was their love and admiration.

I couldn't cope outside; ever since I was 16 I've been in and out of prison. But I hate prison—I want another kind of life, a normal one like everyone else. But I've got no confidence and I feel unworthy and I know that's the main reason I drink. It's a vicious circle though, because when I drink I just get rejected and then I hit out.

Lack of self-confidence was, in fact, the most common problem, and was mentioned by half those interviewed, regardless of their age or offence. Similarly, difficulties in developing or maintaining personal relationships, and an underlying sense of alienation and isolation from the rest of society, were also identified as significant problems by between a quarter and a third of the total sample.

Other types of problems, however, tended to vary according to the age of the prisoner and the nature of his offence. Younger inmates, under 30, were particularly likely to specify drugs and alcohol abuse as a problem and to identify difficulties in controlling their feelings of aggression (see Table 3.8).

Table 3.8. *Age of those citing drugs, alcohol abuse, and the control of aggression as problems*

Type of problem	21–30 years		30 years plus	
	Number	% of age group	Number	% of age group
Alcohol and drug abuse	19	50	9	27
Control of aggression*	21	55	7	21

Note: * $\chi^2 = 7.21$, df = 1, P < 0.01.

Certain types of offences were also found to be associated with those who claimed to have these types of problems. Men convicted of violent offences, which in the main consisted of wounding, robbery, and rape, were twice as likely as non-violent offenders to express concern about their abuse of drink and drugs (see Table 3.9).

Table 3.9. *Type of offence of those citing drugs and alcohol abuse as a problem*

Type of offence	Problem with drug/alcohol abuse	
	Number	% of offence group
Violent	24	45
Non-violent	4	22

However, those who had committed acts of violence did not uniformly admit to having difficulties in restraining their aggressive impulses. Men who had been convicted of offences of wounding and robbery were twice as likely to lay claim to this type of problem as all other offenders. Yet those convicted of sex offences appeared to be particularly disinclined to own up to any vulnerability at all in this area (see Table 3.10).

Table 3.10. *Type of offence of those citing aggression as a problem*

Type of offence	Problem with aggression	
	Number	% of offence group
Robbery and wounding	16	67
Sex offences	5	17
All other offences	7	41

Note: $\chi^2 = 13.97$, df = 2, P < 0.01.

Sexual problems were, perhaps not surprisingly, cited by two-thirds of those who had committed a sexual offence, but by only twelve per cent of all other offenders.[14] Men sentenced for rape, however, were conspicuous by their notable reserve: fewer than

[14] $\chi^2 = 18.03$, df = 1, P < 0.01.

half (42 per cent) felt that they had sexual problems, in contrast to eight out of ten 'other sex' offenders.[15] Yet it is interesting to note that, although the great majority of inmates claimed to have come to Grendon to address their offending behaviour, only thirteen men (18 per cent) included in their list of problems an inability to come to terms with the nature of their crime. Most of these were again sex offenders, typically men who had committed acts of indecency with children.[16]

Initial Impressions of Grendon

Prior to coming to Grendon, inmates had, between them, held a wide variety of ideas about what they thought the place would be like. On arrival, however, most (70 per cent) said that Grendon was different from what they had expected. Some had imagined it would be more like a hospital and had anticipated a different physical structure, typically one which was more modern and in a better state of physical repair. Others had envisaged a more conventional prison and had been surprised by the degree of freedom and the unusually relaxed atmosphere. But irrespective of their expectations, all the men interviewed had something positive to say about Grendon. The majority (70 per cent) focused upon the opportunity which Grendon offered them to obtain help with their problems and to initiate change.

All inmates thought that Grendon was markedly different from a conventional prison and this disparity was thought to be most apparent in the interested and caring approach of the staff. Almost everyone remarked upon the ways in which officers related to inmates as individual human beings, to be helped and listened to, rather than as prison numbers, to be counted and locked away. Their non-authoritarian ways of working were said by two-thirds of the men to foster a relaxed atmosphere on the wing which, for most, and especially for those who had spent time segregated under Rule 43, was unprecedented in the prison context.

The attitudes and behaviour of other prisoners were also claimed by two out of three inmates to be fundamentally different from those found in the conventional system:

[15] $\chi^2 = 5.15$, df = 1, P < 0.05.

[16] Sex offenders constituted fewer than half the total sample but almost two-thirds of those who included among their problems the inability to come to terms with the nature of their offences.

There's no comparison, it's a completely different world. You can talk about your feelings here without putting up an image to survive. In other prisons you feel unsafe—you're always looking over your shoulder. Here you can deal with difficulties by talking—there's no violence. Anyone does anything violent, they're out.

It's strange here, it's really weird. In a lot of respects it doesn't seem like a prison at all. The cons pull together, everywhere else they do the dirty on each other. Here there's no prison culture, no politics.

Men convicted of sex offences, who in other establishments would be segregated for their own protection, were said to benefit particularly from the safe environment and the new-found tolerance of their peers.

Despite these positive testimonies, 86 per cent of the inmates interviewed in the assessment unit said that they had experienced difficulties in coping with life in Grendon. For about a third of the men, these related to difficulties in adjusting to the unconventional relationships and patterns of behaviour which existed on the unit. But for most (73 per cent) the expectation that they should speak openly about themselves to the staff, and to other members of the wing, proved to be the main stumbling block. The men explained their anxieties largely by reference to three specific problems. First, some were inhibited by the sensitivity of the issues and the discomfort they felt about revealing intimate details of their past. Secondly, there were those who feared saying too much lest they 'fail' their assessment and end up facing the consequences back in the system. Finally, some of the men felt they lacked the necessary self-confidence to disclose matters of a highly personal nature to relative strangers.

In general, the men expressed optimism about their future Grendon careers. All but two inmates on the assessment unit anticipated that they would be passed as suitable to stay at Grendon, and two-thirds of the sample envisaged that they would stay in therapy for at least twelve months. As for their plans for the rest of their sentence, nearly three-quarters hoped that they would stay at Grendon until their release, either on parole or at EDR, and would not have to face transfer back into the system.

The Population

To conclude this chapter on getting into Grendon we should briefly document the demographic profile of those who eventually make it through the prison gates. A census of the Grendon population was taken on 2 February 1987, and again two years later, on 2 February 1989. This revealed that, due to some restructuring of the prison, there had been a significant reduction in the numbers of men receiving therapy. In 1987 the four treatment wings accommodated 138 inmates. By 1989 there were only three wings in operation, housing eighty-eight men. However, during this period the assessment unit had increased its population from twenty to twenty-seven. Hence, during the period of the research the capacity of the therapeutic facilities at Grendon was reduced by 27 per cent, from a total of 158 to 115.

Notwithstanding the diminution of the population the profile of the inmates in therapy remained remarkably constant over this period.[17] Most of the men were in their twenties and thirties, the mean age being 30 years, 4 months. In terms of their offending, they represented the 'heavy end of the market', in comparison with the prison population as a whole. Whereas only 50 per cent of the total adult sentenced prison population in 1987 were serving sentences of three years or more, the average length of sentence amongst the Grendon population was 6.5 years, and virtually all of them (97 per cent) were serving sentences of more than three years. Furthermore, as many as one in five of these men were lifers, in contrast to fewer than one in twelve of the national prison population. Their offence profile also differed markedly from that of the wider prison population, demonstrating an over-representation of crimes of sex and violence and an under-representation of the more common property offences (see Table 3.11).

Almost nine out of ten Grendon prisoners had previous convictions: the average score was eight, although over one third of them had eleven or more. This is similar to the national picture. A quarter of the Grendon population had previously been convicted of sex offences and just under one-third had previous convictions for violence. The majority (66 per cent) of men at Grendon had served previous custodial sentences and almost one in five of these men had served more than five years. There are, however, no national figures to compare this with.

Records of institutional behaviour prior to reception at Grendon revealed that two-thirds of Grendon's prisoners had disciplinary

---

[17] The data presented refer to the 1987 census, unless otherwise stated, as this includes most of the men who took part in the fieldwork.

Table 3.11. *The Grendon population and the total sentenced adult male prison population, by offence*

Offence	% Grendon population			% Total sentenced male prison population		
Violence against the person	33	⎫		22	⎫	
Sexual	28	⎬	81	6	⎬	37
Robbery	20	⎭		9	⎭	
Burglary/theft/ fraud	14			41		
Drugs	2			9		
Arson	4			n.a.		
Other	—			13		

offences listed against them. A quarter of the population had committed offences of violence against another inmate, and one in ten had been disciplined for violence against staff. What is perhaps most striking about the institutional history of the men at Grendon is that 40 per cent of them had spent some time during their current sentence on Rule 43 for their own protection. The Rule 43 population primarily included men convicted of sexual offences, but also contained those who had sought protection from the consequences of bad debts and 'grassing'.

The prior institutional behaviour of the men was the only feature which significantly differentiated the populations at the beginning and end of the two-year period of our fieldwork. The inmates on the therapy wings in 1989 had a history of more problematic behaviour in prison. The proportion with a record of disciplinary offending increased by one-fifth to include 76 per cent of the population. The number of men who had been segregated under Rule 43, either at their own request or by order of the governor, also rose by 17 per cent, to include over half (57 per cent) of all the men in therapy.

4

Therapy at Grendon

While Grendon is depicted as a therapeutic community, it is perhaps more accurate to conceive of it as a collection of therapeutic communities which co-operate and share resources within an overall institutional setting. The aim of this chapter is to examine in greater detail how the three treatment wings are structured and to consider what consequences this has for the accommodation of therapy. We begin by describing the ideal typical therapeutic community and discussing its history and theoretical foundations. The focus then turns to the communities in Grendon to examine the extent and ways in which they conform to this ideal type. Attention is directed to the degree of uniformity which exists across the separate communities in the everyday routines and procedures which facilitate therapeutic practice. Procedural and structural differences in the provision of therapy on the three wings are also reviewed and examined in relation to their effects upon two specific areas of interest: first, the length of time inmates spend at Grendon; and secondly, their participation in, and experience of, the therapeutic process.

The Ideal Typical Therapeutic Community

The part of Grendon with which this research was concerned was the three adult treatment wings, which operate as self-contained therapeutic communities. The origins of the therapeutic community can be traced back to the development of group psychotherapy at the turn of the century and, in particular, to the theoretical advances of Alfred Adler. In 1911 Adler broke away from the Freudian school of psychoanalysis to form his own school of individual psychology. This played down the significance of intra-psychic life, past events and deeply-buried unconscious determinants of behaviour that had preoccupied Classical Psychoanalysis, and accorded a far greater significance to the social context of human behaviour and the role of social forces in the origin and maintenance of neuroses. The *social development* of the individual thus lies at the heart of Adlerian theory, the premiss being that man begins life in a state of weak and defenceless inferiority from which he develops by striving for power and evolving a lifestyle which makes his existence within society both meaningful and purposeful. But a deviant path may be followed which fails to overcome the initial experience of inferiority and which leads to the donning of a facade, or false self, and a withdrawal into neurotic behaviour. Neurosis is thus defined as a developmental deficiency, a failure to learn how to overcome the original inferiority state: 'the patient is regarded as discouraged in terms of facing the demands of life and not as suffering from a diagnosable illness'.[1] Within this context, Adler regarded therapy as a re-educative process in which the therapist's role is that of enabling the patient to rediscover and understand the lifestyle he has assumed.

The founder of the concept of the therapeutic community was Maxwell Jones, a key innovator in group psychotherapy during the Second World War.[2] He established the first community at Belmont, later to be renamed the Henderson Hospital, and it is upon this model that the treatment regime at Grendon has been based. As a derivative of group psychotherapy and the Adlerian School of Individual Psychology, the therapeutic community gives predominance to social learning over psychoanalytic methods. In common with other forms of social therapy the concept of the therapeutic community presupposes the existence of a dialectical relationship between the individual and the society in which he lives. In other words, the individual both influences and is influenced by the wider social groups of which he is a member. Self-identity is consequently perceived as being shaped by social interaction and learning is viewed as a social activity which comes about as a result of an individual's relationship with his environment. Most individuals live, work and play in a number of different, and sometimes overlapping, social groups. It follows, therefore, that many emotional, psychiatric, and psychological

---

[1] Bloch, S. (1982), *What is Psychotherapy?* Oxford: Oxford University Press, 74.
[2] Jones, M. (1952), *Social Psychiatry: A Study of Therapeutic Communities*, London: Tavistock, and (1968), *Social Psychiatry in Practice: The Idea of a Therapeutic Community*, Harmondsworth: Penguin.

problems stem from disturbed relationships within these groups and will, in turn, be reflected in group behaviour. Within this theoretical framework the therapeutic community is concerned to deal with the difficulties which exist between people, rather than with the strictly Freudian problematic of the internalized self. The community thus functions to provide both an experimental forum and a social context within which sociopathic disturbances can be expressed, confronted and explored. It permits the opportunity for living-learning processes, whereby people live and work together in a setting where *social analysis*, rather than *psychoanalysis*, is practised and where staff and patients collaborate together and use the resultant group forces for therapeutic purposes. All this takes place within a system which is deliberately organized to promote the psychosocial treatment of mental and emotional disturbance, and in which all resources are mobilized in the interests of therapy.

The therapeutic community regime incorporates a strong behavioural component, whereby an individual's actions are examined with surgical precision and commented upon by the whole community. It entails the detailed and comprehensive assessment and analysis of behavioural patterns, wherein as much significance is granted to the questions of *where* and *when* the problem arises, and *what* maintains it, as is accorded to the questions which have preoccupied the psychoanalytic school of *why* the problem exists and *how* it has come into being. Therapy is goal-oriented and is geared towards the achievement of insight and a greater level of self-awareness. This, it is believed, frees the individual from automatically, and largely unconciously, following entrenched modes of thought and action and enables him to make choices about his future conduct so that ineffective or problematic patterns of behaviour can be avoided and an alternative and more satisfying lifestyle adopted. Equally importantly, however, engaging in therapeutic activities as a member of a therapeutic community also involves participation in mutual and reciprocal relationships with other members. Hence, in addition to furnishing a vivid setting in which problems may be explored and treated, the community also affords a climate in which feelings of isolation and alienation can be dissipated and a sense of belonging engendered. The therapeutic community, therefore, is designed to operate at the outer supportive levels, as well as the deeper exploratory levels, of psychotherapy.

The therapeutic process within the community is facilitated by group meetings, most notably by the small group and by assemblies involving the entire community. The *small group* usually consists of between six and eight members and is traditionally seen as the main forum of psychotherapeutic activity. Although shaped by a diverse set of operating principles, drawn from a range of theoretical schools, the particular form of group work practised within the therapeutic community has been most influenced by the interactionist, or interpersonalist, approach. This orientation derives from the work of Harry Stack Sullivan and the neo-Freudians, who adhere to the belief that human personality is largely the product of an individual's interaction with other significant people. In consequence, they hold that a person's psychological growth entails the development of a self-concept which is largely based on how he perceives the appraisal of himself by others.[3] The small group thus provides a setting in which members learn from one another, within a system of relationships in which interaction will inevitably be more varied and complex than in individual therapy. A wider range of life experiences may be drawn upon and an array of responses and attitudes received.

The *community meeting* differs from the small group not only in terms of its composition but also in terms of the purpose it is designed to fulfil. The community meeting serves a dual function: it provides a forum in which the routine practical functioning of the unit may openly be discussed, and it affords an opportunity to extend and incorporate a wider community participation in the therapeutic activity which originates within the small group.

Ideally, staff members of the therapeutic community regularly meet independently of these settings in order to share and clarify their understanding of events and to take any necessary decisions or formulate contingency plans. They may also meet to discuss practical issues and to air and confront their own interpersonal tensions and conflicts. Another common feature of the therapeutic community is the 'crisis meeting', comprising either the whole unit or one of the small groups. This is an irregular event which may be called at any time, by any member of the community, and is contrived to examine a crucial occurrence, such as an argument or an episode of destructive behaviour, in an honest and supportive manner. Finally, there may be a provision for 'family groups' and

[3] Sullivan, H. S. (1953), *Conceptions of Modern Psychiatry*, New York: Norton; Bloch, S. (1982), *What is Psychotherapy?* 99–100.

for psychodrama. Family groups may be initiated periodically by inviting a member's partner, parent, child, or other significant relatives to a meeting of the small group. This allows at least a three-way discussion and feedback on the member's problems, progress, and family relations, between the member, the partner or relative, and the rest of the group. In contrast, psychodrama facilitates the psychosocial re-creation of an individual's problems, by providing a context in which conflicts can be re-enacted, confronted, and examined by means of role play.

Three important structural elements characterize the organization and functioning of the ideal typical model of the therapeutic community, and set it apart from most other treatment-oriented institutions. The first is *permissiveness*, which ensures that rules and regulations are kept to the absolute minimum necessary for the safety and well-being of community members. The second is *democracy*, wherein the manifestation and operation of a formal hierarchy are played down and decision-making and responsibility are shared by the community as a whole. The third is *communalism*, whereby autonomy is extended as far as possible to the community to control its own boundaries and to develop its own culture and conditions. Together these three elements facilitate a dynamic environment which allows for disturbed feelings and relationships to be expressed and enacted, and for individual responsibility to be developed, through open communication and the shared examination of problems.

Throughout the 1950s and 1960s a widespread and enthusiastic idealism developed about the therapeutic community, and social psychotherapeutic methods were extended into wider rehabilitative ventures, such as the Richmond Fellowship hostels for psychiatric patients and hostels for drug addicts. In recent years, however, this idealism has waned, with the result that few contemporary therapeutic communities reflect the characteristics of the ideal typical model. This is due, according to Brown and Pedder, to a recognition of the limitations of social therapy and to a more general move in society away from permissiveness.[4] They cite the example of hostels for former drug addicts which, they claim, have retained, at least to some extent, the principles of democracy and communalism, but have replaced permissiveness by an authoritarian structure in which conformity is induced by means of a system of punishment and degradation.[5] The imposition of authoritarian structures within treatment-oriented institutions has been defended by the argument that staff must be afforded the freedom to make unilateral decisions in order to cope with emergencies and to maintain a safe structure and environment for all concerned. Safety and security are as pertinent for staff as they are for patients or clients, and an authoritarian framework, with a clearly defined order and accompanying rituals, can represent an attractive and additional defence against the anxieties which frequently arise from working within an institutionalized treatment setting.

Similarities in the Organization of Therapy on the Three Wings

Structural Organization

The three adult therapy wings demonstrated a number of similarities in their structure and organization. They had a regular staff of eight officers and aimed to maintain a population of between thirty-five and forty prisoners. Most interaction occurred among members of the same community, although opportunities for inter-wing contact occurred at work, in education, and during outside exercise periods or at the gymnasium. There was, however, no single timetable of events which operated throughout the institution. In order to ensure that essential jobs in the prison were adequately staffed, and that all inmates were afforded equal time for therapy, the wings were paired to operate alternating timetables. This ensured that while one wing was at work its partner wing was running groups or community meetings. It may be helpful, therefore, to describe a typical weekday programme which operated on one of the wings during the course of the research.

The day began at approximately 6.30 a.m. when the men, all of whom were accommodated in single cells, were unlocked by one of the duty officers. There were no alarm bells to signal this event. The men were required to make their beds and were then free to wash or shower in the communal recesses, have their breakfast, and, if they had time, to carry out small chores and to make any necessary applications to see the governor, doctor, probation offi-

[5] See above, 155–6.

cer, or any other service personnel in the prison, or to receive letters, visiting orders, or spend private cash. At 8.00 a.m. they had
to be ready to go to work. A few men remained on the wing,
employed as the wing cleaners, but most inmates left for jobs in
the prison kitchen, in the laundry, outside in the gardens, or in
other parts of the prison as cleaners or orderlies. At 10.00 a.m.
they arrived back on the wing and group therapy commenced. The
small groups sat for an hour, and group feedback lasted for a further half hour. Between 11.30 a.m. and midday the tables and
chairs were set back in place in the dining hall ready for dinner,
and the food trolleys were wheeled in. The men queued up to
receive their meal, which was served 'canteen style' from behind a
counter by inmate servers. They took their food to one of the
tables, where they sat and ate, chatting in pairs or in small groups.
At 1.00 p.m. exercise was called, the wing doors were opened and
those who were so inclined trooped out to the exercise yard, where
they ran, jogged, or walked at a leisurely pace talking to one
another. Those who declined to go outside could remain on the
wing watching television, listening to the radio, reading, writing
letters, or chatting with other inmates or staff.

Exercise came to an end at approximately 1.40 p.m. and by 2.00
p.m. the men were back at work, where they remained until 4.00
p.m. During this time staff caught up with paperwork or met to
discuss wing business. Tea arrived on the wing at 4.30 p.m., after
which the men were free to engage in a variety of activities until
lock-up at 8.45 p.m. Some watched television in the communal
television room; others played darts or snooker in the dining hall;
attended evening classes; read; or wrote letters in their cells; listened to music; or participated in hobbies, which ranged from
woodwork to writing poetry. Throughout the day the men engaged
freely in conversation with prison staff, discussing anything from
their own therapy to the day's football results. It was not uncom-
mon, for example, to see a prisoner sitting casually on the corner
of the officers' desk in the staff office, chatting in a relaxed and
amicable manner. The uniformed staff, in turn, could be observed
playing darts or snooker with the inmates, or simply talking with
them in the corridor or at the back of the television room.

At about 8.00 p.m. the men had a light supper, usually a hot
drink and a cake, before being called to return to their cells. Most
of the inmates took a flask of hot water back with them to make a

cup of tea or coffee later in the evening. They were then alone in their cells, where they could listen to their radios or read until lights were turned out at 10.00 p.m.

Importance was attached to the fostering of links with the outside world and, although the men were rarely able to leave the prison, efforts were made to bring outsiders in. Inmates who did not have regular contact with friends or relatives were encouraged to volunteer for a prison visitor, who would be contacted by the prison chaplaincy. But the most innovative way in which outside links were forged was through the wing social evenings, which were organized by the inmates every three months, and to which prison staff, their families, and other guests were invited, although the prisoners' own friends and relatives were not included.

Organization of Therapy

In keeping with the ideal typical model of the therapeutic community each wing had two formal therapeutic forums: the small groups, consisting of between six and eight inmates, which met three times a week for one hour; and the wing or community meetings, which were also scheduled for one hour and took place twice weekly.

Small Group

The small group was intended to provide an intimate forum in which all members actively participate in the exploration of their individual and collective problems. At Grendon the groups were of the 'slow open' type, in that membership gradually changes as individuals leave and are replaced by others, as opposed to the 'closed' type, where all participants start and finish at the same time. A recognized consequence of the 'slow open' group was that all inmates experienced movement from the position of newcomer to that of elder member. This progression was described by the wing staff as being extremely important in helping inmates to develop a sense of personal responsibility, which was a central feature of therapeutic development at Grendon.

On all wings allocation to the groups was random, in that new arrivals were assigned to whichever group had a vacancy. Inmates were not free to choose their own group and once allocated they could not change from one group to another. This procedure generally ensured a heterogeneous membership, representing a variety of offence and problem types, which broadened the range of experiences upon which the therapeutic process could draw.

Each small group was nominally allotted one or two uniformed officers, who were part of the group, yet different from other members. Their role was typically that of facilitator, rather than group leader. Their task was concerned less with structuring or defining the agenda and content of group meetings, and more with encouraging the development of a therapeutic atmosphere. In this way the staff could be seen as facilitating the emergence of group solutions to the inevitable tensions of group work. This was particularly apparent where difficulties arose in the process of communication, such as when individuals deliberately avoided issues, or allowed themselves to be ignored. At such times the officer could intervene by making an observation, asking a clarifying question, or providing an interpretation. Because the officer sat with the group, the chairs being arranged in a circle or around the walls of a cell or small office, he represented a structural and integral part of the group. He was one of the 'inner circle' and was expected to participate in the therapeutic process and to reveal, to some extent at least, aspects of himself and his own feelings. Clearly there was a fine line which each member of staff had to draw between being involved in the group work of inmates and utilizing the therapeutic process for his own personal needs. In practice, the active collaboration of uniformed officers with their groups had the effect of enabling prisoners and prison staff to relate to each other as individuals, reducing social distance and facilitating the development of trust, the building of confidence, and the promotion of an atmosphere of safety.

Within the communities emphasis was ubiquitously placed upon a policy of no confidentiality, whereby each man was expected to be open and candid about his own life and not to withold information about himself or other group members. Secrecy was defined as being in direct conflict with the process of therapy and potentially injurious to the integrity of the community. Hence, what took place in the small groups was perceived as a matter for communal review. After each group meeting all proceedings were communicated to the wing via feedback sessions, in which one member from each group presented a verbal report.

Characteristically, group therapy permits an analysis of the 'here and now' through the evolving network of relationships in the group. The premiss is that a man's behaviour in the group can be observed and reacted to, and that his conduct in this context reflects, at least to some extent, his conduct elsewhere. There are, however, some types of group therapy that place a greater emphasis upon an individual's past experiences, particularly those which occurred in childhood and adolescence, in the belief that these reveal information which is crucial to understanding the original causes of his current behaviour. At Grendon an individual's past may be viewed as particularly relevant, in that all the men are united by the common fact that it is, at least in part, their previous criminal activities which have led them to their current situation. The degree to which the past or the present was accentuated, however, differed considerably between the three wings.

On all the wings the work which was undertaken in the groups inevitably became routinized over time and assumed a pattern in which a number of fundamental themes could be identified. In common with all insight-oriented psychotherapy, the themes which emerged were: self-esteem; personal identity; personal relationships; interpersonal conflict; the expression and control of feelings; and a sense of direction and purpose.[6]

At Grendon the men's *self-esteem* and sense of *identity* were addressed by identifying and reinforcing what they, or other people, perceived to be their strengths, as well as tackling their weaknesses. The issue of *personal relationships* focused in particular upon three specific elements: the men's relationships with women, their relationships with figures in authority, and their relationships with one another. The *expression and control of feelings* was closely linked to the theme of *interpersonal conflict*, in that the therapeutic process was geared towards minimizing those behaviours which brought the individual into conflict either with others or with himself. Hence emphasis was placed not only upon learning to be assertive, and to express hitherto suppressed and frustrated emotions, but also upon the ability to control the acting out of fears, desires and fantasies. Such an approach at Grendon clearly reflected a recognition of the violent and sexual nature of the men's crimes. But an additional and dominant theme of the therapeutic process, which was incorporated within, and underpinned all the other themes, was that of *personal responsibility*.

[6] See Bloch, S. (1982), *What is Psychotherapy?* Oxford: Oxford University Press, 100.

Men were encouraged and expected to accept responsibility for their own actions, both in the present and in the past.

Each wing had a set of written guidelines which outlined what was expected of inmates as members of a therapeutic community. They detailed the ways in which individuals should behave on the wing and gave particular guidance about what was required when participating in the small group and community meetings. Everyone was encouraged to engage in therapeutic activities, which contributed not only to their own progress, but also to the therapy of others. Active participation was believed to furnish the individual with an opportunity to discover and confront the personal and interpersonal difficulties which underlay his immediate symptoms, and enable him to provide help and guidance to others.

The overriding belief was that, the greater a man's participation in therapy, the more he would gain from it. This included being increasingly open about himself and his own problems, but also increasingly responsive to and involved with others. It was recognized, however, that some individuals, silent for a while, could still benefit from being in a group, so long as they allowed themselves to relate intellectually and emotionally to what was happening around them. At Grendon, however, tolerance of such passive participation was limited, as was evidenced in the case of an inmate on C wing.

Harry was a man of Romany background who severely lacked confidence and self-esteem and whose speech was rapid and virtually incomprehensible. During his first four months at Grendon he said hardly a word in the group, and was eventually presented with an ultimatum to contribute to the group sessions or risk being ousted from the community. Harry did not change his behaviour and his group took the issue to a wing meeting, with the recommendation that he be 'voted out' of therapy and thus transferred to another prison. When asked at the meeting to comment on what his group had said about him, Harry gave a faltering yet impassioned speech in defence of his case for staying at Grendon. As a result, a compromise was reached whereby the group agreed that they would continue to work with Harry so long as he reinforced his efforts at active participation by taking on the task of presenting the feedback of the group work at the community meetings.

Full and active participation in therapy required the forging of a therapeutic alliance with fellow group and community members, some of whom might initially be feared, held in disdain, or simply disliked. Certain individuals might be rejected by their group or by the community, while others might themselves reject those around them. The situation was relatively clear-cut when the rejection emanated from the individual and was directed at the group or the community. If a man refused to forge a therapeutic alliance he would eventually leave or be transferred from the community. Joe, whose teenage daughter had been viciously raped, had received his sentence for seriously assaulting a man who had previously been convicted of a sexual offence. Throughout his short time at Grendon he trenchantly declared his abhorrence of all members of the wing who had committed sex offences, refusing to work with any of them. For two months the community withstood his aloof and aggressive behaviour, in the belief that once he had been able to express his anger he would be able to build the necessary therapeutic alliance and begin to engage in the therapeutic process. Joe, however, continued to maintain his aggressive stance and was transferred from Grendon after he had threatened another inmate with violence.

The position was more complex when it was the group or the community which refused to form an alliance with a particular individual. Men who had committed especially violent sex offences against children frequently evoked animosity from fellow group members, particularly in the early stages of their time at Grendon. Usually these feelings of disdain and hostility were dissipated over time as the individual expressed remorse for his actions and demonstrated a desire to tackle the problems associated with his criminality. It was argued that an important distinction had to be drawn between feelings about the offender and feelings about his offence. But this did not invariably occur: eventual acceptance was not always guaranteed. This was demonstrated in the case of Nigel, whose sexual abuse of disabled children shocked and alienated his fellow group members. Having listened to a comprehensive account of his offences they refused to work with him further. It was roundly denied, however, that this decision was taken solely on account of the nature of his offences. Instead, it was claimed that the matter-of-fact and cold-blooded way in which he recounted his offences was insufficiently remorseful, and that he was insincere in his commitment to change his behaviour. While a demonstration of commitment to the therapeutic endeavour was a fundamental requirement of community membership, it was evident that the hurdles were being set higher in some cases than others.

Another man who never managed to overcome his group's initial antipathy towards him was Mick. He had been convicted of the manslaughter of his girlfriend's baby son, whom he had savagely bitten and beaten to death. Central to the group's rejection of Mick was his constant protestation that the child's death was an accident. This attempt to minimize his own culpability, and thus the seriousness of his offence, was viewed by his fellow members as clear evidence of his lack of genuine remorse for what he had done. Mick's situation was further compounded by his perpetual portrayal of himself as a 'career victim': the victim of violent and abusive parents, authoritarian teachers, cruel peers, exploitative girlfriends, and a homosexual rapist. His recitals of the sufferings and blows he had been dealt in life were interpreted by the group as a manipulative strategy, designed to avoid talking about his killing of the child. As time progressed, Mick's relationship with his group, whose sympathies lay not with him but with his child victim, deteriorated rather than improved, and he was 'voted out' of therapy after being at Grendon for nine months.

It was possible, however, for the process of rejection to be halted, or at least slowed down, by the intervention of a group officer or an inmate member of the group. Paul, a car thief, had incurred the dislike of his fellow group members who were unable to tolerate what they perceived as his obsessive lying and lack of 'moral fibre'. He was a timid man who was forever changing his story and presenting different accounts of the same event, in order to avoid conflict and attain popularity. In an attempt to integrate Paul into the group and out-manœuvre the other members' rejection of him, the group officer suggested that one meeting should be devoted to 'clearing the air' by each individual speaking candidly about each fellow member. Partly as a result of this Paul's relationship with the group improved, but the effect was not sustained and after six months he was 'voted out' of therapy by the community.

Men at Grendon were urged to face up to the fact that therapy can be a painful process, but that the acceptance of criticism and the acknowledgement of sensitive and painful episodes was a necessary part of the 'healing' process. Men learned a great deal about themselves and their relationships with others by feedback from other group members. In this way they were able to discover how their behaviour and attitudes were perceived by others and, in consequence, see how their actions were often self-defeating. Sometimes such feedback was positive and hence reassuring and confidence-building. At other times, however, it could be negative and experienced, initially at least, as hurtful and threatening. Peter was shocked and angered when members of his group, with whom he thought he had a close and positive relationship, told him that they did not trust him, but feared him, and found him to be aggressive, insensitive, and arrogant. He responded by accusing the group of being disingenuous and operating according to double standards because they had kept their feelings hidden from him. It was only after he had reflected on the matter that he realized how his own stance had effectively restrained the group from criticizing him in the past. At the next group meeting Peter apologized for the verbal attack he had launched on the group and asked to use the session to discuss these inimical aspects of his personality. In so doing, he was understood to be expressing a desire to confront this painful issue and to further his understanding of himself and his relationships with other people.

There were times when inmates experienced particular difficulties in relating to specific members of their group because the individual concerned displayed or represented unwelcome aspects of their own personality or situation. This again could be a painful event and could seriously inhibit therapeutic activity. It became clear within a short time of Andy arriving at Grendon that he was avoiding any interaction with Robert, one of the members of his group. Whenever the group was focusing on Robert's problems Andy would 'switch off' and become completely passive. One day Andy announced to the group that he detested Robert, accusing him of being sick and perverted, and calling into question the validity of his problems and his commitment to therapy. In the course of the discussion it emerged that Robert's proclaimed homosexuality represented a terrifying threat to Andy's fragile sexual identity. A central feature of Andy's problems, which was to be addressed in therapy, was the difficulties he experienced in his sexual relationships with women. He had been brought up in the care of the local authority and had nurtured the prospect of a stable and happy family life as an adult. Yet he found that he was sexually attracted to men rather than to women. He had managed to keep these feelings a closely guarded secret until he came to

Grendon, where Robert's blatant homosexuality provided a mirror for his own latent homosexual inclinations and thus represented for him the ultimate threat to his dream of family life.

Wing Meetings
The wing meetings were attended by all inmates and as many staff as possible. They were chaired by an inmate who had been elected by the community, and usually there was a deputy chairman or secretary who recorded the events of the meeting in a Wing Book. The meetings took place in the television room, where chairs were arranged in a large circle to enable face-to-face communication. In keeping with the ideal typical model of the therapeutic community, two major purposes were served by the wing meetings: first, the facilitation of the day-to-day functioning of the unit; and secondly, the development and extension of the therapeutic process. On most occasions there was a strong practical focus on routine domestic issues, such as the allocation of prison work, the planning of sports and social events, and the dissemination and clarification of information about the wing, or about the prison as a whole. Discussion of mundane practicalities of communal life was not, however, divorced from the therapeutic function of the meetings. Virtually any topic could be examined in ways which enabled practical concerns to be redefined in therapeutic terms. For example, applications for specific jobs or positions of responsibility on the wing were discussed in relation to the man's motives, fears, and expectations. The vote of the community was based less upon an evaluation of who was the 'best man for the job' and more upon an assessment of who would be most in need of the job, or most likely to benefit from the post.

Wing meetings also provided a forum for the airing of grievances or relational difficulties, and for praising or criticizing individual members of the community, be they staff or inmates. But, in addition, community meetings played an explicit therapeutic role in raising and debating matters of immediate concern to an individual's therapy. Thus, it would be misleading to depict the small groups as the arena for therapeutic discussion and the community meeting as the arena for practical matters: both were pivotal elements of the therapeutic community.

Staff in the Therapeutic Community

As members of a therapeutic community all staff, including the uniformed officers, probation officers, psychologists, and doctors, operated as individuals within a multi-disciplinary team, each contributing his or her personal and professional skills to the shared therapeutic endeavour. It was not uncommon, for example, for the wing psychologist and probation officer to sit in on meetings of the small groups and to act as facilitators. Indeed, on two of the wings they were assigned to particular groups in the same way as the uniformed staff. In addition to group-work, all members of the staff team were available to counsel prisoners on an individual basis. Care was taken, however, to ensure that these one-to-one encounters did not circumvent the group process. The 'no confidentiality' rule required inmates to feed back to their groups the nature and purpose of these individual sessions.

Among the staff the usual pyramid of authority was to some extent flattened, reducing the social distance between the groups of civilian staff, as well as between the senior and junior ranks of officers. This was intended to enable all staff to participate equally in the therapeutic process, to speak candidly to one another, and confront tensions and conflicts in an honest and productive way. This democratic and multi-disciplinary approach was designed to limit the power of any one group of staff and to ensure that decision-making was a collective exercise shared between staff of different disciplines. The prison governors, however, did not participate in this process and were structurally divorced from the therapeutic communities. Their sphere of operation was designed to manage the institution as a prison, in such a way as to enable the other staff members and the prisoners to function effectively within a therapeutic community.

Regular meetings of the staff team were held three times a week on each of the wings. These were attended by all the officers on duty at the time and, whenever possible, by the wing doctor, wing psychologist, and wing probation officer. Two of these weekly meetings were set aside for the discussion of business matters, such as parole reports, applications for home leave, assessments of inmates' progress in therapy, the allocation of work, and any other issues relating to the organization and management of the wing. The third meeting, sometimes referred to as the 'staff sensitivity group' or 'staff support group', was strictly reserved for non-business matters. During this time the staff were encouraged to talk about any difficulties or anxieties they were experiencing, whether at work or at home; to confront inter-personal tensions; and, where necessary, to lend each other support.

Limiting Parameters of Gender

The ways in which issues were formulated and addressed in the small groups and wing meetings were inevitably structured by the highly specific context in which the men at Grendon were operating. Within Grendon there were established conventions which circumscribed how inmates defined and articulated their problems, and a set of normative values which specified the range of possible solutions. To some extent this is true of all therapeutic settings, but at Grendon it was particularly apparent. The range of experience upon which inmate members of the communities could draw was limited by the fact that all of them were male and over the age of 21; all had been convicted of serious criminal offences; and all of them were prisoners, sharing the common bond of punishment associated with their loss of liberty. Hence the extent to which the therapeutic communities at Grendon could reflect the 'human condition in miniature' was severely restricted.

The significance of this limitation was most clearly manifested in terms of the sexual composition of the communities. Grendon was and is an overwhelmingly male environment, in relation not only to the prisoner population but also to the civilian and uniformed staff. Throughout the period of this research the only women with whom the men had regular contact were two probation officers, one psychologist, and one part-time psycho-dramatist (all of whom were attached to particular wings), and the teachers within the education department. The first female prison officers were introduced into Grendon in 1988. Since then the numbers of female staff have gradually increased as the Prison Service's policy of cross-sex postings has taken effect. However, although this has been an important development, the relative numbers of women are still very small. The lack of routine daily contact with women has major implications, both for the therapeutic process itself and for those women who are present and actively participate in it.

During the research it was possible to discern a distinct male ethos, which was prevalent throughout the institution, and which categorized and stigmatized women on the basis of sexual stereo-types. Such stereotyping provided a central framework within which the inmates sought to understand their relationships with women and develop new forms of behaviour. It was not uncom-mon for women to be depicted as male property. One male mem-ber of staff, for example, stated empathetically to a prisoner whose partner had recently left him for another man, that he too would be angry if someone had 'stolen' his wife. Closely associated with this form of chauvinism was the characterization of women as 'the weaker sex', physically vulnerable and therefore in need of male protection. The notion of vulnerability, however, extended beyond the risk of physical harm to incorporate assaults upon female sensi-bilities. An exaggerated form of chivalry emerged, whereby inmates would apologize for swearing in front of a female member of staff, or others would remind the speaker to 'watch' his language and to remember that there were ladies present.

Not all women, however, were ascribed the status of a 'lady'. The ways in which women were spoken about and treated pro-duced extreme stereotypes, wherein they became either objects of worship, placed reverently on a pedestal, or victims of abuse, degraded and reduced to the gutter. Both staff and inmates tended to judge women according to whether or not they were thought to possess certain ideal typical feminine qualities which were broadly seen as natural or inherent endowments. Adulation or denunciation frequently depended upon a woman's perceived success in fulfilling a nurturant role. One category which aroused particular condem-nation comprised mothers who had left their families, 'abandoning' their husbands and children. Such judgements were less frequently, and less vehemently, dispensed to absent fathers.

But it was a woman's sexuality, and in particular her sexual fidelity, that dominated the process of evaluation, and which pro-duced the crude caricatures that devolved from the concepts of Madonna and whore: the former to be revered; the latter to be deprecated. An example of this form of stereotyping occurred dur-ing a group session when one of the men attempted to justify his offence of rape by referring to his victim as the 'village bike'. As such, she was, in his view, a whore, a woman who had already violated her own feminine character and who had, therefore, relin-quished any claim to be treated with respect. He stated that, had she not been the 'village bike' he would not have forced himself upon her, and that he had never before forced a woman to have sex with him. To this revelation a fellow group member retorted that she might have been the 'village bike', but that this did not automatically deny her the right to say 'No'. It would, therefore, be misleading and inaccurate to suggest that all the men at Grendon unanimously, and in every circumstance, adhered to these stereotypical views. But the overwhelmingly male environment undoubtedly produced a milieu in which such portrayals of women frequently went unquestioned and, in consequence, provided fertile conditions for the reinforcement and perpetuation of distorted and invidious stereotypes.

Women working within the communities were particularly vulnerable to the effects of these stereotypes. Along with the men's mothers, wives, and girlfriends, they were expected to be sympathetic, nurturant, and loyal. On the occasions when they were perceived as fulfilling these expectations they were praised, revered, and respected. When, however, they were thought to have veered from such ideals they fell from grace and were vilified. The descent from the heights of the pedestal to the depths of the gutter was not a gradual process, but could occur rapidly and as a result of a single incident. On one occasion on which a female probation officer refused to support a prisoner's application for a period of home leave, she was publicly denigrated in a community meeting for being a 'hard, cold bitch'. On another occasion the same probation officer told one of the men that he would have to wait to see her later that afternoon, because she had to finish her paperwork by midday in readiness for a lunch-time meeting. This time she was accused of being 'power hungry' and more authoritarian than the male staff in a conventional prison.

Being few in number, female staff were seen as a scarce resource and were thus in constant demand. Ironically, this made it even more difficult for them to fulfil the men's idealized expectations of them. Apart from any professional skills these women possessed individually, their value to the communities was assessed in relation to their presumed ability to represent 'the female point of view'. In other words, there was an assumption that women's attitudes and beliefs are consistent and undifferentiated, and that female staff could thus be relied upon to speak not just for themselves but on behalf of all womankind. An example of this occurred when Danny attempted to explain to his group that he could not express his fears and anxieties to his wife because he knew that women despised men who cry. Another member of the group queried this, saying that he had heard that women did not object to men crying so long as they did so only in front of them, and not in front of anyone else. A debate ensued, but was suspended when one of the inmates suggested that, in order to settle the issue, they should ask the female probation officer.

It can be seen from the foregoing description that the therapeutic process at Grendon is not a free ranging and anarchic experience, but one which is prescribed by the idiosyncratic environment of the institution and by certain didactic precepts which are informed by a liberal political perspective. The opportunities for inmates to test out new forms of behaviour are similarly limited by the social reality of the therapeutic communities. There are obvious impediments to practising alternative ways of relating to women and children. Hence, the validity of certain 'solutions' which are claimed to derive from therapy, have to be taken on faith, since their applicability and relevance can only be known by the individual after his release into the 'real' world.

Differences in Wing Organization

Despite the overall similarities in the regimes of the three wings, important differences remained. These served to reinforce the distinct identities of the wings as individual and self-contained communities which varied in respect of: their reputations; their inmate populations; wing policies; procedures for assessing inmates' progression in therapy; the roles of the civilian staff in the treatment process; the content of group work; and the relationship between the group work and the community meeting. What follows is a brief description of the three communities.

C Wing

At the time of research C wing was unique, in that it was the only wing to receive prisoners directly from other prisons, rather than from the assessment unit. As a result, its population differed from the populations of B and D wings in two related respects. First, inmates on C wing were significantly more likely to have served less than two years of their sentence.[7] Secondly, they were signifi-

<hr>

[7] $\chi^2 = 12.02$, df = 4, P < 0.01.

cantly more likely to have been at Grendon for shorter periods of time: almost half of them had been at Grendon for less than six months, compared with fewer than one in ten on B and D wings.[8] Apart from these distinctions, however, the nature and structure of the population on C wing did not differ significantly from those on the other two wings.

Throughout the prison C wing had the reputation of being the most inflexible and least tolerant of the three adult treatment wings. To some extent this reputation was borne out by the existence of formal structures within the community, which were designed to discipline communal conduct and thus minimize disruptive and antisocial behaviour. On C wing the guidelines or policies informing inmates about the behaviour required of them as members of a therapeutic community took the form of a written constitution, drafted originally by the men themselves and only approved and verified by the staff. This document specified a series of formal rules which strictly governed inmate conduct and incorporated a system of mandatory penalties for specific offences. Hence any member who used illicit drugs, engaged in homosexual activities, or committed any act of violence was required to be 'voted out' out of the community and thus transferred from Grendon. The inmates had an elected council, called the Cabinet, which was formally responsible for introducing new arrivals to the functioning and policies of the wing, imparting the spirit and content of the constitution, as well as ensuring that the rules were strictly maintained, and that sanctions were imposed in the event of their breach. A system of 'compacts' or 'contracts' had also been designed which provided a means of formally cautioning those inmates whose 'commitment' to the community had been questioned. The terms of these 'contracts', which could be drawn up by a man's group or by the community as a whole, required the individual to agree to, and comply with, the imposition of certain conditions upon his behaviour. A refusal to conform to these prescriptions would result in the man becoming liable to transfer from Grendon. Where serious constitutional violations occurred which risked expulsion from the community, or even where relatively less serious rules had been broken but where the man stood in danger of being transferred because of a demonstrable lack of

[8] $\chi^2 = 23.76$, df = 4, P < 0.0001.

'commitment' to therapy, the judicial process took place at the wing meeting. All members acted as both judge and jury, voting to determine guilt in disputed cases and to decide whether or not a guilty party should suffer the ultimate penalty and be transferred out of the prison. During the period of research on C wing the inmate community operated a rigorous and unbending adherence to the letter of the constitution, although the final decision regarding transfer was always made by the staff team.

The assessment procedure on C wing was continuous in that once a week a number of inmates would have their progress assessed by the entire community. For each prisoner this would take place after he had been at Grendon for one month, then at three months, again at the six-month stage, and thereafter every six months. There was no requirement that an inmate undergoing assessment should submit any written report, but he was expected to make a verbal presentation to his group and later to the whole community, in which he had to explain why he felt he should remain at Grendon. Both his group and the community would be expected to comment upon his progress and both would vote on whether he should continue in therapy. The democratic decision of the community, however, was read by the staff only as an indication of peer support and did not bind their authority. The staff held their own separate assessment meetings to which a written report was submitted by the group officer, who was required to complete a standardized form, scoring an inmate's performance on a scale of one to ten in relation to a number of criteria which were similar to those used by other wings. There was no formal structure by which all members of the staff team had an opportunity to comment on each individual inmate. In effect, assessment on C wing was left in the hands of those members of staff who happened to be on duty at the time of the meeting. The consequence was that some inmates could be assessed in the absence of their group officer and the wing psychiatrist. The primary purpose of the assessment was to discern whether a prisoner should remain at Grendon. Little emphasis was placed in this process upon the formal development of a future treatment programme and there was no requirement for the prisoner to produce a written goal schedule or treatment plan. Typically, the principal officer who chaired the meeting fed back to the prisoner comments which had been made about him and pointed out areas in which staff believed progress should be made.

Unlike the other units, there was no psychologist attached to C wing at the time the research was carried out. The only civilian staff operating within the community were the doctor and the probation officer. Neither of them regularly attended the small groups but both would sit in on group sessions on an *ad hoc* basis if specifically requested to do so by the prisoners. Both of them would see prisoners individually, although, in the case of the doctor, this did not constitute a separate programme of treatment, but was usually an isolated event initiated by the inmate seeking clarification or guidance about a specific issue.

As already mentioned there was some variation in the content of group work between the three units in terms of the significance accorded to past or present events. The groups on C wing tended to emphasize a historical perspective. Considerable importance was attached to men telling their life stories and recalling past events and experiences, particularly in relation to their childhood and adolescence. C wing was also distinctive in that of the three units it had the most structured lines of communication between the small group and the total community. As with the procedure followed at the Henderson Hospital, each community meeting began with feedback reports from the groups, followed by a period of questions and comments. This ensured that all members were aware of what was going on in each of the groups and provided an opportunity for communal discussion of any issues arising.

B Wing

Prisoners on B wing were not received directly from other prisons, but were randomly allocated from the assessment unit, where, typically, they would have undergone a process of evaluation and induction over a period of approximately eight weeks. Partly as a result of this they were more likely than prisoners on C wing to have been at Grendon for longer and to be further into their sentences.

In contrast to C wing the written guidelines which specified the behaviour required of inmates did not represent a formal constitution, with mandatory penalties for breaches, but provided a series of policies which permitted a greater degree of discretion in the decision-making process. On B wing there was no elected Cabinet and no system of 'contracts' to impose specific standards. Instead, relatively minor breaches of wing policies tended to be handled at the small group level and were only discussed at wing meetings on an *ad hoc* basis. In consequence, the public display of self-policing, which was very much in evidence on C wing, was far less apparent.

B wing was accorded the reputation of being a highly structured and closely supervised unit. As such it was deemed to be a particularly suitable location for those prisoners who were suspected of being capable of manipulating the therapeutic process for their own illegitimate ends. The procedures for assessing the progress of inmates on B wing were in some ways more formal than those in operation on C wing and incorporated less involvement from the entire community. Two weeks were set aside every four months, during which time staff involvement in groups and wing meetings ceased and staff meetings were held to review every inmate in the community. The purpose of these 'assessments' was to decide, first, whether the man should remain at Grendon; and, secondly, if he should stay, to identify and clearly define a treatment programme which would be discussed and agreed with the individual prisoner. All members of the wing staff, including civilian attachments, were consulted in advance of the meetings for their opinions and were required to cast a vote on each prisoner's continued stay at Grendon. In addition, each inmate was required to submit a 'goal schedule', which he should have drafted in the light of discussions with his group. This schedule would outline specific problems he wanted to confront; the ways in which he intended to set about doing this; and the means by which he might gauge his own progress. Each assessment meeting was attended by all staff on duty and was routinely chaired by the psychologist, who would present the staff with a summary of all written reports received on the inmate. Towards the end of the meeting the prisoner would be called in to hear the views of the staff and to discuss his progress. The assessment decisions were not routinely discussed at the wing meeting and would be brought to the attention of the whole community only if an individual member chose to put it on the agenda.

On B wing there was a greater involvement of a wider range of civilian staff in both group work and the assessment process. The psychologist, doctor, and probation officer all regularly attended the small groups and education staff frequently involved themselves in the therapeutic activities of the wing, sitting in on groups and contributing to the assessment process. As on C wing, all the civilian staff would have individual contact with prisoners, but again most of these sessions were instigated by the inmates and fuelled by the desire to discuss single events or highly specific concerns.

In striking contrast to C wing, the group process on B wing tended to be rooted in an analysis of the 'here and now'. Less emphasis was placed upon uncovering the past and, instead, group time was typically devoted to discussing a man's behaviour on the wing, his relationships with other inmates and members of staff, and his attitudes towards living within the rules laid down by the community. There was also a less formal structure to the wing meetings, in that there were no fixed arrangements for group feed-back at every session. This is not to say that group activities were never discussed during community meetings, but that they were spontaneously raised or placed on the agenda at the initiative of individual members. In general, the non-business content of these meetings tended to focus upon matters defined by the community as being of immediate concern, irrespective of whether they had come to light through the group, through an individual's behaviour on the wing, or by any other means.

D Wing

In many respects D wing more closely reflected the organization of B wing rather than C wing. Its population was randomly allocated from the assessment unit and hence closely mirrored that of B wing. There was no formal constitution, no Cabinet, and no sys-tem of inmate contracts. Indeed on D wing, there was a marked absence of 'house rules' in the written guidelines and the commu-nity tended to operate with a minimum of formal regulations.

D wing had an assessment period every four months, although, unlike B wing, all other therapeutic activities continued during this time. There were two phases to D wing's assessment process, both of which involved the staff. The first of these took place in the small groups where inmate members and the group officers were joined by the psychologist, the wing probation officer, and, when-ever possible, the doctor and the wing principal officer. All group members participated in the evaluation of each other's progress, according to a set format which reviewed a man's behaviour and relationships on the wing, at work, in education, and with people outside the prison. A specific focus of these assessments was the prospect of recidivism. In every case consideration was given to whether any therapeutic progress made by an individual had any relevance to his offending behaviour. In general, however, the primary objectives of this phase of the process were to identify outstanding areas of concern and to formulate an action plan for the next four months. In effect, this was equivalent to the written 'goal schedule' produced by the inmates on B wing.

The second phase of the D wing assessment was conducted at staff meetings, wherein the deliberations of the group were reported back and all members of staff in attendance had an opportunity to comment. The meetings were structured primarily to evaluate and develop the therapeutic objectives which had been identified for individuals in their groups and did not routinely assess whether a man should keep his place at Grendon. It was not part of the assessment routine for staff to vote on whether an inmate should stay at Grendon: such questions were raised by individual members of staff only when the issue of a man leaving seemed relevant. A summary of the group assessment and the staff's discussion would be fed back in writing to each inmate, who would then be expected to work on these issues with his group over the next four months. The prevailing presumption that an inmate would remain in therapy, rather than be expected repeatedly to justify his place in the community, may be seen as responsible, at least in part, for D wing's reputation as the most supportive and easy-going of the three treatment wings.

Like their colleagues on B wing, the civilian staff, including the teachers, regularly and actively participated in both group work and the process of assessment. With the exception of the doctor, they also had contact with the men on an individual basis. Again this was usually at the behest of the inmate, although the psychologist on D wing tended to be more proactive than any of the other therapists in adopting an interventionist approach and initiating contact. In contrast, the doctor on D wing was significantly less likely than the doctors on B and C wings to have seen men individually.[9] While not totally at odds with his colleagues, he adhered more strictly to the view that individual work was antithetical to the principles of the therapeutic community.

In terms of the content of group therapy, D wing tended to occupy the middle ground, demonstrating no obvious emphasis

---

[9] $\chi^2 = 11.26$, df = 2, P < 0.01.

upon either the past or the present events of an inmate's life. The community meetings, however, were similar to those on B wing, in that they tended to adopt an informal structure, facilitating the spontaneous raising of issues by individual members.

The question which has to be addressed is whether these differences in the organization of the wings had any consequences for the ways in which inmates experienced therapy at Grendon. This will be examined in relation, first, to the length of time individuals stayed in therapy at Grendon; and, secondly, to the way in which inmates engaged in the therapeutic process, and what they felt they derived from it.

Time Spent in Grendon

A census was taken of the population *transferred* from Grendon over a twelve-month period, between 1 March 1988 and 28 February 1989. This clearly showed that, although similar proportions of men left the three treatment wings, significant differences existed between the wings in the length of time the men had spent at Grendon. On average, inmates stayed for fourteen months on C wing; for seventeen months on B wing; and for twenty months on D wing. The men on C wing were more likely than those elsewhere to be transferred within their first twelve months, whereas those transferred from D wing were more likely than the men from B or C wing to have stayed at Grendon for more than two years (see Table 4.1).

Two reasons may be advanced to explain the variation in the lengths of time the men stayed on the different wings: the first relates to the disparities which exist between the different wing

Table 4.1. *Time at Grendon, by wing*

Time at Grendon	B wing		C wing		D wing		Total	
	No.	%	No.	%	No.	%	No.	%
Less than 12 months	5	18	13	46	5	19	23	28
12 months up to 24 months	19	68	11	39	11	42	41	50
24 months plus	4	14	4	14	10	39	18	22
TOTAL	28		28		26		82	

Notes: Mean = 16.96 months.
   $\chi^2 = 12.59$, df = 4, P < 0.01.

policies; and the second relates to dissimilarities in the wings' procedures for assessment.

The written constitution on C wing placed deviant members in a far more vulnerable position regarding transfer than their counterparts on either B or D wing. The fact that it identified an explicit set of rules; provided a structure for their enforcement; and designated specific sanctions, ensured that inmates had more formal opportunities to breach the code of conduct; were more liable to be policed by their peers; and were more likely to be subjected to a system of mandatory penalties. During the nine months spent in research on this wing, every man who was deemed to have broken one of the three fundamental rules which carried the mandatory penalty of transfer were, without exception, expelled from the community. In addition, the staff group on the wing did not overturn a single decision which involved an inmate being voted out by his peers for a disciplinary offence.

The guidelines which existed on B and D wings allowed for a higher level of tolerance and permitted a greater degree of discretion in the decision-making process. Hence, on these wings the question whether a man should be expelled from the community was less frequently placed on the agenda and, on the relatively rare occasions when this did occur, the decision was not bound by statutory proscriptions. During the period of research on B and D wings, the inmate communities failed to expel a single person for lacking 'commitment' by violating the more trivial house rules. Indeed, even where more serious breaches had taken place, the operation of discretionary decision-making permitted a culture in which men were routinely given the benefit of the doubt and maximum penalties were rarely enforced.

Differences in the assessment procedures may also have accounted for some of the variance in the mean lengths of stay on the three treatment wings. The most relevant distinction here related to the lack of emphasis which D wing staff placed upon the question whether or not a man should stay in Grendon. As was mentioned earlier, the major purpose of the D wing assessment process was to develop therapeutic objectives and to consider whether any therapeutic progress made by the inmate reduced the likelihood of his reoffending. Neither the staff nor the inmates routinely voted on whether or not someone should remain in the community; this issue was only discussed if a member of the staff team, or the inmate himself, raised the possibility of his leaving. In consequence, the presumption in favour of an individual staying in therapy reduced the likelihood of men on D wing being assessed as unsuitable for Grendon, particularly in the early stages of their career. In contrast, a major focus of the assessments on C wing was the decision whether a man should stay in therapy or be transferred out. Staff and inmates routinely voted on the issue and it was a question uppermost in everyone's mind when an assessment took place.

But differences in the timing or scheduling of the assessments on the three wings also made it more likely that men would be assessed out of treatment earlier in their careers on C wing than on either B or D wing. The mass assessment every four months on B and D wings operated so that a man's first assessment was largely routine and non-controversial, encouraging him to settle in and to develop, with his group, a more clearly defined set of objectives for his next assessment. In practice, a man could be on the wing for almost eight months before undergoing a serious evaluation of his place in therapy. In contrast, the procedures on C wing ensured that each man's progress was reviewed at specific points in his career. Thus everyone was assessed after he had been on the wing for one month, three months, and again at six months. C wing also had the not infrequently used provision of interim assessments, whereby inmates who were thought to be under-achieving were subjected to special review prior to their official date of assessment.

The Experience of Therapy

Men on the treatment wings who took part in this research were generally not newcomers to psychiatric treatment. More than two-thirds had a history of psychiatric intervention and for the vast majority (92 per cent) this had involved some form of psychotherapy. Thus, this study focused not upon a group of men who were unfamiliar with psychiatric practice, but with a population which had on previous occasions been identified as needing to counter its psychological dysfunctioning.

Definition of Problems

All the men interviewed believed they had problems with which Grendon was helping them, and for the majority (60 per cent) these problems focused upon their inability to develop and maintain satisfactory personal relationships. Significantly, this was the most common category of problem mentioned on all three wings, regardless of age or type of offence. Four out of ten of the men claimed to have a problem in controlling their aggression, and a similar proportion felt that they lacked self-confidence. Again, these difficulties were found among all age and offence groups, although, perhaps not unexpectedly, problems of aggression tended to be more frequently cited by men under thirty and by those who had committed offences which involved some element of violence. Alcohol and drug abuse were identified as problems by about one-third of the sample, as were sexual problems and difficulties associated with facing up to the nature of their crimes. But whereas problems with drink and drugs were evenly distributed across the population, sexual difficulties and an inability to come to terms with the nature of their offence were significantly more likely to be cited by men who had been convicted of sex offences.[10] Indeed, men who claimed to have difficulties in accepting the reality of their crimes were made up almost entirely of those who had committed murder, rape, and sexual offences against children.[11] Interestingly, only about one in ten of all the men interviewed felt that the problems they needed to deal with at Grendon were associated with coping with life in prison.

The majority (84 per cent) said that their perception of their problems had changed since coming to Grendon. Most (68 per cent) claimed that they had found problems they did not know they had, or that they had discovered their problems were considerably more complex than they had previously realized. In this respect, however, there were significant differences across wings. Inmates on D wing were less likely than men on B and C wings to see their problems as more numerous and more complicated: fewer than half (46 per cent) the inmates on D wing perceived their problems in this way, in comparison to 88 per cent of B wing and 70 per cent of C wing.[12] The reason for such variance between the wings is not immediately apparent, or obviously reducible to a single structural difference. It may, however, have been related to

[10] Sex offenders were more likely to cite sexual problems: $\chi^2 = 21.66$, df = 1, P < 0.01. Sex offenders were more likely to be unable to face the nature of their crimes: $\chi^2 = 5.19$, df = 1, P < 0.02.

[11] $\chi^2 = 24.24$, df = 8, P < 0.01.   [12] $\chi^2 = 15.37$, df = 4, P < 0.01.

the less critical and confrontational procedures, and the general ethos of tolerance, which prevailed on D wing.

Group Work

Although group therapy may be defined as a distinctive process the ways in which individuals experience this process are likely to be influenced by the structure and social contexts in which it takes place. As might be expected the men's participation in, and feelings about, group work varied to a certain extent across the three wings. These differences, whilst limited and insufficiently consistent to constitute defining features of the men's experience of group therapy, nevertheless appeared to be in keeping with specific wing characteristics, and most particularly with the more tolerant climate on D wing.

Typically, it took the men at least a month to settle into the wing before they started to discuss their problems in the group. But again, there were significant differences between the wings, with inmates on D wing being more likely to talk about their problems earlier than those on the other two wings. More than a third (39 per cent) of the men on D wing had launched into group work within their first week, in comparison to 16 per cent on B wing and 9 per cent on C wing.[13]

Three-quarters of all the men interviewed, however, claimed to have experienced some difficulties in talking about themselves in their group, although again, this was less likely to be mentioned on D wing than on either B or C.[14] Yet the sources of these difficulties were remarkably similar regardless of which wing the men came from. For the majority (59 per cent) these anxieties were primarily related to the complexity and sensitivity of the highly personal issues they felt they had to discuss. Indeed, for some, these were subjects about which they had never previously spoken to anyone. About one-quarter of the men thought that their difficulties in talking to their group stemmed from their own lack of confidence and general sense of inhibition in speaking in front of other people. Only 17 per cent attributed their uneasiness to any lack of

---

[13] $\chi^2 = 13.07$, df = 6, P < 0.05.

[14] Difficulties in talking in the group were mentioned by 63% of men on D wing, 85% on B wing, and 79% on C wing. $\chi^2 = 14.44$, df = 8, P < 0.07 (approaching significance).

trust they felt in particular group members or in the group as a whole.

Notwithstanding these obvious anxieties, the majority (80 per cent) of the men claimed to have been sufficiently assertive and to have brought issues they wanted to discuss to the attention of their group. But about half these men said that this was not a one-way process and that other members of their group would also turn the spotlight on them and initiate the debate. Two out of three men interviewed, however, admitted that prior to taking matters to their group they usually 'tested the water' and discussed the issues with at least one other member of the wing, although typically these were individuals selected from within their own group. The extent to which matters were rehearsed in this way varied considerably between the different groups and was related to other indices of group cohesion. None the less, it is important to note that, regardless of these differences, the majority (80 per cent overall) of all groups, on all three wings, felt that most members of their own group were supportive of them, and fewer than one in ten expressed a preference for changing their group. In general, it was held that the small groups operated within a supportive framework and that group members tended to suppport one another against other inmates on the wing.

Perceptions of the Officers' Role in Therapy

The presence of uniformed officers in the groups was generally welcomed by the inmates, although about a third of them said that they had some mixed feelings about it, or that they approved of only specific members of staff being group officers. Overall, the uniformed staff were perceived to be active participants in the group but were not seen to assume the role of group leader. Inevitably the men's perceptions of the role played by the group officer varied from group to group. But, again, the most significant differences occurred between the wings. The depiction of an active but non-directive participant was common only to B and D wings. On C wing inmates were more likely to depict their group officer as a passive presence (see Table 4.2).

Inmates were evenly divided as to whether or not they thought the group worked differently when the group officer was not in attendance. Among those who believed their group changed, half thought that it became more open and more relaxed, and half said

Table 4.2. *Inmates' perception of group officer's role, by wing*

Perceived role	B wing	C wing	D wing	Total
Leading/directive	4	7	7	18
	13%	20%	22%	18%
Active but not directive	23	10	23	56
	74%	29%	72%	57%
Passive	4	18	2	24
	13%	51%	6%	24%
TOTAL				98
	31	35	32	100%

Note: $\chi^2 = 29.4$, df $= 6$, P < 0.001.

that the group abated its work and did not use the time as constructively as when the member of staff was present. Men who felt
that their group officer played a leading and directive role were
particularly likely to claim that the group was different when he
was absent but, again, their views varied about whether the group
was more open or whether it was less productive.

Most inmates (86 per cent) on all three treatment wings thought
that all, or at least the majority, of officers at Grendon were fundamentally different in their attitudes and behaviour from those
they had encountered in other prisons. The nature of these differences was largely related to the quality of relationships which the
men felt existed between themselves and the staff. Officers at
Grendon were seen as more informal and less authoritarian than
their colleagues in other establishments and all but a tiny group of
inmates (6 per cent) felt that these differences were genuine and
not superficial. Only about a third of the men thought that there
were basic dissimilarities in the intrinsic characteristics or personal
qualities of the staff. Instead, most thought that it was the environment at Grendon which permitted and encouraged officers to adopt
ways of working and relating with inmates which were outside the
range of conventional practice.

Most inmates (86 per cent) said that they felt it was possible to
talk to the officers about personal matters, and three-quarters said
that they had done so with more than one member of staff. It was
clear, however, that the men carefully selected the officers they
spoke to, usually choosing a particular officer because he possessed
personal qualities they valued and admired. Different men were

attracted by different characteristics, and so most staff on all wings engaged in this type of contact, although it was apparent that certain individuals were targeted more frequently and made themselves more available. Inmates on all wings, however, were divided about whether or not they would talk to these same officers if they were to meet them in another prison, largely because they doubted whether the conventional prison culture would permit either side to foster a relationship of this kind. Yet, even within Grendon, where widespread inter-personal communication was common place, two-thirds of the prisoners said that there were limits to the sorts of things they would be prepared to discuss with the staff. In the main, these issues focused upon illicit activities on the wing and matters which individuals felt were too personal and not necessarily relevant to their therapy. There were, however, significant differences between inmates on different wings, with those on B wing being more likely to say that they felt able to talk to the staff about anything and those on D wing claiming to feel most inhibited about illicit activities (see Table 4.3). These variations are not readily explained by differences in the structure and organization of the wings but are most probably a reflection of the personal relationships which existed on the wings at one particular point in time.

Table 4.3. *Whether inmates would discuss illicit activities with staff, by wing*

Wing	Would talk about anything	Would restrict discussion and exclude illicit activities	Would restrict discussion but not specifically exclude illicit activities	Total
B	16	8	8	32
	50%	25%	25%	100%
C	9	10	15	34
	27%	29%	44%	100%
D	10	17	6	33
	30%	51%	18%	100%
TOTAL	35	35	29	99
	35%	35%	29%	100%

Note: χ^2 10.83, df = 4, P < 0.02.

Assessment of Therapeutic Gain

Virtually everyone (94 per cent) on all the wings felt that they were benefiting from the therapeutic regime at Grendon and great value was placed, in particular, upon the work carried out in the small groups. Indeed, four out of ten inmates believed that, for them, the most useful therapy occurred within the group context. Most typically the men said that their participation in the group had enabled them to gain a greater understanding of themselves and of their own problems, both by talking about themselves and by listening to, and identifying with, the experiences of other members. About a third of the inmates also claimed to have gained in self-confidence and similar proportions said that they had become more skilled in communicating and socializing with others; felt less isolated and alienated from the rest of the world; and had a better understanding of, and empathy with, other people and their problems.[15] Moreover, about four out of ten men felt that the benefits they had accrued from the group work reflected demonstrable changes in their behaviour.

I was a total wreck when I came here. I'd spent the last three years in virtual isolation—I spoke to no-one unless I had to. I never looked at people's faces. I recognised the officers by their shoes and their boots. I was too ashamed and disgusted to look at anyone. I still feel disgusted with what I've done and I still feel deep down that I shouldn't be on this earth for what I did. But we don't have capital punishment in this country and so I shall just stay in prison—I don't want to ever be released. But I realise that I have to come out of my shell in prison otherwise I'll probably go completely mad. So now I try and mix more and I look at people. I go in the television room and sometimes I'll go in the office and chat to whoever's in there.

Well I know it's working for me. I've learnt to control my temper a lot more and walk away from situations which before I would have just powered into.

One of the most important things I've got from the group is a sort of realization that I've brought a lot of my problems on myself and that instead of blaming other people, especially Linda, I should take a look at myself first. They made me realize too, what it must have been like for Linda all these years. . . . Since I've been here I've written to her and put it all down on paper and she came up on a visit and we talked a lot, really for

---

[15] The proportions in these categories were not mutually exclusive.

the first time. And we both feel now that I've changed a lot. I'm more considerate, I listen to what she's got to say rather than just try and be the boss all the time.

Clearly, the therapeutic process at Grendon is not confined to what takes place in the group meetings, but concerns the entire day-to-day experience of living and working within the community. One of the central features of community life at Grendon is the opportunity for individual contact and one-to-one therapy, both with other inmates and with members of staff, which is afforded by the high level of open association on the wings and relaxed social relations. The value attached to this facility is evidenced by the fact that one-quarter of the men believed that they had derived more benefit from the sessions they had had with individuals than from those they had had with their group. About eight out of ten inmates had participated in at least one individual session with the wing doctor or psychologist and, as was mentioned earlier, the majority of men had discussed their problems with specific officers. But it was not the individual therapy with members of staff which was perceived by the inmates as most advantageous. Only about 30 per cent thought that the most useful sessions had been with either the wing therapist, the probation officer, or a uniformed member of staff. Instead, it was the one-to-one contact which inmates had with one another, both with members of their own group and with members of the wider community, which was the most highly prized.

There were, however, important differences between the wings in respect of the therapeutic value which inmates attached to the small groups and one-to-one sessions. Men on C wing were significantly more likely than those on B and D wings to say that the most beneficial therapy they had received at Grendon had emanated from individual sessions rather than from the groups.[16] There may be a number of different explanations for this divergence of opinion. The organization of community meetings on C wing, which promoted analysis and discussion of the work in the small group, may have led to deeper and more intimate relationships amongst the wider community and consequently provided greater opportunities for more meaningful one-to-one sessions

[16] 49% of C wing, 12% of B wing and 15% of D wing said that their most useful therapy had occurred on a one-to-one basis. Conversely, 49% of B wing, 47% of D wing and 27% of C wing said that their most useful therapy had occurred on the group: $\chi^2 = 22.52$, df = 6, P < 0.001.

among a wider range of inmates. It is, however, more likely to have been due to differences in the nature of the populations on the three wings, rather than to any organizational or ideological differences between them. At the time of the research C wing had a higher proportion of men who had been at Grendon for less than six months and, as will become apparent in Chapter 6, the men's perceptions of the benefits they accrued from the group work varied according to the length of time they had spent at Grendon. Hence, what appears here as a difference between the wings is more probably due to differences between the phases of an inmate's therapeutic career.

Other aspects of the therapeutic regime at Grendon tended to be evaluated less in terms of their therapeutic content *per se,* and more in relation to the opportunities they afforded inmates to build upon and extend the work they were doing in the group and in one-to-one sessions with other members of the community. Wing meetings represented one important forum in which the whole community met and had an opportunity to comment on the behaviour and attitudes of individual members. But despite wing differences in the purpose, use, and content of these meetings, markedly similar opinions were expressed by inmates throughout the institution regarding their contribution to the therapeutic process. For the most part, the community meetings were deemed to have only occasional value because most of the time was said to be taken up with petty domestic issues of little or no therapeutic relevance. Where these meetings were thought to be beneficial was in facilitating the development, testing out and reinforcement of self-confidence and assertiveness through the practice of talking in a public setting. And, in addition, they were also thought to provide a useful forum in which a man could be exposed to more varied questioning and comments, based upon a wider range of experience than would be available from his group.

Another important therapeutic activity at Grendon was work, although the range of employment was limited and primarily focused upon the essential maintenance of the institution. Not unexpectedly, the men's assessments of the best jobs in the prison were influenced to a large extent by their interest in, and the perks associated with, particular tasks. Yet, about half the men who cited a 'best' job also gave what can be described as 'therapeutic' reasons for their choice. In other words, they considered a job as being particularly valuable if it contributed to particular therapeutic objectives. In general, the therapeutic value of work was articulated in terms of the opportunities it provided to test out, modify, and practise new attitudes and behaviours learned on the wing. However, particular themes tended to be associated with specific tasks. For example, most inmates thought that the best jobs were the 'red band' positions because the nature of the work permitted a considerable level of freedom to move around the prison unescorted and to mix with civilian staff and visitors. This, it was said, enabled them to test out their capacity to act in a responsible way and to practise their social and communication skills with 'normal' people. Kitchen work, on the other hand, although considered less popular, was said to be attractive because it provided good pay and extra food, as well as constant opportunities, afforded by the pressures of the job and working environment, to test out their levels of tolerance.

In addition to the men's paid employment there were a series of tasks, known as 'reps'' jobs, which serviced the community and were carried out by nominated inmate representatives. In contrast to the evaluation of paid employment, the reps' jobs tended to be valued mainly because of the perks which were associated with them. Therapeutic considerations tended to be referred to only when the men were defining what constituted the most unpopular tasks. For example, the 'sports rep', which involved the setting up of various recreational events, was most frequently cited as a popular job because it was said to enable the post-holder to make maximum use of the sporting facilities in the prison. Ironically, the job of 'television rep', which carried the weighty responsibility of organizing a daily vote to establish which television programmes would be shown that evening, featured among both the most popular and the most unpopular jobs. The power afforded the elected representative to bring his interests to bear in deciding the evening's entertainment made it an attractive post for some, while others were repelled by the thought of the inevitable public challenges and confrontations which invariably went along with it. Notwithstanding this, however, the majority (between 71 per cent and 85 per cent) of men on all wings had held a rep's job of some description and most of them felt that they had gained therapeutically from it. The degree to which they felt they had benefited and the nature of the benefits they cited were none the less considerably varied.

Being TV rep was an opportunity for me to put into practice some of the things we'd talked about on the group. It put me up-front and under a lot of pressure and it was down to me to handle it. It proved to me that I could deal with situations without violence and that was a big boost to my confidence.

I went for the sports rep because I like sports and I wanted to be involved in whatever I could. I thought I could handle the job better than the previous blokes and so I put up for it. I knew I could do it, but I suppose getting the tournaments sorted out and matches set up proved the point.

Difficulties in Therapy

The therapeutic experience at Grendon was, at one and the same time, reassuringly supportive and threateningly turbulent. Eight out of ten men described particular difficulties they had encountered in adjusting to life in the wing communities. Like the men interviewed within the first few weeks of their reception, most (60 per cent) of them felt that the major stumbling block was in being able to speak openly about themselves in front of others. Such anxieties have already been discussed in the context of the men's fears of self-disclosure within the group setting. But it is interesting to note that, although men on D wing reported less concern about talking on the group than those on B and C wings, they were just as likely to state that they had experienced some trepidation in speaking openly about themselves within the community as a whole. In fact there were no significant differences across the wings in this respect, which is perhaps surprising in that it might have been expected that men on B and D wings, who had undergone a process of induction on the assessment unit, would have been less likely than those on C wing, who had largely been received directly from other prisons, to have experienced such difficulties. This, however, was not the case.

Nearly a third of the men also claimed to have found difficulty in coping with what they perceived as the constant pressures of undergoing therapy, and the inability to escape and switch off the search-light. Adjusting to relationships with other inmates, and managing the problems which arose from close personal contact with those they might otherwise have chosen to avoid, was mentioned by about a quarter of the men as being a major source of concern. Interestingly, this was not mentioned more frequently by sex offenders than by any other prisoners, despite their experience of the traditional patterns of abuse and degradation. Becoming accustomed to the more liberal attitudes of staff, and the more intimate relationships between inmates and officers, was also found to be a formidable task by about one in six inmates. But again there were no significant differences by wing, and men on C wing, despite their lack of a separate induction programme, were no more likely than inmates elsewhere to find this problematic.

Despite these adversities everyone, with only a sole exception, felt able to identify specific advantages of the Grendon regime. Most notably, comments were tinged with a mixed sense of relief and gratitude in having the opportunity to engage in therapy and to address their problems and find resolutions to them. About a third of the men also claimed that the mutually supportive relationships at Grendon, both among inmates and between inmates and staff, were particularly valuable commodities. A similar proportion claimed that the general atmosphere of safety which prevailed was a unique and highly-prized aspect of life at Grendon. Interestingly, this was mentioned most frequently by men who had committed offences involving some element of violence and among those who had committed sex offences.[17]

The Critical Elements

An important question which this chapter has addressed is whether an inmate's allocation to a particular wing influenced the nature and extent of his participation in therapy. The conclusion which has been reached is that structural and organizational differences, which persisted during the period of research, significantly influenced the length of time for which men on the different wings stayed at Grendon, but did not fundamentally affect their assessment of their experience of therapy. Variations in the procedures for assessing inmates' progress in therapy, and differences in the structure and application of systems of community regulation, resulted in the average length of stay ranging from fourteen months on C wing to twenty months on D wing. Yet, despite some differences in their participation in group work, men on all three wings demonstrated markedly similar patterns of community

---

[17] A general atmosphere of safety was mentioned by 43% of violent offenders and 19% of non-violent offenders, and by 47% of sex offenders and 29% of non-sex offenders.

involvement and reported analagous benefits from the therapeutic process.

This uniformity of experience is perhaps remarkable, given the notable variation across wings in the content and nature of the small groups and community meetings, differences in the relationship between these two therapeutic forums, and the differential involvement of civilian staff. Thus, it would appear that the similarities are more important than the differences. An inmate's experience of therapy would seem to be primarily influenced by those factors which determine the therapeutic milieu, rather than those which structure its organization. Five characteristics may be identified as elemental in the creation of the therapeutic environment common to all three wings. The first is the existence of mutually supportive relationships between inmates. Each man's therapy can be seen to be facilitated by his involvement with others and his contribution to the life and well-being of the community. Secondly, there is the free flow of communication between inmates and staff. Both sides are encouraged to conceive of themselves as playing for a single team, the shared goal being the health of the community and the pursuance of therapeutic objectives. Third, there is the general atmosphere of safety, largely fostered by the 'no violence rule', which enables individual expression without fear of physical retribution. Fourth, permission and encouragement are given to all inmates to confront and find solutions to problems which underpin their current situations. Finally, all of this is contextualized for the inmates by their prior knowledge of the prison system. They have all encountered the culture of a conventional prison which extols the maxim of 'every man for himself'; promotes the necessity of a 'them and us' mentality; encourages the suppression of personal identity; and imposes compliance through the rule of force. Thus, the therapeutic milieu at Grendon is experienced, interpreted and appreciated by inmates in relation to their shared understanding of what they have known before.

5
Issues of Order and Control

The preceding chapters have discussed the organization of Grendon as a collection of therapeutic communities, but they have largely deferred any consideration of the fact that these communities are located within the walls of a prison. So far, the role of the establishment has been portrayed in terms of its treatment dimension, that is, the opportunity it affords inmates to understand their problems and to identify alternative and socially acceptable ways of coping with them. But it must be remembered that Grendon is also charged with a duty to contain in secure conditions, and maintain control over, a population of men who have been convicted of serious crimes and who have received some of the most severe penalties which the criminal justice system can impose. Essentially, Grendon may be conceived as embodying two separate institutions: on the one hand, the therapeutic community and, on the other, the prison, each with their own principles, aims and practices co-existing under one roof. This chapter seeks to examine how Grendon attempts to achieve the dual task of treatment and control, and what consequences this has for the functioning of the therapeutic communities and for the order and security of the prison. In this respect, it will address three specific issues. First, the fundamental characteristics of the two institutions will be compared and the major points of conflict identified. Secondly, the ways in which the two institutions co-operate in order to facilitate their mutual co-existence will be explored. And finally, the nature of the social order which is produced, and how this is maintained and controlled on a day-to-day basis, will be examined.

Two Institutions: Conflict and Co-operation

At face value, the prison and the therapeutic community appear to be highly incongruous cohabitees: a partnership destined for conflict. In the first place, the primary stated objectives of the two institutions are at variance. The major task of the prison is to contain a population of conscripts under conditions which are conducive to the maintenance of good order and control, defined in this instance as the avoidance of any kind of disruption to routines and regulations. Within a therapeutic community attendance is voluntary and the primary objective is treatment, which may be designated as the alleviation of pain or suffering. The very enactment of treatment, however, may require, and even demand, the expression of symptomatic attitudes and behaviour, which could well threaten order and question discipline.

The two institutions also differ fundamentally in terms of their principles and working practices. Prisons tend to be socially divided and hierarchically organized societies, producing a 'them and us' social structure in which the staff monopolize the legitimate power. Regulation is typically imposed by means of a system of explicit and non-negotiable rules, which seeks to bring about conditioned obedience, by coercion if necessary. As such, the prison operates to de-personalize the individual and seeks to inhibit the expression of personal choice. The therapeutic community, on the other hand, aspires to encourage the development of personal identity and to facilitate its expression. Unlike the prison, it is organized to minimize social divisions and to enfranchise all members in the democratic exercise of power. Within this structural context, regulation is achieved by means of a process which permits negotiation: rules are made by the community and may therefore be changed by the community. In this way, compliance is fostered by a commitment to the rules, facilitating the development of a system of internalized norms rather than a system of externalized rules.

The question which must be addressed is how these two seemingly incompatible institutions manage to co-operate in order to function within the same establishment, particularly in the light of the fact that this co-operation is not between equal partners. Grendon's primary identity is that of a prison and, as such, it is subject to the same formal rules as the rest of the system. In consequence, whatever level of co-operation the prison extends to the therapeutic community, it must reserve the right to step in and seize control whenever the security and discipline of the establishment are perceived to be under threat. Thus, within the communities, the staff team, in which the uniformed officers form the majority, retains the ultimate authority to make or revoke decisions in the name of the prison. Hence, the question of co-operation essentially refers to the level of tolerance which the prison is able to extend to the therapeutic community, while preserving its commitment to the goal of good order and discipline.

This research suggests that co-operation between the two institutions is made possible by the fact that they share two common features. Both institutions are designed to regulate deviant behaviour and both are concerned to maintain conformity in order to preserve the interests of their respective organizations, albeit that there are differences in the precise nature of the conformity required and the means by which it is achieved. In other words, it would be misleading to conceive of the prison as monopolizing all legitimate interests in the maintenance of order. Secondly, the extent to which the two institutions are able to co-operate to produce a social order which is acceptable to both is facilitated by the fact that those who live and work within the prison and the therapeutic community are one and the same. Prison officers are both custodians and therapists, and inmates are both prisoners and clients. This common ground enables the prison to relegate much of the day-to-day control of deviant behaviour to the therapeutic community. But control can only be achieved within the therapeutic community by negotiating compliance to an agreed set of norms. The extent to which the communities are able to maintain an acceptable standard of control through discourse is almost entirely dependent upon the degree to which the officers and inmates are able to modify their traditional prison roles, in order to break down the social divide between the 'keepers' and the 'kept', and to facilitate co-operative relationships and alternative working practices.

Staff Working Practices

Prison officers were acutely aware of the dual functions they were expected to perform. Virtually all (94 per cent) of them felt that working at Grendon was different from working anywhere else in the system. The routine measures of prison security, such as cell searching, landing patrols, and the escorting of prisoners, although present, were accorded a relatively low profile. But it was the level of contact and the nature of their working relationships with inmates which they thought fundamentally differentiated their job from that of their colleagues elsewhere. Their relationships with inmates tended to be characterized by three specific qualities: individualism, permissiveness and trust. In general, officers and inmates related to one another as individuals, calling each other by their first names and exercising personal choice over whom they spoke to and the level of affability they extended to one another. Their interactions permitted the mutual expression of dissent, in that inmates were allowed to voice dissatisfaction with the behaviour of the staff, as well as being expected to accept the criticism which staff levelled at them. In essence, these relationships were used as vehicles for inmates to entrust their personal problems to the discretion of individual members of staff. Such trust was, in turn, fostered by the willingness of officers to go some way toward sharing their own feelings and personal opinions with inmates.

Social relations between staff and inmates were facilitated by a range of working practices which collectively constitute one of the defining features of the Grendon ethos. To begin with, there was a flattening of the formal staff hierarchy, a bridging of the usual divide between the civilian and uniformed groups, and an emphasis upon multi-disciplinary democratic teamwork. Although the formal management structure of the prison service was present, everyone was expected to engage in the therapeutic activities of the wing and to participate as a full and equal member of the staff group in the process of decision-making. Typically, staff meetings were characterized by a pooling of resources and a sharing of skills and expertise. All officers, including those who had only recently been recruited to the service, felt that their views were taken into account and that all members of the staff team had an equal right to be heard.

The basic training which all prison officers receive does little to equip those who are posted to Grendon to assume the role of 'therapist'. In the words of one officer who had recently arrived from the Prison Service College:

I feel like I've been trained as a plumber and given a job as an electrician.

Although almost all of them had attended an introductory course in group work which was run at Grendon, and had found this helpful from a theoretical perspective, the majority (82 per cent) felt that the most significant training they had received had been 'on the job' under the guidance of more experienced staff. In playing the role of 'therapist' officers were required to tread a narrow line between, on the one hand, making themselves available to the men and encouraging them to talk about their problems and, on the other, imposing their own moral judgements or becoming 'over-involved' in particular cases.

Standards of professional conduct within the Service require prison officers to treat all prisoners equally and without discrimination. But at Grendon, this requirement becomes particularly demanding because of the close working relationship they are expected to have with inmates. The uniformed staff must act as guide, arbiter and protector to men towards whom they may personally feel considerable antipathy, either because of the abhorrent nature of their crimes or because of inimical aspects of their personalities. One group officer, for example, spoke of the difficulty he had experienced when he had been required to listen to the details of a particularly shocking crime, which had been recounted by a man who displayed little recognition of the atrocities he had committed and no remorse for the suffering he had inflicted upon his victims. This officer felt that he had not only to suppress his own feelings of disgust but also to temper the highly charged atmosphere which had been created within the group.

A key feature of staff working practices at Grendon is the high level of tolerance which officers extend toward behaviour which their formal training in prison discipline requires them to define as insubordination. The use of abusive language to an officer and the refusal to obey an order are among the most common disciplinary charges recorded against inmates in other prisons. Yet at Grendon such behaviour rarely results in formal adjudicatory proceedings and the subsequent imposition of punishments. This does not mean that swearing at members of staff and refractory behaviour are acceptable, but that alternative means of controlling them are employed. In essence, officers are expected to exercise control through therapeutic means and to interpret such behaviour as the manifestation of a man's problems and thus, as material for discussion rather than as an offence requiring a formal hearing. One man routinely tried the patience of wing staff by what were considered to be his arrogant demands for attention. He was seen to treat the officers as if they were his personal menservants, employed solely to cater to his needs. One morning he walked into the office where incoming letters were being censored and demanded his mail.

When he was informed that the post was not yet ready to be distributed he hurled a tirade of abuse and accused the officer of dereliction of duty and gross incompetence. The officer concerned responded by calmly apologizing for the delay and politely informing him that, contrary to his expectations, the Prison Department had still not issued instructions to suspend all other duties in the interests of expediting the delivery of his copy of *The Australian*. Implicit in this was the recognition by the officer that it would be counter-productive to challenge this man's abusive manner there and then. Instead, the issue would be taken up for discussion on his group or during a community meeting.

The success of these working practices, however, largely hinges upon the extent to which prison officers approve the aims and objectives they are being asked to work towards. Nine out of ten of the officers who were interviewed believed that the purpose of Grendon was to provide inmates with an opportunity for social and criminal rehabilitation, and three-quarters of them thought that the institution achieved at least some measure of success in attaining these goals. Overall, more than three-quarters of the officers stated that they found their work at Grendon to be rewarding and fulfilling.

Almost all (94 per cent of) the officers thought that in some respects working at Grendon was more difficult than working elsewhere in the system. They felt that different skills were required of them which, in the main, demanded that they gain compliance through a process of discourse, relying upon the force of their own personal resources, rather than upon the authority of their uniform. Eight out of ten officers stated that there were notable conflicts in the dual roles they were expected to play. They spoke of the incongruity of being expected at one moment to talk with a man about painful and intimate experiences and, at the next, to subject him to a routine search for contraband. They experienced a sense of inconsistency in their approaches to inmates, on the one hand, offering relationships based upon trust, and on the other, upon suspicion. An example of this was observed one evening when an inmate was sitting on the desk in the staff office and chatting about the guest list for the forthcoming wing social. At one point during the conversation the inmate leaned forward to look at the list to see who else had been invited. The officer, a new recruit, awkwardly shielded the list and told the man that he was bound by the Prison Rules and could not allow him to see it because it contained some private addresses. Almost two-thirds (60 per cent) of these officers, however, felt that the conflict between their discipline and therapy roles was not difficult to resolve: they were prison officers first and therapists second.

The Inmate Code

It is difficult to imagine that the working practices of Grendon's prison officers could be sustained if there were not parallel changes in the behaviour of the inmates. Traditionally, a code of conduct exists among prisoners, which demands loyalty and solidarity and condemns any fraternization with the staff, who tend to be seen as members of an opposing force. At Grendon the conventional inmate culture is largely dismantled in order to accommodate the therapeutic relationships with staff, as well as the therapeutic relationships between inmates. In line with the adaptations made by the uniformed staff the men modified their code of conduct in three fundamental ways, which permitted the erosion of stereotyped images and facilitated the development of relationships based upon assessments of the individual rather than upon preconceived notions of status.

The first of these represents a flattening of the customary hierarchy which exists among prisoners. The development of a therapeutic milieu within a prison setting is clearly dependent upon the breaking down of barriers between specific groups of inmates. At Grendon, the concept of a 'pecking order' is systematically eroded, being either obliterated altogether or re-constructed upon entirely different criteria. Seventy per cent of the men said that there was no place within the communities for the typical system of inmate stratification. Deference towards those who control the illicit supply of goods and services and toward prisoners convicted of 'respectable' and 'elitist' crimes, such as armed robbery and other offences connected with a professional criminal career, were largely abandoned. Frequently, these men were referred to as 'plastic gangsters' because their images as 'hard' men came to be seen as little more than a veneer of toughness, masking precisely the same fears and anxieties shared by everyone else. Instead, status and kudos were achieved by commitment to the community, which was demonstrated by a man's ability to use the therapeutic process constructively, not only for personal gain but also for the benefit of others.

On each of the wings the men whom other inmates identified as being most respected within the community were those who were seen to have made considerable personal progress in therapy, often undergoing a great deal of painful introspection and readjustment, and who were recognized as possessing a high degree of personal strength which enabled them to make their own decisions and to stand out against the crowd when necessary. Such men were described as valuable resources because their judgement was trusted and their ability to give unbiased and genuine advice was respected.

The general ethos of the communities was said to enable the men to experience an increased sense of safety, and to feel less threatened and more able to lower their defences and drop the protective image previously seen as so essential for survival in the system. The great majority (87 per cent) of the men interviewed stated that their relationships with other inmates at Grendon were substantially different from those they had experienced in other prisons. More than three-quarters (79 per cent) of those who had been there for less than six months claimed that they were able to relate more openly and, in consequence, more meaningfully than ever before.

The second and related way in which the traditional inmate culture is modified at Grendon concerns the subversion of those ritualistic practices which formally oppress those inmates who occupy the lower strata of the conventional hierarchy. At the bottom of this pecking order are those men who have committed sex and/or violent offences against women and children, and who have been segregated from other inmates under Rule 43 for their own protection. Four out of ten men on Grendon's treatment wings would be considered to fall into this category and most (88 per cent) of them claimed that in other parts of the system they had experienced either physical violence, frequently in the form of a 'beating in the showers' or a PP9 battery in a sock aimed at the back of their head, or verbal abuse. Indeed, half of them said that they had suffered such abuse from prison staff. At Grendon the majority (58 per cent) of inmates would, in a conventional prison, constitute the potential aggressors, from which the others would be expected to seek protection. One in five of these men had previously physically assaulted 'Rule 43' prisoners, a further 17 per cent had shouted abusive remarks to them, and just over a third (36 per cent) said that, while they had not actively engaged in any hostilities, they had ostracized these men and avoided any contact with them. Yet, within less than six months of being at Grendon, three-quarters of them claimed to have changed their behaviour towards the 'Rule 43' prisoners. Such reported behaviour was borne out by the patterns of friendship which existed on the wings. These indicated a high degree of integration between the 'Rule 43s' and the rest of the population: only one in five sex offenders identified friends exclusively amongst other sex offenders; and only one in four non-sex offenders failed to name a sex offender as a friend. Such individualization within the inmate culture acts not only to change the ways in which prisoners relate to one another, but also serves to reinforce the working practices of staff which hinge upon a receptiveness among inmates to personal communication.

This is not to suggest that sex offenders, who have traditionally occupied the role of social pariah, suddenly become totally integrated into the social fabric of Grendon. Indeed, half the men interviewed said that these offenders were not fully accepted within the community. What seemed to emerge, however, was a degree of tolerance and acceptance which was dependent partly upon the nature of the offence, but also upon the level of remorse the offender appeared to express about his crime. Those who recounted their offence in an emotionless way, who peppered their accounts with inconsistencies, and who attempted to justify their crime or negate or reduce their responsiblity for it, would be in line for an extremely uncomfortable therapeutic ride. In keeping with the approach adopted by the officers, inmates took the view that, however depraved and perverted the offence, these men needed some kind of help, and that there was a moral obligation to leave no therapeutic stone unturned—if not for their sake then for the sake of future victims. But in return for this, such members of the community were required to conform to behavioural expectations which were applied to them more rigorously and energetically than to any other category of offender.

The reasons which the majority (68 per cent) of inmates gave for their changed behaviour towards sex offenders focused upon the belief that they had gained a better understanding of the circumstances which led up to these men's crimes and that, in consequence, they were able more successfully to divorce their feelings about the offence from those about the offender. The men also argued that the regime at Grendon enabled and encouraged them to abandon aggressive practices, to which they had never been wholly committed but to which they had simply conformed because of pressures within the culture to do so. Half the men, however, maintained that, to some degree, they had been forced into accepting and working alongside sex offenders. Failure to tolerate their presence and reversion to previous practices were recognized by them as being counterproductive to their own interests. This would merely guarantee a reserved window-seat on the bus and the loss of their own place in therapy.

It is perhaps worth noting that, although three-quarters of the non-'Rule 43' population said that their behaviour towards sex offenders had changed since coming to Grendon, two-thirds of them said that this would not be sustained if they were transferred to a conventional prison. Most of these (79 per cent), however, insisted that any reversion on their part would not represent a backsliding to old attitudes, but would essentially be a survival tactic employed to protect their own position within a traditional prison culture. Only one in five of them maintained that they still harboured extremely negative feelings towards such men and merely conformed at Grendon in order to ensure the continuance of their own therapy.

To some extent the 'Rule 43' men experienced a greater sense of acceptance than was perhaps intended by their peers. Virtually all of them said that they were treated differently at Grendon and 70 per cent said that they felt completely integrated into the community and not discriminated against by either staff or inmates. Most (72 per cent) put this down to the ethos of the establishment, which they thought facilitated a degree of tolerance for the offender, if not for the offence. But, as with the majority of the population, half these men recognized that the regime at Grendon not only facilitated, but also enforced, a level of permissiveness by guaranteeing that an inmate's failure to conform would seriously jeopardize his place in therapy.

The third, and arguably most radical, aspect of the dismantling of traditional prison culture is the expectation that the inmate communities will engage in a degree of self-policing to control the illicit, and thus destructive, activities of their members. The wing constitutions and guidelines, for example, make it clear that it is each individual's responsibility to feed back to the community any information he may have about the use of violence, or about the supply and use of illicit drugs. In essence, prisoners are being asked to breach a cardinal rule of the inmate code of conduct, that is, to become 'a grass'. However, even in the earliest stages of their time at Grendon, very few men considered that taking action to enforce the 'no violence rule' represented grassing. Ninety per cent said that they would do something to control such behaviour and for most this meant either bringing it to the attention of the community at a wing meeting, or informing the perpetrator's group. The line which inmates drew between 'grassing' and 'therapeutic feedback' was determined by their assessment of the damage which certain kinds of behaviour could wreak upon the therapeutic activities of the community. At Grendon, tolerance of violence was low and there was a general recognition by staff and inmates alike that the 'no violence' rule represented a valuable and indispensable source of security within the therapeutic community. It was accepted that every man, regardless of his previous malevolence, should be afforded the opportunity to engage in therapy and to speak of his past behaviour without fear of physical retribution.

The control of drug use, however, was an area of conventional prison culture which proved less amenable to immediate change. Inmates were, for example, divided in their views about the ban on smoking cannabis. Most of them did not regard this type of drug use as damaging to therapy since, although drug supply in many other prisons tended to be associated with corruptive and intimidatory practices, they claimed that this was not the case at Grendon. It was roundly denied that distribution was associated with baroning (racketeering) or with the accumulation of debt and, in consequence, it was said that, as there were rarely any victims, the smoking of cannabis was something which was already sufficiently regulated by the community. This, however, is not to suggest that the inmates never revealed information about cannabis, rather that they tended to do so only on those relatively rare occasions when they perceived a man's therapy or the functioning of the community to be impaired or in jeopardy. Sixty per cent of inmates interviewed said that they would not take any action at all about the use of cannabis. However, the situation was reversed when 'harder' drugs, such as heroin, were considered. Only one in three inmates said that they would do nothing at all under these circumstances.

Faced with such reluctance on the part of inmates further to regulate the use of cannabis, the staff are effectively dispossessed of their power to maintain control within the terms of the therapeutic community. If they are to control the illicit use of drugs by community rules, they are required to respond to each case on its individual merits; to search for underlying causes, rather than manifest symptoms; and to use their discretion in the application of sanctions. But in order to do this they need to have the co-operation of the inmate members, who must share the staff's definition of the problem and be willing openly to discuss their own behaviour and the behaviour of others. If they refuse to conform in this way, the staff have no room for manœuvre within the therapeutic process and, in consequence, community control is suspended. This inevitably sparks a crisis of confidence on the part of the prison, which cannot tolerate the abandonment of control in this area, and subsequently steps in to impose its own order.

During the course of fieldwork, an example of this process occurred on C wing when there was an influx in the supply of cannabis which led to a more conspicuous pattern of use and a suspicion of profiteering and intimidation, which heightened the anxieties of staff and inmates alike. Officers urged those involved, in either the supply or the use of these illicit drugs, to come forward and own up. The inmates, however, felt that they were in a 'no win' situation, in that, if they admitted responsibility they would automatically be shipped out under the terms of the wing constitution. Those men who were not personally involved were similarly reluctant to provide information, either because they feared retaliation if, or when, they were returned to the system, or because they felt that the decretive penalty was out of all proportion to the offence. Staff argued that the constitution had been drawn up by the community and that all members had a duty to abide by it. If, in the light of these events, the community wished to alter the rules, a new constitution should be negotiated. In the meantime, staff maintained that the present game should be played according to the established rules. What ensued was a stalemate, in which the staff blamed the inmates for acting like conventional prisoners and concluded that they had no option but to abandon the role of therapist and assume the role of prison custodian. A list of suspects was unilaterally compiled and approved at the staff meeting, and the 'nominees' were duly transferred without any further reference to the community.

But the power relationship between the prison and the therapeutic community was not always this absolute. The therapeutic community could reassert its authority by challenging the efficacy and legitimacy of the prison's solution. There were, for example, occasions when the power of the prison was defused by the actions of the civilian staff and, in particular, by the wing doctors and psychologists who would identify the consequences and costs of adopting a particular line of action. In one case, a doctor responded to a list of suspected drug abusers whom the uniformed staff wished to 'put on the bus' by suggesting to the officers that there might be alternative ways of dealing with the impasse. He pointed out that, by pursuing a rigid line, and acting solely upon suspicion, they ran the risk of appearing unjust and hypocritical, and that this could seriously undermine their credibility within the community. He called the officers to account for their own behaviour by asking them to clarify their objectives and by encouraging them to assess whether the imposition of penal sanctions would further what they had already achieved through denunciation. In this instance the prison officers were persuaded that further confrontation would be futile and they abandoned the battle in the interests of winning the war. Thus, the civilian staff play a crucial part in the reconciliation of competing interests between the prison and the therapeutic community. Unlike prisoners and prison officers in the front line of combat, the civilians on the wing are free to play the role of mediator, because they have no prison uniform to parade and no divisional code to uphold.

It would be misleading, however, to suggest that the prison is willing to relegate all issues of control to the therapeutic community. During the period of research, a number of incidents occurred which seriously threatened the security and discipline of the establishment, and over which the prison refused to relinquish any power whatsoever. In one case a man sexually assaulted a woman visitor; in another, a female member of the administrative staff was threatened in the prison's kitchen with a knife; in a third, a man was charged with attempting to escape from Grendon. In all these instances, the threat to the good order and control of the prison was perceived to be so great that the men concerned were immediately transferred from the establishment, without any reference to their treatment interests or the therapeutic community. The priorities of the prison were clear-cut, non-negotiable, and immune to any consideration of therapy.

But the therapeutic community, too, is capable of taking unilateral action to protect its interests. In the course of the study, situations were observed in which certain inmates threatened community stability, not by breaking specific rules, but by challenging the assumptions which underpinned the legitimacy of the rules. Typically, they refused to accept that commitment to the therapeutic process necessarily required them to conform to all the community's prescriptions for their treatment. The response of the community to such men was determined not only by the nature of their challenge, but also by the persistent way in which they communicated it to others, particularly the way in which they communicated it to the staff. In effect, they refused to play the game of therapy according to the established rules. For example, in one case a man challenged the view of the community that his close friendship with one of the younger men was damaging either to this man's therapy or to his own. The community view was that, by focusing his attention and efforts upon his friend's difficulties, he was effectively avoiding dealing with his own problems. The democratic conclusion was that the two of them should spend less time together, and it was prescribed that he should change his job to allow this to happen. The man concerned denied that by helping his friend he was engaging in any kind of avoidance strategy, and although he did change his job, he did so reluctantly and refuted the validity of such a remedy. Throughout the course of these events he succeeded in continually shifting the grounds of debate away from the issue of his own compliance and acceptance and on to the issue of the staff's competence to make these decisions. In so doing, he implicitly questioned the community's right to assume authority over his best interests. In the face of this, the community, and more particularly the staff, were at risk of becoming outmanoeuvred and, in consequence, vulnerable to a loss of control over the definition of therapy.

When an individual's defiance is perceived to reach this level of threat, the staff take the decision, with or without the consent of other inmates, to expel him in order to maintain control within the therapeutic community. This was the fate of the man in the example. In such cases the prison has no vested interest to preserve, since these men only threaten the good order of the community and, in other respects, are frequently model prisoners. Thus, the exercise of control in these instances represents a manipulation of power by the therapeutic community alone.

The Human Element

Despite the fact that Grendon accommodates two separate institutional concepts, which appear to possess divergent and potentially conflicting principles and objectives, the maintenance of order and control is largely uncontroversial and is typically achieved by means of co-operation. The security of the prison is in large measure dependent upon the success of the therapeutic community in modifying relationships and facilitating new working practices between prisoners and prison officers. The accomplishment of this, however, hinges upon all parties agreeing that it is both a valid and an appropriate course of action. The constant need to engage in this kind of interaction was said to be a demanding and, at times, stressful experience. The informality of the relationships which officers had with inmates was simultaneously perceived both to threaten and engender their personal safety. It was said to be all too easy to become complacent about the men in their charge and to overlook the seriousness of their offences and the risks they were deemed to pose society. Yet, conversely, the officers also argued that it was the personal quality of the relationships they had with the men which afforded them their greatest personal security. The permissiveness, individualism, and trust, which characterized their interaction with prisoners, were believed to reduce the risk of physical assault by dismantling the traditional barriers of hostility and facilitating alternative strategies for dealing with inter-personal conflict.

However, the willingness of staff to modify their traditional ways of working was based not only on their view that such practices were an efficient means of maintaining order and security, but also on their commitment to the objectives of the therapeutic community. Notably, the staff reported a high degree of job satisfaction which was, in the main, related to their conviction that there was an end-product to their work and that what they were attempting to achieve was socially worthwhile. Typically, they focused upon the satisfaction they felt when they were able to observe significant improvements in the attitudes and behaviour of particular inmates, and the credit they could claim for the progress which had been made.

The staff's optimism about their work and their commitment to the aims of the regime were, to some degree, matched by a similarly positive attitude among inmates, who largely believed that it was a privilege to be at Grendon. The fact that all men are free to choose whether or not they come to Grendon and whether or not they stay, and that all those received into the institution are specially selected, reinforces the concept of privilege. The maintenance of this perspective is, of course, only possible so long as Grendon is seen to function within a system which provides a wealth of unattractive alternatives. Risk of premature transfer to other prisons hangs over the inmates like the Sword of Damocles and undoubtedly contextualizes their willingness to comply with the demands of the establishment.

It may be argued that as a prison Grendon represents 'a paradigm for good prison management'.[1] It is highly successful in maintaining security and control over a population of serious offenders with a minimal use of force and coercion. At the same time it provides some opportunity for the realization of the rehabilitative ideal embodied in Rule One of the Prison Rules, which states that the aim of the prison is:

to hold [securely] those people admitted to custody and to encourage and assist them to lead a good and useful life.[2]

Clearly, the case for more prisons like Grendon is compelling. But it has to be remembered that the extent to which the entire prison system could be run on the Grendon model is inevitably limited by the need to preserve the concept of privilege. It is, however, important to note that no single element provides the key to Grendon's success in maintaining order and control. Rather, it is the interaction between these elements which is crucial.

[1] Gunn, J. and Robertson, G. (1987), 'A Ten Year Follow-Up of Men Discharged from Grendon Prison', *British Journal of Psychiatry* 151, 674–8, at 678.
[2] Home Office (1964), *The Prison Rules*, London: Home Office, s. 1, no. 388.

6
Therapeutic Achievements

This chapter seeks to address how it might be possible to evaluate the therapeutic achievements of Grendon. The issue will be examined by posing a number of sequential questions. First, is there any indication that an inmate's experience of, and reaction to, therapy constitute a graduated process, whereby specific and related stages of development are achieved within certain periods of time? Secondly, is there any evidence that the formal assessment of an inmate's progress in therapy is structured by the concept of a staged process of development, or a 'therapeutic career'? Finally, how might it be possible to identify a 'Grendon success' and thus evaluate the therapeutic achievement of the establishment?

The Therapeutic Process

In 1978, John Gunn and his colleagues published *Psychiatric Aspects of Imprisonment*, in which they evaluated the psychotherapeutic effect of Grendon upon a sample of 107 men received into the prison between 1971 and 1972.[1] They concluded that while these men were in Grendon 'massive changes' took place in their social attitudes and psychiatric state. By means of psychiatric interviews and psychological testing they demonstrated a highly significant reduction in neurotic symptoms, such as anxiety, tension, and depression, and a decrease in the amount of hostility and antagonism felt by the men towards other people, but particularly towards those in authority. In addition, the study showed that there was a marked increase in the self-confidence and self-esteem of inmates, who reported a significantly greater degree of social participation and a lessening of anxiety about social interaction. Most of these changes, it was said, took place within the first three

[1] Gunn, J., Robertson, G., Dell, S., Way, C. (1978), *Psychiatric Aspects of Imprisonment*, London: Academic Press.

months of an inmate being at Grendon, but the authors noted that 'some changes, whilst they occur quickly, require more time for consolidation and reinforcement'.[2] Indeed, the men in their study reported that they found the treatment more useful as time went on, so that the proportion who felt they 'had learned a considerable amount about themselves' rose from 66 per cent at three months, to 85 per cent at nine months.

Seventeen years later, and approximately 1,800 inmates further down the line, this study similarly found that men reported significant changes in their attitudes and behaviour which they attributed to the therapeutic regime, and particularly to the group work. But the issue to be addressed here is whether these changes tend to be achieved within specific periods of time. For example, is it possible to identify a staged therapeutic process? Our sample of 102 inmates, who were interviewed during their period of therapy on the treatment wings, was divided into three groups: those who had been at Grendon for less than six months; those who had been there between six and twelve months; and those who had stayed for twelve months or longer.[3] The responses of these groups were compared, in the light of contemporaneous observation of the content and social dynamics of the small group and community meetings, in relation to three specific areas of change: modifications in the inmates' adherence to traditional prison culture; developments in their perceptions of their problems; and changes in their assessments of the benefits they had derived from therapy.

Inmate Culture

Consistent with the earlier research, the sorts of changes reported by the men on the three treatment wings varied according to the

---

[2] Ibid., 122.

[3] There were no major differences between the groups in their criminal and demographic histories, or the reasons they offered for coming to Grendon. All the men were asked whether they felt they had gained from being in therapy and, if so, what particular benefits they had accrued. Given the similar profiles of the three groups, and the fact that they had been subjected to the same therapeutic programmes and penal regime, the assumption was made that, if a staged process existed, the responses of any one of these groups at a particular point in time could be expected to be representative of the responses of the other two groups at the same moment in history. For example, it was anticipated that the responses of inmates who had been at Grendon for less than six months would broadly reflect those of inmates in the other two categories, had these men been asked the same questions within the first six months of their therapy.

lengths of time they had been at Grendon. There were a number of significant developments which seemed to be manifested almost immediately, although these appeared to have been consolidated and reinforced among those inmates who had stayed longest at Grendon. The previous chapter demonstrated that modifications to conventional attitudes and behaviours, which traditionally under-pin relations among inmates and between inmates and staff, are clearly a prerequisite for the initiation of any therapeutic activity within a penal context. But the dismantling of such conventions may in itself also signify therapeutic achievement. This study has shown that within the first six months of arrival at Grendon almost three-quarters of the men (71 per cent) had abandoned adherence to the conventional inmate pecking order and had low-ered the barriers between the traditional insider and outsider groups, thus enabling them to step outside their 'image' and relate as individuals.

The 'them and us' mentality which rigidly separates staff and inmates in many other establishments was also seriously eroded during this time: two-thirds (68 per cent) of the men who had been at Grendon for less than six months said that they had been able to overcome their initial resistance and talk to prison officers about personal matters. However, the proportion of men who reported this was significantly greater among those who had spent longer in Grendon: within the group that had been there for between six and twelve months, more than eight out of ten felt able to discuss per-sonal issues with at least one prison officer, and of those who had been there for more than twelve months the proportion rose to more than nine out of ten (see Fig. 6.1).[4] But it was only among those who had been there for six months or longer that a majority of men said that they had spoken to a larger number, and broader range, of uniformed staff. In the first six months only about a quarter of the men had spoken on this level with more than one member of staff, whereas two-thirds (68 per cent) of those who had been there for between six and twelve months, and nine out of ten of those who had been at Grendon in excess of a year had done so.[5]

Opposition to the presence of uniformed staff in the group was also much lower among those who had spent longer at Grendon.

[4] $\chi^2 = 8.58$, df = 2, P < 0.01.   [5] $\chi^2 = 23.17$, df = 4, P < 0.0001.

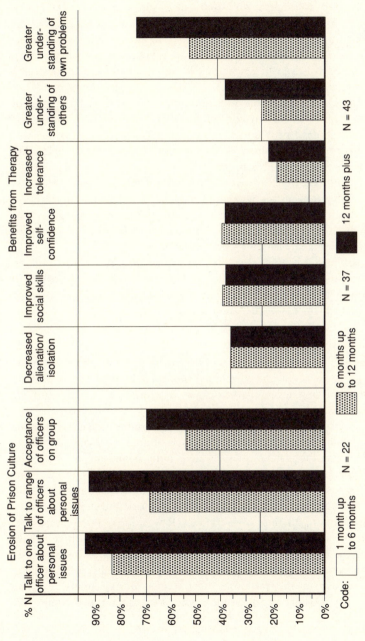

Figure 6.1. *Erosion of prison culture and benefits from therapy by time at Grendon*

In the first six months only four out of ten men were in favour of officers listening and contributing to discussions in the group. Of those who had been in therapy for six to twelve months, however, just over half approved of this practice, and this proportion increased to seven in ten among those who had been there over a year.[6]

There was also some indication that the extent and nature of inmate intervention to control illicit activities and, in particular, their attitudes towards the supply and use of heroin, varied according to how long the men had spent at Grendon. It was only among those who had been there for more than a year that a majority (60 per cent) said that they would intervene if they suspected the presence of heroin on the wing, and that they would do so by recourse to formal measures, such as informing the staff or bringing it to the attention of the whole community. In the context of therapeutic development, this may be indicative of an increase, over time, in the men's confidence to 'stand out against the crowd' and in their preparedness to assume personal responsibility in order to control, not only their own behaviour, but also the social conduct of other members of the community.

Perceptions of Problems

Observational work on the assessment unit and on the three treatment wings revealed that, almost immediately after their arrival at Grendon, inmates embarked upon a process of redefining their problems, whereby they were encouraged to look beyond the surface of symptomatic features of their difficulties and to search for underlying causes. This process constituted a 'dynamic' force, mobilizing the men to question their motives and to face up to the harsh realities of their situation and unpalatable truths about themselves. Individuals were left in no doubt that the community would not tolerate members who hid behind excuses and denied personal responsibility for their own conduct. It was, for example, unacceptable for sex offenders to blame their victims for provocative behaviour, or for violent offenders to explain their aggressive outbursts as a consequence of excessive drinking. These observations were borne out in the responses of the men during interview. The majority (85 per cent) of men who were interviewed while still

[6] $\chi^2 = 14.19$, df = 6, P < 0.02.

within the first six months of their therapy claimed that their perception of their problems had already changed since coming to Grendon, and all but one of these felt that they had either discovered new problems or realized that their difficulties were more complicated than they had previously thought.

Inmates carried on redefining their problems throughout the therapeutic process as they continued to seek clarification and greater insight. When comparisons were drawn between men who were interviewed within a few weeks of reception and those interviewed at varying points in time during their period of therapy, it was evident that certain differences of perception existed. For example, amongst those men who had been at Grendon for more than six months there was some decrease in the proportion who claimed that their problems emanated from alcohol or drug abuse; and this appeared to be sustained amongst those who had been in the institution for more than twelve months. Conversely, among those who had been at Grendon for between six and twelve months, there was a significant increase in the proportion who felt that their problems stemmed from their difficulties in establishing and maintaining personal relationships (see Table 6.1).[7] It is, however, noteworthy that whilst a high proportion of men who had remained at Grendon for more than twelve months continued to attribute their problems to relational difficulties there was some reduction in their numbers in favour of more complex explanations.

Table 6.1. *Definition of problem, by time at Grendon* (%)

	Reception sample (n = 71)	Main sample on treatment wings (n = 102)		
		less than 6 months	6 months up to 12 months	12 months plus
Problem with drink/drugs	39	45	32	26
*Problem with personal relationships	25	36	73	60

Note: * For main sample: $\chi^2 = 7.71$, df = 2, P < 0.02.

[7] An individual inmate may appear in more than one problem category if he defined his problems as multi-faceted. Similarly, if he mentioned numerous benefits derived from therapy he will be represented in more than one category of benefit.

Over time, the men also demonstrated a heightened awareness of their own feelings of aggression. At the point of reception into Grendon this was a problem which was identified almost exclusively by inmates under the age of thirty and by those who had committed a violent offence.[8] On the treatment wings it was apparent that a wider range of offenders recognized that they too had problems in dealing with aggression. This was found to be particularly the case among men convicted of rape, who, as a group within the reception sample, tended to ignore or deny the aggressive features of their behaviour. Among the receptions only 17 per cent of this category of offender admitted to such a problem, in comparison with half of those who were interviewed within the communities.

Perceived Benefits from Therapy

The benefits inmates claimed to gain from the process of therapy also appeared to be related to the lengths of time they had spent in Grendon. Something which seemed to be achieved immediately, however, was a reduction in their sense of alienation. When the men were asked what they thought they had gained so far from being at Grendon, a similar proportion, irrespective of the time they had been in the establishment, spontaneously said that they felt less isolated and less alienated from other people (see Figure 6.1).[9] This is clearly consistent with the principles of social therapy and with the emphasis which is placed at Grendon upon encouraging all inmates to see themselves, from the moment they arrive, as full members of the community. As Schilder has pointed out: in a group, individuals 'realize with astonishment that the thoughts

[8] See Chapter 3.

[9] The issue here is the identification of a process. What is of interest is whether the proportion of men spontaneously mentioning particular benefits continues to rise over time, or whether there is a point after which there appears to be no further increase. We are not concerned here with identifying whether a majority of men have either succeeded or failed to achieve specific benefits at particular points in time. Indeed, the data do not allow for this interpretation, since the men were not asked specific questions relating to each benefit cited. Rather, the analysis is based upon spontaneous responses to an open-ended question about gains from therapy. Thus, omitting to mention any specific benefit may be interpreted in a number of different ways and does not necessarily indicate therapeutic failure, e.g. a man may not mention that he feels less isolated because he has never experienced a sense of isolation, or because other benefits predominated in his mind at the time of the interview, or because his sense of isolation has not been affected.

which have seemed to isolate them are common to all of them'.[10] By sharing and facing up to the problems of living together as a community, inmates were able to move away from feelings of isolation and alienation and from the sense of abnormality which many of them had hitherto experienced. Their initial feelings of emotional and psychological distance became bridged by the dawning recognition that many of their problems, which they had hitherto defined as uniquely pathological, were in fact shared with fellow inmates.

There were, however, other benefits which, while mentioned by some men within the first few months of being at Grendon, appeared to be much more frequently cited by those who had been there for over six months. For example, between six and twelve months there was a markedly higher proportion of inmates who reported an increase in self-confidence, an improved ability to communicate and socialize, and a higher degree of tolerance towards other people. But there was no increase in the proportion of men reporting these changes who had been in Grendon longer than a year. Among this latter group, however, there was a notably higher proportion of inmates who said that they had gained some insight into their own problems, and a greater understanding and degree of empathy with the problems faced by others (see Figure 6.1).

The Phasing of the Therapeutic Process

All this would appear to indicate that the therapeutic process at Grendon follows a series of phases, whereby specific changes tend to be achieved within certain broad time periods. There is, however, an alternative interpretation which could account for these findings. For example, it may be contended that the different responses of the three groups merely reflect a process of distillation, whereby the 'best bets' remain longer in therapy and thus increasingly weight the positive responses of the longer-serving groups. These two, rather different, interpretations need not necessarily be contradictory or, indeed, mutually exclusive. Detailed observation of the daily functioning of the therapeutic communities demonstrated the existence of distinct phases of therapeutic development. Yet, at the same time it would not be unreasonable to

---

[10] Schilder, P. (1939), 'Results and Problems of Group Psychotherapy in Severe Neurosis', *Mental Hygiene* vol. 23, 87–98, at 91.

anticipate that, for various reasons, certain types of men will stay longer at Grendon than others.

In keeping with the interview data, the observational work suggested that the first six months may be conceived as a settling-in period, in which the *'ancien régime'* of traditional prison culture is dismantled and replaced with the 'new order'. During this time inmates reassess their problems and appear to undergo a process of acclimatization to the therapeutic community, which enables them to experience a sense of acceptance, belonging and social integration. By the end of twelve months a process of resocialization appears to have been effected, in which the men review their social skills and revise their modes of social interaction. Such reformulations lead them to experience a greater degree of satisfaction in their relationships with others and particularly with those in authority. But after the first year there seems to be a consolidation of achievements and a furtherance of the intellectual component of therapy. There is a continued increase in the numbers of inmates gaining confidence and trust in staff, in the numbers moving towards greater acceptance and exercise of social responsibility, and in the numbers developing insight into the interrelated nature and underlying causes of their own problems.

The Assessment of Individual Progress

The identification of a phased therapeutic process begs the question of how it might be possible to assess each individual's progress in therapy. In this respect it is necessary to question whether the evaluation of individual therapeutic achievement at Grendon is based upon a presumption of graduated development and the concept of a progressive career. One way of assessing this is to examine the criteria employed in the routine assessments carried out by staff on the three treatment wings. Observation of the various assessment procedures revealed that, within each of the three treatment wings, there were certain conditions which an inmate was required to meet in order to qualify as someone who was making progress in therapy.

At the bottom line, the individual was required to accept the fact that he had committed his crime and must now take responsibility for it. What this meant was that he had to acknowledge that his offence had consequences for himself and for other people, such as the victim, the victim's family, or even members of his own family. In doing this, he had to accept that his behaviour had been socially harmful. This required him to display an appropriate level of remorse, both at an intellectual level, whereby he recognized that he should feel regret for his actions, and at an emotional level, whereby he actually experienced contrition.

The inmate also had to demonstrate a motivation for change, a desire to be different, and to provide evidence that he had the aptitude to put this into practice. What this usually amounted to was that he could identify his problems, and express some understanding of how they were interlinked to produce socially harmful behaviour. What was being evaluated was his ability to absorb and fit together ideas: in other words, his capacity for learning. Being able to show that he could withstand the rigours of the therapeutic process was also a feature of the evaluation. What was often looked for here was the ability to accept criticism and not avoid addressing painful issues. The assumption was that, if done properly, undergoing therapy at Grendon was the 'hardest way to do time' because pain was an inevitable consequence of the therapeutic process. True progress was marked by using these painful experiences constructively, without becoming overwhelmed and destroyed by them.

Linked with such robustness was the expectation that the individual should demonstrate 'commitment' to the therapeutic process. This was usually represented by the inmate conforming to certain expectations which had been placed upon his behaviour by the community. In practice, the requirements placed upon the individual could be wide ranging: from being expected to talk more on the group; to changing his job; or even being urged to alter certain aspects of his relationships with people outside the prison. In essence, what was required was a willingness to accept the medicine which other members of the community had prescribed. But inevitably, there came a time when what was looked for from the individual was a change in his behaviour, especially in those domains which had been defined as most difficult for him. For example, if a man was seen to suffer from an inability to stand up for himself in situations of conflict, thereby internalizing his anger to his own detriment, any sign of greater assertiveness on his part would be deemed to indicate significant progress.

The assessment process judged how far an individual had

succeeded in meeting some or all of these conditions. If he was thought to be making progress, he was defined as deserving of his place at Grendon. Conversely, if he had failed to meet the necessary conditions, he risked being defined as a non-deserving case, and his transfer back to the system became imminent. It was, however, possible for inmates to fail to meet these requirements yet still be defined as deserving of a place at Grendon. These may be termed the 'special cases', in that the decision to keep them was based not upon the standard criteria of therapeutic progression but upon other factors. For example, some men had been kept at Grendon because their crimes were seen as so dangerous, and their potential risk to society so great, that the communities experienced a sense of obligation to push the boundaries of their tolerance to the limits. The same was true of men who were perceived as being so vulnerable that they represented a serious risk to themselves. In all these cases, Grendon provided a service not only to the individual but also to the rest of the prison system. Prisons are charged with the duty to protect society from dangerous criminals and to contain them in conditions which permit the least disruption to the management of the system. The therapeutic regime at Grendon, with its back-up of professional staff, serves as a useful resource for the surveillance, assessment, and ultimate control of these prisoners.

What has been described so far indicates that the regular assessments carried out on the treatment wings embody an expectation of staged therapeutic development. But what is also implicit throughout this process is the concept of a progressive therapeutic career, whereby inmates are expected to progress through three distinct therapeutic modes, moving from the role of novice to that of elder member. When men first arrive on the treatment wing they are permitted a degree of lattitude to sit back and observe the community at work. Participation at this stage is expected to take the form of studied attentiveness, purposeful enquiry and comment. After this, the men are expected to engage in a process of high therapeutic activity. This is gauged by their candid participation in the group and community meetings; by their search for new testing grounds for their behaviour, exemplified in their applications for new jobs and responsibilities on the wing; and by their concerted efforts to contribute to the therapy of others. The final stage is marked by an expectation that inmates will embark upon a process of detachment from the intensity of therapeutic work and prepare for eventual flight from the nest. By this time it is anticipated that they will have become an established source of guidance and support for less experienced members of the community.

The Therapeutic Achievement of Grendon

The discussion so far has suggested, first, that there are discernible and sequential stages in the therapeutic process at Grendon; and secondly, that the evaluation of individual progress is predicated upon an expectation of graduated advancement through a therapeutic career. The question remains, however, whether it is possible to identify, and thereby measure, the therapeutic achievements of the establishment. One of the problems which has dogged Grendon's history is its inability to evaluate its own performance. From its inception in the 1960s there has been a notable absence of agreed criteria whereby the impact of therapy upon the inmate population might objectively be evaluated and the success of the therapeutic regime adjudged.

Research into psychotherapy has been notably reluctant to engage in any objective evaluation of the effects of such intervention. Most evaluative studies have worked from the basis of clients' subjective reports of their own achievements, and these have shown that most forms of such treatment are approximately 50 per cent more likely to produce an improvement than would otherwise occur.[11] Howarth has attributed the lack of attention to objective assessment of psychotherapeutic outcome to the existence of two false beliefs.[12] The first relates to the assumption that there is no need for objective studies since psychotherapists themselves can assess effectiveness through their own clinical practice. Howarth argues, however, that this type of learning 'requires feedback which is faster and more reliable than any which is available to a practising psychotherapist'.[13] In other words, the difficulty with this type of assessment is said to be the lengthy time periods over which psychotherapy usually operates, and the fact that the

[11] See e.g. the analysis in Smith, M. L., Glass, G. V., and Miller, T. I. (1980), *The Benefits of Psychotherapy*, Baltimore: Johns Hopkins.
[12] Howarth, Ian (1989), 'Psychotherapy: Who Benefits?', *The Psychologist*, vol. 2, no. 4, April, 150–2.
[13] Ibid., 150.

available knowledge is based upon a subjective construction of social reality formulated within the therapist–client relationship.

The second belief is that 'scientific evaluation is not appropriate for procedures which deal with existential, rather than factual, matters'. They require, it is suggested, 'a phenomenological or hermeneutic approach'. Howarth suggests that this type of argument is flawed because it assumes that 'clients should only be interested in their own perceptions and beliefs' and not in the reality which is experienced by others, or in 'more objective measures of their well-being'. The need to move beyond this is justified in that:

The belief that one has been helped by a psychotherapist is unlikely to be self-validating for most people. Most people's beliefs are not strong enough to enable them to walk on water or to get a better job if their behaviour is inappropriate.[14]

All this, however, raises two crucial points regarding the assessment of the effectiveness of therapy. First, any measurement of 'success' must be predicated upon a clear statement of objectives. And secondly, any statement of objectives must be predicated upon a judgement as to what it is reasonable to expect of psychotherapy. An evaluation of Grendon's 'success' must therefore be based upon criteria which relate to the achievement of its stated task, and not upon those which pertain to matters beyond its influence. The objective of the therapeutic communities has been clearly stated in the 1987 Circular Instruction:

The aim is to create an atmosphere in which an individual can explore and acknowledge his pattern of behaviour, understand the motives underlying it, and modify his behaviour both during sentence and in the longer term when he is released to the community at large.[15]

In other words, it is expected that Grendon will enable men to engage in therapeutic activity in order to achieve specific benefits which will ultimately facilitate changes in their behaviour. Implicit in this is a concern with the future criminality of inmates. But prior to any evaluation of Grendon's success in reducing rates of recidivism, it is essential to assess how far the establishment succeeds in facilitating the therapeutic progress of individual inmates.

---

[14] Howarth, Ian (1989), 'Psychotherapy: Who Benefits?', *The Psychologist*, vol. 2, no. 4, April, 151.
[15] Home Office (1987), Prison Department Circular Instruction 21/1987.

The Therapeutic Career

In order to measure Grendon's success in relation to the therapeutic progress of its inmates, it is not enough simply to record how far an individual reports that he has attained specific benefits within specific periods of time. Such an analysis would overlook the possibility that, for example, a man who reported an improvement in his ability to communicate with other people might already have been relatively functional in this area. While it could be argued that it is advantageous for individuals to undergo an experience which leaves them feeling more positive about themselves and their relationships with others, this is clearly not the main objective of the therapeutic communities. Men are selected for Grendon because it is believed they have specific problems which are amenable to the sort of therapy available within the communities. Any evaluation of individual progress must, therefore, be based upon an assessment of change which is related to each inmate's particular problems.

Detailed observation of the ways in which the staff formally assessed the progress of each member of the community enabled us to identify broad therapeutic expectations and provided a basis upon which we were able to construct a five-stage career model that could constitute a framework within which to evaluate more objectively what individuals are achieving in therapy (see Fig. 6.2).

Stage I	Recognition	—	Definition of problem
Stage II	Motivation	—	Expression of desire to change
Stage III	Understanding	—	Recognition of inter-connected and related aspects of life
Stage IV	Insight	—	Identification of solution to problems
Stage V	Testing	—	Putting into practice new ways of coping

Figure 6.2. *The Therapeutic Career Model*

The first stage is that of *recognition:* the man has to recognize that he has problems and he has to be able to define at least some of their constituent elements. The second is the stage of *motivation*, in that, having recognized that he has a problem, the inmate has to experience a desire to change. The third stage may be considered to mark the beginning of therapeutic activity, in that the man has to acquire some *understanding* of how his problems have arisen, and how they are interconnected, and relate to other aspects of his life. For example, a man who recognizes he has a problem in controlling his feelings of violence may associate such outbursts with periods of heavy drinking. But, at the same time, he may need to recognize that both his violence and his drinking may only be symptoms of other underlying problems, such as his low self-image and lack of ability to relate to other people, which, in themselves, may be rooted within difficulties in his childhood experiences. The fourth stage represents the point of *insight,* whereby the individual has to achieve some understanding of what he has to do, or change, in order to bring about some resolutions to his problems. So to continue with the earlier example, the man may perhaps decide that he needs to become more assertive and less aggressive in his approaches to other people and learn to accept criticism and rejection without allowing them to overwhelm his concept of himself. Finally, there is the *testing* stage, at which point the inmate has to test out, in practice, at least some of the new and alternative ways of coping. This may take place either inside the prison or, more importantly, outside, if he has been granted a period of home leave.

Our assessments, based upon detailed and lengthy interviews with men about to be released or transferred to another prison, indicated that progression through these stages was highly correlated with the length of time they had spent in therapy. The longer their period in therapy the more likely the inmates were to have progressed to the final stage. Inevitably, different individuals move through the process at different speeds, but the interview data suggest that there is a critical period, at or after eighteen months, when the majority of men who are leaving Grendon have progressed to the final stage. In other words, they will have met the intellectual requirements, by having achieved an understanding of their problems and insight into how they may resolve them, and they will have met the behavioural requirements, by having tested out and modified some of their ideas in practice. It is significant that only 19 per cent of men who were leaving after having spent less than twelve months in therapy reached this final stage, in comparison with 33 per cent of those who were leaving after a period of between twelve and eighteen months, and a staggering 88 per cent of those who were going after eighteen months or more.[16]

[16] $\chi^2 = 23.84$, df = 2, P < 0.001.

Less than 12 months	19%
12 months up to 18 months	33%
18 months plus	88%

Figure   6.3.   Completion   of   Thera-
peutic Career

Looking at it in another way, this means that of the thirty-two men who had completed all five stages, two-thirds had stayed for eighteen months or longer. It was very rare for someone to achieve all stages and leave within six months.

If the objective of the therapeutic regime at Grendon is to help an inmate to develop understanding and insight into his problems and to assist him in changing his behaviour, the application of this framework could provide a systematic means of demonstrating the therapeutic process at Grendon and of assessing the performance of the establishment. In particular, it opens up the possibility of being able to identify specific groups of prisoners who seem to progress further in therapy than others and, conversely, those who seem to make very little progress at all. It should be borne in mind, however, that the model is essentially progressive and that a failure to reach the final stage does not necessarily indicate failure *per se.* Someone who, on leaving Grendon, has not progressed beyond the third stage will still have identified his problems and will have recognized how the various aspects of his life are interrelated to produce certain outcomes. Nor does leaving Grendon necessarily mark the end of the process. It is possible for individuals to continue therapeutic activity after they have left the institution.

So, what does this study reveal about those men who are most likely to be 'Grendon successes', that is, those who stay eighteen months or longer and who would be expected to progress to the final stage of their therapeutic career? A census was undertaken of the entire population *transferred* from the three treatment wings between 1 March 1988 and 28 February 1989. This represented a total of eighty-two men who left Grendon at different points in their careers and for varying reasons. The purpose of this exercise was to query whether there were any significant differences in the personal characteristics of those men who stayed less than a year, those who stayed between twelve and eighteen months, and those who stayed for eighteen months or longer. One methodological point which should, however, be made is that the small size of the sample inevitably limited the range of factors which could be correlated. This is particularly pertinent in relation to any analyses of the effect of a man's offence and, perhaps most importantly, of the factors associated with the length of stay on any particular wing.

The first point to emerge from the census data was that, contrary to the view of many doctors responsible for the initial referral of inmates to Grendon, the age of the prisoner appeared to be unrelated to the length of his stay. It has to be remembered, however, that the age span of the men on the three adult treatment wings was already largely restricted to those aged between twenty-five and thirty-five. There were, however, a number of factors related to the men's personal and institutional background which, although they did not reach a level of statistical significance, appeared to be associated with their careers at Grendon. Men who stayed for eighteen months or more tended to possess fewer previous convictions and to have fewer disciplinary offences listed against them from other prisons, especially for offences of violence against inmates. There was also some indication that particular offences were associated with the lengths of time the men spent at Grendon. At the top end of the scale, nine out of ten of those convicted of murder who had left Grendon did so after eighteen months, although this may be related, in part, to the difficulty of moving life-sentenced prisoners within the system. At the other end of the scale were those who had been convicted of rape: two-thirds of these offenders who had left had done so within six months of their arrival. It is important to note that again this finding differentiated these men from other sex offenders, only 16 per cent of whom had left within this time period.

There were, however, a number of factors which were significantly related to the lengths of time men stayed at Grendon. The first of these was sentence length: the longer the sentence a man was serving, the longer he tended to stay at Grendon. The mean length of stay for men serving between three and ten years was eleven months, in comparison with a mean of twenty-four months for those serving determinate sentences of ten years or more, and a mean of twenty-two months for those sentenced to life imprisonment.[17] The men's psychological test scores were also significantly

[17] $\chi^2 = 20.40$, df = 8, P < 0.01.

related to the lengths of time they spent at Grendon. Inmates who stayed longest were the more intelligent, those who demonstrated high levels of guilt, and those who tended to be highly self-critical, rather than blaming others for their situation.[18] In addition they tended to be the more introverted men, to have low scores of actual and paranoid hostility, low psychoticism ratings, and to direct their feelings of hostility inwardly towards themselves rather than 'acting out' towards other people.[19]

All this, however, begs the question why these particular factors appeared to be significant. Is it possible to identify some internal meaning and reason for these particular findings? Is it, for example, the case that these men are, by virtue of their personal characteristics, more amenable and responsive to therapeutic intervention than those who did not manage to stay the course, and left before they had completed all five stages of the career model? There is clearly some consistency between the personal characteristics of the men who remained at Grendon for longer then eighteen months, and the requirements encapsulated in the routine processes on the wing for assessing inmates' progress in therapy. For example, high guilt and self-criticism scores in the psychological tests are compatible with the expectation that a man should accept responsibility for his crime and demonstrate remorse. Similarly, a higher level of intelligence is likely to assist the inmate in dealing with the intellectual component of therapeutic progression.

But, as has already been demonstrated, an inmate's career at Grendon is not solely determined by the formal processes of assessment: it is also shaped by processes of decision-making which have to do with issues of control rather than considerations of treatment. Both the prison and the therapeutic community contain their populations within certain limits of tolerance. When these are breached, or even suspected of having been exceeded, the respective institutions step in to protect their boundaries, and expel the deviants who threaten the maintenance of therapeutic activity

[18] Intelligence $\chi^2 = 8.45$, df = 2, P < 0.01
Guilt $\chi^2 = 12.49$, df = 2, P < 0.001
Self-criticism $\chi^2 = 6.68$, df = 2, P < 0.05
Criticism of others $\chi^2 = 7.53$, df = 2, P < 0.02.
[19] Introversion $\chi^2 = 8.09$, df = 2, P < 0.01
Actual hostility $\chi^2 = 4.94$, df = 2, P < 0.08 approaching significance
Paranoid hostility $\chi^2 = 8.80$, df = 2, P < 0.01
Psychoticism $\chi^2 = 11.36$, df = 2, P < 0.001
Direction of hostility $\chi^2 = 18.15$, df = 2, P < 0.0001.

and/or the security and control of the prison. Hence, the ways in which institutional interests are defended may well explain the tendency for those who have records of more serious prison indiscipline, and those whose psychological profile suggests that they tend to direct their feelings of hostility outwards, to have shorter careers at Grendon. It is perhaps worth pointing out that, when treatment considerations are excluded from the decision to transfer a man from Grendon, one consequence may well be that an individual's career is foreshortened and he is expelled for displaying symptoms of the problems which prompted his referral to Grendon in the first place.

The concept of therapeutic success in Grendon, or indeed elsewhere, is socially constructed by, and hence represents a product of, a complex process of interaction between the idiosyncratic characteristics of the individual and the structural features of the therapeutic environment. At Grendon this environment is produced by a negotiated settlement between two potentially competing institutions: the prison and the therapeutic community. Career progression at Grendon is thus contingent, not only upon the individual satisfying the expectations inherent in the therapeutic process, but also upon the ability of the social processes at work, within both the prison and the therapeutic community, to tolerate the expression of his deviance.

Future Criminality

The assessment of Grendon's therapeutic achievements in relation to the progression of individual therapeutic careers begs the important question whether this process leads to a redirection or abatement of criminal activity. It has to be remembered that this was at least part of the symptomatology which motivated the men's referral for treatment in the first instance. It must be borne in mind, however, that this is not seen to be a relevant issue in all cases, since there are some inmates who, it is generally believed, would be unlikely to re-offend, with or without the intervention of therapy. But notwithstanding this, what can Grendon realistically be expected to achieve? In this respect, it has to be remembered that the therapeutic process occurs within a highly specific environment which is circumscribed by the institutional presence of the prison. Moreover, is it feasible to expect Grendon, or any form of psychotherapy alone, to induce changes in an individual's personal and social functioning which, in and of themselves, result in changes to his social situation or structural position in society?

In 1987 John Gunn and Graham Robertson published the results of a study in which the reconviction rates of men discharged from Grendon ten years previously were compared with a matched control group.[20] This showed somewhat disappointing results, at least from Grendon's point of view, in that more than eight out of ten men in both samples had been reconvicted during this time. Moreover, there were no significant differences in either the frequency or severity of their post-discharge convictions. The authors were, however, at pains to point out a number of inherent limitations in the use of reconviction rates for a comparative evaluation of the effectiveness of the Grendon regime. They noted that 'official records are a crude and dubious measure of offending behaviour', not least because of the important distinction which must be made between committing offences and being caught and convicted of them. But they also questioned the appropriateness of such measures of Grendon's performance, arguing that any variance in the men's reconviction rates must be interpreted in the context of the totality of their previous experiences and not merely by reference to whether or not they have undergone treatment in prison.

It was argued that a fixed and limited period of time spent in prison X, as opposed to prison Y, constituted a tiny fraction of the variance which might be held to contribute to the criterion measure of reconviction and that the measurement of its contribution was confounded by lack of control over these more potent contaminating variables.[21]

In consequence Gunn and Robertson stated that 'to view the prison as "treatment", analogous to the criterion variable in a physical experiment, is inappropriate and misleading'.[22]

If, however, it is accepted that therapy at Grendon assists the men to understand their problems, and to define alternative strategies for coping with situations which have led them into difficulties in the past, then it could be argued that a consequence of this may well be some degree of change in their criminal activities. But, irrespective of these arguments, as long as the stated objectives of Grendon incorporate an expectation that the therapeutic regime

[20] Gunn, J. and Robertson, G. (1987), 'A Ten Year Follow-Up of Men Discharged from Grendon Prison', *British Journal of Psychiatry* 151, 674–8.
[21] Ibid., 674.   [22] Ibid., 677.

should lead to a reduction in criminal conduct, then recidivism must continue to be one of the criteria by which Grendon's achievements are evaluated. Some indication could be gained from a study of reconviction rates, but this should focus upon a study of men who have successfully completed their therapeutic career, rather than upon a random population which includes some men who will have failed even to embark upon the therapeutic process. Thus, Grendon's success as a therapeutic community should be measured, at least in the first instance, in terms of an individual's progression along a clearly defined career path. This study has demonstrated the existence of such a process, and has defined criteria by which it might be possible to construct a therapeutic career model and thereby evaluate Grendon's therapeutic achievements.

Shortly after we had completed the research, our tentative therapeutic career model was used to inform a preliminary analysis of the reconviction rates of men passing through Grendon.[23] Data were collected on a randomly selected sample of 214 men who were serving determinate sentences and who had been in therapy at Grendon between January 1984 and December 1989. By subjecting these data to a range of statistical tests and comparing them with the Home Office Prison Statistics for England and Wales, it was found that the general rate of reconviction was lower (although not significantly so) amongst these men than amongst the wider prison population: 33.2 per cent of the Grendon sample had been reconvicted within two years of being released from prison in comparison with between 42 and 47 per cent of all adult males who had been released during the same period. However, this broad comparison was found to mask important distinctions within the Grendon sample. When account was taken of the length of time that the men had spent at Grendon, it emerged that a significantly smaller proportion of those who had completed eighteen months or longer in therapy had been reconvicted (20 per cent) than those who had spent less than eighteen months in therapy (40 per cent). The probability of reconviction was reduced further when the men had been released directly from Grendon (16 per cent) and when they had been rated as a 'success' in therapy (7 per cent).

Whilst this appears to be encouraging from Grendon's point of view, it does not provide conclusive proof that Grendon works to

[23] Cullen, E. (1993), 'The Grendon Reconviction Study Part I', *Prison Service Journal*, 90, 35–7.

reduce reoffending, even in the short term. First, as Cullen acknowledges, reoffending is associated with a number of features, including the age of the offender, the type of offence committed, and the length of sentence served. The fact that, at the time of our research, the average age of the men at Grendon was 30 years, 4 months; that, in comparison with the wider prison population, a greater proportion of these men had been convicted of offences against the person and were serving long sentences; and that the longer the sentence a man was serving the longer he tended to stay at Grendon, may explain, at least in part, the lower rates of reconviction amongst the Grendon sample, and, in particular, amongst those who had spent eighteen months or longer in therapy. In order to control for these features, a second phase of analysis has been proposed in which the sample of men from Grendon will be compared with 'matched' samples drawn from the wider prison population.

It is likely, however, that the Grendon men will still differ from other prisoners, irrespective of how closely they are matched, because of their motivation to modify their behaviour. Thus, even if the Grendon sample continued to demonstrate a lower rate of reconviction, it would be impossible to determine from any statistical analysis based solely upon prison records whether this was due to a predisposition to stop offending or to the influence of Grendon. It would, however, be reasonable to speculate that, at the very least, the successful completion of therapy at Grendon would reinforce any prior disposition based upon motivation. However, a further problem remains in the use of reconviction rates to measure reoffending, since a man might reoffend, yet not be caught or convicted. One way of overcoming these difficulties would be to incorporate a more qualitative dimension into the analysis by interviewing the men. This would enable both a more accurate assessment of reoffending rates and an exploration of the relationship between the role played by motivation and the influence of the prison environment upon subsequent criminal behaviour.

7

Leaving Grendon: Back in the System

This chapter examines how and why inmates leave Grendon and seeks to describe the post-Grendon experiences of those men transferred back to other prisons. Where do they go? Why do they leave? Who makes the decision? And how do they adapt to the change? First, we identify the men's destinations and describe the reasons which underlie the decision-making process which leads up to a man's transfer out of Grendon. We then examine how the men feel they have benefited from their time in therapy, and what consequences they believe this will have for them in the future.

So far this research has demonstrated that while inmates are at Grendon important and beneficial changes take place in their attitudes and behaviour. But are these changes simply adaptations to a therapeutic environment or are they sustained once the men are transferred back into the milieu of a conventional prison? Given that many of those who leave Grendon are returned to other establishments to finish their sentences, it should be questioned whether their period of therapy has had any lasting consequences, either for themselves or for those who manage the system. The remainder of the chapter reports on the experiences of a sample of ex-Grendonians who were followed up in other establishments. It describes how they readjusted to life back in the mainstream prison system, and considers the extent to which conventional patterns of inmate behaviour continued to be modified, and what consequences this had for prison management. In addition, it examines some of the costs of the Grendon experience for those who failed, for whatever reason, to complete their therapeutic career. In order to gain as clear a picture as possible, these issues are explored in relation not only to what the men say about their interaction with staff and other inmates, and how they report dealing with difficult situations, but also in terms of the official records of their prison behaviour. An important purpose and continuing theme throughout this chapter is to discover whether there are any notable differences in what happens to inmates who have spent varying lengths of time at Grendon and who are, therefore, likely to have progressed to different stages of their therapeutic career.

It is, of course, notoriously difficult to assess the effects of any single intervention in a person's life. Each individual is routinely exposed to a wide range of experiences, which may be singly or collectively influential in producing certain kinds of outcome. Given this situation it is impossible to set up a controlled experiment and, at best, all that can be hoped for is a series of indications which form a pattern, and from which general conclusions may be drawn.

The Destination of Men leaving Grendon

Between 1 March 1988 and 28 February 1989 a total of eighty-two inmates left Grendon from the three treatment wings. About three-quarters (73 per cent) of these men were returned to the mainstream prison system and only a quarter (27 per cent) were released, either at their EDR or having been granted parole. This represents a complete reversal of the practice revealed in John Gunn's study seventeen years ago. His analysis of a cohort of 107 men demonstrated that only a quarter (25 per cent) were transferred to other prisons and that three-quarters (75 per cent) were released or paroled directly from Grendon.[1]

Clearly there are problems associated with comparing data based upon a population of transfers with those based upon a population of receptions.[2] But these difficulties are unlikely to explain such a dramatic shift of practice. Rather, the increase in the number of men being transferred back to other prisons is most likely to be accounted for by the fact that Grendon is now serving a very dif-

---

[1] Gunn, J., Robertson, G., Dell, S., and Way, C. (1978), *Psychiatric Aspects of Imprisonment*, London: Academic Press, 71–2.

[2] The former are likely to yield a greater proportion of men who leave Grendon earlier in their careers. An attempt to overcome this methodological difficulty was made by drawing a census of men received over a twelve-month period, 1985–6. This showed that there had been a substantial shift of turnover and length of stay between 1985 and 1989 so these data could not be used as representative of current practice (see Chapter 2).

ferent sector of the prison population than it was in the early 1970s. At that time, the majority of men received at Grendon were serving relatively short terms of under three years, and they were transferred toward the end of their sentences in the expectation that they would be released directly from Grendon. We have already demonstrated that, at the time of our research, Grendon was receiving a high proportion of long-term and life-sentenced prisoners. Inevitably, the process of decategorization required to prepare these inmates for release will significantly reduce the numbers of prisoners who could realistically be expected to be discharged from Grendon. In fact, all the men who were released on parole during the census period were serving determinate sentences of less than ten years and, within this group, those most likely to be paroled were serving sentences of less than five years (see Table 7.1).

Table 7.1. Sentence length, by whether released, paroled, or transferred

	Released on EDR	Paroled	Transferred	Total
1 year up to 5 years	1 (4%)	10 (44%)	12 (52%)	23
5 years up to 10 years	2 (5%)	7 (18%)	31 (78%)	40
10 years plus	1 (14%)	0	6 (86%)	7
Life	—	—	11 (100%)	11
TOTAL	4 (5%)	17 (21%)	60 (74%)	81*

Note: * Data missing for one man.

The Effects of Therapy

Implicit in the research by John Gunn and his colleagues is the assumption that those who were returned to the system were 'Grendon failures', in that they were transferred 'prematurely, i.e. before their release or parole date'. This can no longer be said to be an accurate reflection of the current situation. Of the sixty men who were transferred to other establishments during the census period, eighteen (30 per cent) had spent eighteen months or longer in therapy and would have been likely, therefore, to have progressed through all five stages of their therapeutic career (see Table 7.2). Indeed, of all those who had stayed for eighteen months or longer, more than half (56 per cent) were transferred back into the system, although the majority of these were lifers. But even among the determinate-sentenced men who had remained at Grendon for eighteen months or longer, more than a third (36 per cent) were returned to other prisons (see Table 7.3). If an inmate had spent less than eighteen months in therapy he was almost certain to be transferred to another establishment: more than eight out of ten were sent back to other prisons, even though a number might reasonably be expected to have completed their therapeutic career.

Table 7.2. Time spent at Grendon, by whether released, paroled, or transferred

	Released on EDR	Paroled	Transferred	Total
Less than 18 months	1 (2%)	7 (14%)	42 (84%)	50
18 months plus	4 (13%)	10 (31%)	18 (56%)	32
TOTAL	5 (6%)	17 (21%)	60 (73%)	82

Note: Mean length of stay for those paroled = 19 months.
   $\chi^2 = 8.38$, df = 2, P < 0.005.

Table 7.3. Time spent at Grendon, by whether released, paroled or transferred (Determinate-sentenced men only)

	Released on EDR	Paroled	Transferred	Total
Less than 18 months	1 (2%)	7 (14%)	41 (84%)	49
18 months plus	4 (18%)	10 (45%)	8 (36%)	22
TOTAL	5 (7%)	17 (24%)	49 (69%)	71

The policy of transferring men from Grendon is based upon the principle that all inmates should be returned to the prison whence they came. Indeed, for the most part, inmates were transferred back to the establishment from which they had come, or to one of a similar type and security classification. This clearly limits the opportunity for decategorization from the institution. Only four men (8 per cent) were reallocated to a prison of lower security than they had previously been used to, and all these were life-sentenced prisoners transferred from category B to category C training establishments. In line with Grendon's policy of receiving determinate-sentenced inmates towards the latter part of their sentence, those transferred to other prisons had relatively short periods left to serve before their release: 90 per cent of the men returned to the system had less than two years to run before their EDR.

The Decision to Leave Grendon

The ultimate decision that the time has arrived for a man to leave Grendon is often the consequence of a complex process of negotiation between the prison, the therapeutic community, and the individual. In practical terms such decisions may involve any number of participants from within the community. For example, a man may take himself out of therapy; he may be 'voted out' by the staff group and/or by his peers; or he may leave as a result of a combination of these factors. A major problem associated with locating and classifying inmates within this, or any other, interactive process is that different interpretations may frequently be given to the same event by the different individuals involved.

The Staff's Perception

An exercise was conducted in which staff were asked to recall what had prompted the transfer of each of the 102 inmates who had been returned to other prisons over the preceding twelve months. As might be expected varying perceptions were held by different members of staff regarding the circumstances leading up to the departure of the same individual. Nevertheless, it was possible to discern some broad areas of agreement which divided the inmates roughly into two general categories, according to whether the staff attributed the prime cause of their transfer to therapeutic or disciplinary factors.

Approximately four out of ten (44 per cent) of the inmates were said by most staff to have been transferred solely for therapeutic reasons. In these cases the decisions were said to have been based upon an assessment of therapeutic progression, and to have been reached through a process of negotiation between members of the wing, acting as representatives of the therapeutic community, and the individual, in his role as client. Within this category more than half (55 per cent) of the inmates were described, by at least one member of staff, as having successfully dealt with their problems and reached the end of therapy. A further 38 per cent were said to have made some progress, but had reached a stage in their therapy where they were unlikely to make any further advancement. Only three men were considered by *all* the wing staff to have been unsuitable for treatment.

Disciplinary offending was claimed by most staff to have contributed to, if not secured, the removal of a further 41 per cent of men, and a small number (7 per cent) of others were said to have been ousted for displaying disruptive behaviour which overstepped the limits of tolerance within the community.[3] It is interesting to note that inmates whose transfers were categorized in this way were not necessarily defined by staff as having failed in therapy. Indeed, when staff were asked to assess the therapeutic achievements of these men, only one-third were consistently rated as failures; half of them were described, by at least some, as moderate successes; and a small proportion (4 per cent) were defined as unreserved successes. Overall, the responses of staff clearly indicated that only nineteen men, fewer than one in five of the population, were regarded as having failed in therapy.

The Inmates' Views

Interviews conducted with a sample of sixty-nine inmates immediately prior to their leaving Grendon shed further light upon the intricacies of the decision-making process leading up to a man's transfer from the treatment wings. One of the most striking features of the Grendon regime is the opportunity it affords inmates to make their own decision to opt out of therapy and leave the institution. As many as one-third of the fifty-three men who were leaving Grendon to be returned to other prisons claimed that they had exercised this right and instigated their own transfer. The reasons they gave for leaving were varied: six of these seventeen men believed that it was time for them to go because they had successfully dealt with the problems they had come to solve; four felt that the therapy offered at Grendon was unable to assist them in finding solutions to their particular difficulties; four had become disillusioned with the ways in which the communities operated; and three felt that they were no longer able to cope with the pressures and demands of the therapeutic regime. But regardless of the

[3] It is important to bear in mind the distinction between a population of transfers and a population of receptions, in that the former is likely to yield a higher proportion of men who leave earlier in their careers. A transfer cohort is, therefore, likely to include a greater number of men who are transferred for reasons of disciplinary offending, or disruptive behaviour than would be expected if the data were drawn from a population of receptions.

reasons the men gave for wanting to leave, it was clear that their decisions had not been taken lightly or in isolation. For the most part they had discussed the issue and sought the opinions of prison officers, peers, and, in particular, other members of their groups. In consequence, these decisions tended to be characterized by a high level of agreement among members of the community.

However, the remaining two-thirds of the inmates who were returning to other prisons felt that they had been given no say in the decision. Included in this group were not only those who had been 'voted out' for reasons associated with the maintenance of order and control, but also those who were being transferred for therapeutic reasons, including those who were leaving because they were said successfully to have completed their treatment. But notwithstanding their lack of participation within the decision-making process, almost half (47 per cent) of these men agreed with the decision that they should leave Grendon, although the extent of this agreement varied considerably according to the reasons the men had been given for their departure. All but one of those who were said successfully to have reached the end of their treatment agreed that it was time for them to move on, and half the men being shipped out for disruptive or delinquent behaviour also accepted the appropriateness of the 'penalty'. However, inmates notably disagreed with the decision to transfer them when it was based upon the view that they were either unsuitable for the treatment available at Grendon, or were unlikely to make any further progress in therapy. The majority (67 per cent) of prisoners in these categories disputed such assessments and were opposed to their return to the system.

As would be expected, the men who had stayed for eighteen months or longer were the most likely to say that they were being transferred for therapeutic rather than disciplinary reasons, and in most cases (71 per cent) they were leaving because they thought they had successfully reached the end of their treatment. Conversely, those departing within twelve months of their arrival were more likely than other inmates to say that they were leaving for disciplinary reasons.[4] However, the inmates' lengths of stay at

[4] 35% of those transferred within twelve months of arrival were removed for disciplinary offences or other disruptive behaviour, in comparison with 27% of those who were transferred after being at Grendon for between twelve and eighteen months, and only 6% of those who were transferred after eighteen months.

Grendon did not affect the proportion of men who made their own decisions to leave. Nevertheless, the reasons the men gave for these decisions did vary according to how long they had been in therapy, and whether or not they had completed their therapeutic career. Those who had been at Grendon for less than eighteen months, and were leaving without completing their career, tended to have opted out for what could be described as negative reasons: because they felt unable to cope with the pressures of therapy, or because they had become disillusioned with the regime. Men who had spent eighteen months or longer in therapy, and who had completed all five stages of their career, tended to have taken more positive decisions to leave, and had initiated their transfer because they felt they had completed their therapy.[5]

Approaching Departure

The overwhelming majority (91 per cent) of inmates who were leaving, for whatever reason and irrespective of how long they had stayed, thought that they had benefited from the time they had spent at Grendon. And most (82 per cent) believed that their therapeutic experience would remain with them and help them to cope with the vicissitudes of life when they eventually left prison. Over half the men (59 per cent) said that they had learned new ways of behaving, which they anticipated would better equip them to avoid the sorts of difficulties which had led them to their current situation, and more than one-third (39 per cent) claimed that Grendon had provided them with a sense of direction and hope for the future. Regardless of whether the men were about to be transferred back to other prisons, or were being paroled, or released into the community, the descriptions they gave of the benefits they had derived from their stay at Grendon were remarkably similar, and in line with those cited by the inmates who were interviewed while still in therapy.[6]

---

[5] All five men who had stayed eighteen months or longer and who chose to leave, did so, because they felt they had reached the end of treatment. Among those staying under eighteen months, one man chose to leave because he felt he had competed therapy; four felt Grendon was unable to help them; four were disillusioned with the regime; and three could not cope with the pressures of therapy.

[6] See Chapter 6.

Few of the men who were approaching their return to the mainstream prison system were looking forward to the 'impending day of reckoning'. This is perhaps not surprising, given that as many as three-quarters of them had experienced difficulties in previous establishments. Among this group were men who, according to the established norms of traditional prison culture, had been located at the bottom of the inmate hierarchy and had become regular victims of verbal threats, intimidation, and even physical abuse. At the other end of the spectrum were the potential perpetrators of this violence. These were men whose anti-authority attitudes, aggressive behaviour, and subsequent indiscipline had secured them a place on the roundabout of constant conflict and confrontation with prison staff. Finally, there were those for whom the prison experience had proved totally overwhelming, and who had withdrawn into an isolated world, suffering severe depression, alienation, and even paranoia.

Most of the inmates (79 per cent) awaiting transfer, however, thought that what they had learned at Grendon would influence how they approached the rest of their sentence. Three-quarters of them believed that the main advantage would be in terms of their relationships with other inmates, and half of them anticipated improved relations with prison staff. It was widely believed that their new-found ability to be reflective, discerning, and to 'think things through' before acting would enable them to avoid trouble. In this respect, it is significant that about two-thirds of the men who had experienced problems on account of their anti-authority behaviour in the past believed that they would now be able to avoid such trouble. A similar proportion of men who had previously been the victims of abuse said that they felt they would be better equipped to stave off victimization. And again the same proportion of men who had suffered some kind of psychological trauma in the mainstream system felt that they would be better prepared to cope with their feelings in the future.

Overall, half the inmates anticipated that their time at Grendon would make the rest of their sentence easier to live through. As would be expected, this group mainly consisted of men who were leaving on a positive note, either because they had come to the end of their therapy, or because they were thought to have progressed to their limit. Once again, men who had spent eighteen months or more at Grendon were significantly more likely than those who had stayed for shorter periods to believe that their time in the system would be eased.[7]

Only a quarter of the men who were returning to other prisons said that they did not intend to change the ways in which they had previously approached their imprisonment. Almost invariably, this was founded upon the belief that they had to 'fit back' into the system, and the fear that any modification in their behaviour that might set them apart from their peers would create difficulties which they were not prepared to confront. Indeed, such problems were acknowledged even by those men who had successfully completed their treatment at Grendon, and who intended to change their behaviour. As many as two-thirds were concerned about both the stigma that would be attached to them as 'ex-Grendonians' and the problems they felt they would have to confront in attempting to eschew the roles and behavioural expectations inherent in traditional prison culture.

Back in the System: Inmates' Perceptions of the Therapeutic Effects of Grendon

A total of forty ex-Grendonians were interviewed in twelve different establishments representing all categories of security and a wide range of prison conditions.[8] More than three-quarters of the men were serving long sentences of five years or more, and seventeen were lifers. The over-representation of life-sentenced prisoners, and long-termers in general, was due largely to the fact that these men were easier to locate because they tended to remain in the system for longer periods of time, and were less transient. Half of the sample had stayed at Grendon for at least a year and almost a third had remained for eighteen months or longer. Among those who had stayed for under a year there were three men who had been transferred within less than three months of their arrival and who, therefore, were unlikely to have even begun to embark upon a therapeutic career. The men had been back in the system for varying periods of time, ranging from two months to five years,

---

[7] 78% of men who had been at Grendon for eighteen months or longer thought the experience would make it easier for them to complete their sentence in comparison with 43% of those spending twelve to eighteen months and 35% staying twelve months or less: $\chi^2 = 9.56$, df = 4, P < 0.05.

[8] See Appendix 3.

although half of the men interviewed had been away from Grendon for more than twelve months, and 10 per cent had left more than three years ago.

Adjustment to the System

Most (80 per cent) of the men, regardless of how long they had spent at Grendon, continued to feel that they had benefited from the therapeutic experience and only one man believed that it had been a wholly negative experience. Nonetheless, a majority (60 per cent) of inmates had experienced some difficulties in readjusting to life in a conventional prison. It is, however, interesting to note that none of these men said that their difficulties had anything to do with there being a stigma attached to having been at Grendon. Although some inmates said that they had been the butt of a number of jokes and had been required to put up with some jibing about Grendon being a 'nonce prison' and a 'funny farm', they had not interpreted this as a personal attack and therefore had not seen it as a major problem. In the main, comments made by other prisoners were enquiring and interested and virtually all ex-Grendonians had spoken to other inmates about the regime at Grendon and the purpose of therapy.

The main difficulties the men experienced in adjusting to a conventional prison environment can be divided into three broad categories. First, there were difficulties associated with getting used to new routines and practices, particularly in local prisons where the men typically experienced severe restrictions upon their freedom of movement and constraints upon their opportunities for varied activities. Some inmates, for example, used to being unlocked all day at Grendon and enjoying free association every evening, were moved to establishments where they were held in their cells for twenty-three hours a day without any employment and with the possibility of evening association once every three days. The second type of difficulty was linked to the men's psychological adaptation to their sentence. For example, some found that they had spent a lot of their time at Grendon focusing upon events—past, present, and in the future—outside the prison walls, and that returning to the 'real world' of the conventional prison only emphasized their confinement and their sense of frustration.

Before I went to Grendon I accepted prison as my fate—I wasn't worth anything else, it was all I deserved. But Grendon gave me a belief in myself—I'm not rubbish and I can make something of my life. Sitting out the rest of my sentence has been hard because I just can't wait to put my life together out there. (John: life: category C prison. At Grendon three years, two months. Returned to system four years.)

But, in keeping with the anxieties expressed by those inmates who were interviewed just prior to their transfer from Grendon, the difficulties which were most commonly experienced were associated with the adjustments the men had to make in order to compromise with the demands of conventional prison culture. Inmates found that they had to come to terms with the fact that the rest of the prison system did not run as a therapeutic community. They had to realize that it was not in their interests to discuss their problems openly or advise other prisoners about aspects of their behaviour which they thought might benefit from some modification. Those men who had previously had a high profile as trouble makers experienced special difficulties, in that returning to the system often involved confronting their old image. Other prisoners and staff made it clear that they expected them to live up to their earlier reputation and, for some, breaking away from this proved highly problematic.

I was determined to put into practice the things I'd learned at Grendon and not to get mixed-up with the bad elements again. But I found I'd got a reputation to live down and some people just wouldn't let it die . . . Some of my old mates think I have been brainwashed and the staff thought I was putting on an act to work the system. It's bloody hard walking against the tide sometimes. (Mick: life: dispersal prison. At Grendon nine months. Returned to system two years, six months.)

Despite these initial difficulties of adjustment, a majority (60 per cent) of inmates felt that their time at Grendon had made it easier for them, rather than more difficult, to serve the rest of their sentence. This was particularly the case among those who had stayed at Grendon for eighteen months or more: three-quarters of these men thought their time in therapy had subsequently enabled them to alleviate the difficulties of serving out their time, in comparison with half of the men who had stayed for less than eighteen months. The main ways in which Grendon was said to facilitate this 'easing of time' was by increasing the men's social skills and enabling them to gain insight into their own behaviour and their interactions with others. Inmates claimed that since being at

Grendon they had gained a heightened awareness of how to get on with other people, and had developed an ability to be more reflective and to understand how certain situations can arise. In consequence, they said that they no longer felt it necessary to expend their energies in maintaining an image in order to 'fit in', and that they felt more able to identify and avoid those situations which would compound their difficulties and lead them to grief.

There was, however, some evidence that men who had previously been on Rule 43 for their own protection were more likely to find that being at Grendon had increased their difficulties in serving the rest of their sentences. More than half (nine) of the sixteen men previously on Rule 43, in comparison with only one in eight of all other prisoners, said that their period at Grendon had made it more difficult for them to complete their sentence. This difference is largely explained by the fact that, for most of these men, returning to the conventional prison system had meant a return to the fear of intimidation, the threat of violence, and the reality of social isolation. Their time at Grendon was generally regarded as a period in which they were treated as individuals, rather than as perpetrators of a particular crime, and one in which they were permitted the freedom of personal expression and the opportunity to participate as equal members of a community. Back in the system only other outcasts were their equal, they existed at the bottom of the pecking order, and were dispossessed of any rights to express themselves, or to have any identity beyond that which was ascribed to them by virtue of their criminality.

Influence on Attitudes to Life Beyond the Prison Gates

Apart from the effects which therapy was thought to have had upon their adjustment to life back in the system, the men were also asked whether they thought that the time they had spent at Grendon would have any consequences for their future in the outside world. Only four out of ten thought that their future plans had been fundamentally influenced by their experiences at Grendon, but opinions varied according to how long the men had spent in therapy. Over half of those who had stayed for eighteen months or longer reported that their plans would have been very different had they not been to Grendon, in contrast to a third of those who had stayed for a shorter period. It should be borne in mind, however, that the influence which is brought to bear at Grendon is not of a kind which structures the practical details of future ambitions but one which tends to facilitate choice and disclose new options. For example, a number of men claimed that because they had gained in self-esteem, improved their self-confidence, and had increased their ability to relate with other people, they had become open to prospects which had hitherto remained out of sight.

Notwithstanding this, a majority (60 per cent) of the men interviewed maintained the belief that their time at Grendon had been influential in reducing the risk of their re-offending. Again, this was mentioned most frequently by those men who had stayed at Grendon for eighteen months or longer: more than three-quarters of them, compared with half of those who had been at Grendon for less than eighteen months, thought that their therapeutic achievements had diminished, if not nullified, their chances of committing another offence. The role which therapy was seen to play in this arena focused upon enabling the men to understand the circumstances which had preceded and contributed to their previous crimes, and to devise ways of avoiding similar circumstances in the future, or to conceive of alternative strategies for coping with these situations should they arise.

It was like I was on a treadmill and I just couldn't see a way off. I was utterly confused about my sexuality—was I gay? Was I straight? I thought I was straight but all I really knew for sure was that I was attracted to kids. But at the same time I didn't want to be: I wasn't at ease with it and I felt awful afterwards . . . I learnt at Grendon that the reason I had no friends was not because I was a loner, which was what I'd thought before, but because I had a real problem in relating to other men. I was frightened of them—not just in prison—and that this really stemmed from my father and the way he terrorised me and my mother. When he died I was sixteen and I sort of felt responsible for my mother who had always protected me from him. I think I felt in her debt and I felt guilty going out without her. I had one girlfriend when I was about eighteen and remember feeling really disloyal to my mother, it was a relief to get back to her. When I started working in the (children's) home I had no friends and I felt really uneasy with the other staff there. The kids were the only friends I had. They didn't threaten me and, in fact, they were like me, in a way, in need of love. (Keith: eight years: local prison. At Grendon nineteen months. Returned to system nine months.)

From what has been said so far, it is evident that the men who had been to Grendon shared a high degree of confidence and optimism about the effects of therapy upon their attitudes and behaviour, both inside and outside the prison walls, and, in this respect, they mirrored many of the views held by those men who were interviewed while they were at Grendon. Three quarters of all the men interviewed after their transfer to other establishments thought that, on balance, they would describe themselves as a Grendon success. More than half felt that it had made a major contribution in enabling them to deal more constructively with the remainder of their sentences, and almost two-thirds anticipated that it would have a positive impact upon their lives after their release. Those men who had been at Grendon for eighteen months or longer consistently held the most enthusiastic and unequivocal views: more than two-thirds of them, in comparison to only a third of the other men, claimed that their time at Grendon had benevolent consequences both for their adaptation to imprisonment and for their eventual reintegration into outside society.

Counting the Costs

But this is not to say that there were no costs attached to the Grendon experience. For many inmates the process of therapy had been a painful experience in which defences, which had taken a life-time privately to erect, were publicly dismantled within a few months. During this process illusions were shattered and the responsibilities which accompanied the new reality were often not comforting replacements, at least not in the short term. For those men who had embarked upon a therapeutic career but who, for one reason or another, had foreshortened the process and left Grendon prematurely, there was a discomforting sense of non-completion. They spoke of feeling ill-equipped to deal with the half-emptied contents of Pandora's box. They could neither dislodge the remainder, nor could they put back what had already been exposed: the lid had been raised but had jammed, refusing to open fully or to slam shut.

All I can say is that it's like going to have your appendix out and they cut you open, take out your appendix, and send you home without stitching you up again. You look at the hole and you wonder what the hell you are going to do with it. (Brian: five years: local prison. At Grendon eight months. Returned to system four months.)

Men who had returned to the system after having been defined as unsuitable for therapy at Grendon were particularly likely to feel that their excursion had been a costly one. For most, their expectations had been raised and they had been disappointed. They returned often frustrated, angry, and with an overriding sense of failure. Regardless of how persistently the staff at Grendon had reinforced the idea that the process of assessment was designed to evaluate whether or not the therapeutic communities could provide a suitable medium for dealing with their problems, and not a means of judging whether or not they were 'good enough' for Grendon, inmates staunchly perceived it in terms of their own personal success or failure.

I still feel very bitter about it. They said I'd be torn apart on the groups and that it would do me more harm than good. But they never gave me a chance, they just rubbished me off. (Ian: life: category B prison. At Grendon two months. Returned to system thirteen months.)

Other men were told that their problems were not amenable to the therapy available at Grendon, but that they could benefit from some other kind of specialist programme, such as an educational or training scheme, or, in some cases, more intensive one-to-one psychotherapeutic intervention. But for the men concerned, this did not sweeten the pill of failure since, in their view, the probability of their ever gaining this help was extremely remote.

I was really disappointed after I'd failed the assessment because I really felt I'd done all I could. What they said at the time was that I needed to gain confidence in myself and that one way of doing this was to get some training or go on some education courses. But it's dead here, there are no opportunities for anything, and I've been told I won't be moved because I'm a Rule 43. Since I've been back I've had to start right at the bottom of the ladder again because they've filled my job, and I was on the list for classes, and I've had to go to the bottom of that. I want help, I don't want to come back to prison, but there's nothing forthcoming, it's a dead-end. (Ron: four years: local prison. At Grendon three months. Returned to system seven months.)

Another important question which needs to be raised is whether returning men to the system, particularly after they have been deemed successfully to have completed their treatment, undermines those changes they have achieved at Grendon. Most inmates who were interviewed during the course of their therapy had expressed reservations about going back into the system, and most had hoped for release or parole direct from Grendon. However, among the men who were followed up and interviewed in other prisons, a more equivocal picture emerged. Overall, they were evenly divided about whether they would prefer to have finished their sentences at Grendon, but interesting differences emerged, depending upon how long the men had spent in therapy. Only one in three of those who had been there for less than eighteen months felt that there had been advantages in being transferred back into the system, whereas seven out of ten of the men who had stayed for eighteen months or longer, the majority of whom might reasonably be expected to have completed their therapeutic career, approved of their transfer, and said that it had turned out to be a useful and valuable experience. The benefits which the men said they had gained by coming back into the system, however, were the same regardless of how long they had spent at Grendon. Most typically they saw their transfer as providing a bench-mark of their own progress.

The biggest impact was when I came back here. I knew I'd made a lot of progress whilst I was at Grendon but I hadn't fully appreciated the full effect. It's like sitting indoors and watching the snow falling outside the window. You see the little pieces come fluttering down, but it's only when you step outside that you realise it's eight feet deep. (Mark: twenty years: local prison. At Grendon twelve months. Returned to system five months.)

At one level I would have liked to have stayed there because it's easier and more humane. But overall I'm glad I came back here. I look around and I see these guys and I realize what I used to be like—it's pointless. It's embarrassing really, but I just never saw it for what it was. (Bill: five years: local prison. At Grendon thirteen months. Returned to system seven months.)

Despite this degree of appreciation, almost all of the men felt that the ways in which the prison system operated had made a negative impact upon their readjustment. Inmates claimed that there were no incentives, other than their own motivations, to put into practice the things they had learned at Grendon, and some inmates even argued that there were notable disincentives.

There are no incentives here, only disincentives. Everyone is highly individualistic—it's every man for himself. Survival is the name of the game and your barriers are maintained at all times. There's no way you can put care and consideration into practice here. (Nathan: life: category B prison. At Grendon fifteen months. Returned to system four years.)

There was one officer who had taken a real liberty with me and so I asked him if I could have a word with him. I asked him why he'd taken my property without me being there and without asking me if I'd already got permission. And he just said that he could do what he liked and that he didn't have to get my permission for anything. I told him that I wasn't expecting him to get my permission, but that he was out of order because I had passed all my property through reception and I was entitled to it. I tried to be really calm and reasonable, but he just stormed off, saying that I wasn't at Grendon now. The next day I went and apologized, and said that I was sorry if I'd upset him, but that I'd just wanted to sort it out face-to-face. I expected him to say he was sorry, too, and that there had been a bit of a misunderstanding, but all he did was shrug his shoulders and say 'I accept' and walked off. I felt like hitting him, but now I just see that he's ignorant and abuses the power of his uniform. (Graham: seven years: open prison. At Grendon sixteen months. Returned to system four months.)

The Impact of the Prison

It became apparent during the course of the fieldwork that there were important differences between the prisons in terms of how they responded to the men, and that these appeared to have consequences for the ways in which inmates acclimatized to their new environment. Although very few of the men felt that they had deteriorated during their period back in the system, a distinction could be drawn between the majority of men who had effectively put their lives on 'hold', and suspended much of what they had learned at Grendon, and a small minority who had continued to progress with the aid of, rather than in spite of, their receiving establishment. This study is too small to say anything conclusive about the nature of the regime and specific establishments which are best suited to accommodate ex-Grendonians, but a number of indications certainly emerged. First, there was a tendency for men who had been transferred to relatively small establishments, or to small units within larger prisons, to speak of the regime having had a positive influence upon their readjustment. This was largely due to the fact that the size of the establishment tended to be related to the degree of informality and level of association between inmates and staff. In these units the men felt that they were known as individuals rather than as numbers and that they were treated according to how they behaved. This was in sharp contrast with those who had returned to very large prisons where they felt as if they had been absorbed into an amorphous population, undifferentiated and unrecognized from the next man. Secondly, the men spoke of the importance of staff expressing a degree of interest in what they had done at Grendon and in listening to their assessment of how they had benefited. For many inmates, therapy at Grendon represented one of the most significant experiences of their lives and, perhaps not surprisingly, a number of men felt a desire to talk about this once they were back in the system. The willingness of staff to pay some attention to their stories, and to give some credibility to them, provided one of the first indications to the men of how far the world outside Grendon was amenable to their reintegration. Thirdly, and perhaps most importantly, some establishments had responded to the men, giving them specific opportunities to build upon, and to put into practice, what they had learned at Grendon and, in the event of success, had praised the men for their achievements. For example, one inmate was given a period of home leave shortly after arriving at the prison; another was given a prized job in the establishment; and another was asked to participate in setting up a joint committee of inmates and staff to facilitate the running of the wing. Interestingly, all of these characteristics: smaller prison units which enable personal identification and interaction; a staff role that balances security and control with humanity and justice; and facilities for prisoners which encourage personal responsibility and reduce institutional dependency, have been identified by Lord Justice Woolf (as he then was) as key requirements of modern prison regimes.[9]

The Consequences for Prison Management

It has to be remembered that the therapeutic regime at Grendon is not only a resource for prisoners but also a resource for the prison system. An important factor in the referral of certain inmates to Grendon has been said to be the disruptive potential which they are seen to pose to prison management, either because they threaten prison discipline or because they threaten their own safety. A legitimate question, therefore, is whether therapy at Grendon minimizes the threat which these men pose to the maintenance of good order and discipline within the prison. This was considered in the follow-up study, first in the light of what the

---

[9] Woolf, Lord Justice H. and Tumim, Judge S. (1991), *Prison Disturbances April 1990: Report of an Inquiry by the Rt. Hon. Lord Justice Woolf (Parts I & II) and His Honour Judge Stephen Tumim (Part II)*, London: HMSO, Cm 1456.

men said about their feelings and behaviour, and secondly, on the basis of a review of recorded information about their conduct prior to, and after, their period at Grendon.

Much of the analysis that follows divides the men into three broad categories: those who have previously disrupted the smooth running of the prison, committing numerous and/or serious disciplinary offences; those who have previously been deemed vulnerable either to themselves or to other prisoners; and those who have presented no particular problems for management. In total, eight were classed as vulnerable prisoners and eighteen qualified as having been a disciplinary problem, although only five of these could be regarded as presenting a serious threat to prison discipline by virtue of the length of their records and the violence of their offending. Inevitably, the small numbers of men involved here precludes a detailed statistical review, but, nevertheless, interesting findings emerged, which raise important hypotheses that could be put to the test in a larger-scale follow-up study.

Perceptions of Impact on Behaviour

Overall, three-quarters of the men felt that their behaviour in prison had been affected positively by their time at Grendon. Again this was particularly noted among those inmates who had stayed at Grendon for eighteen months or longer, all of whom felt that their conduct in prison had been changed by their period of therapy. Those men who had previously represented a problem for prison discipline were more likely than any other group to report specific changes in their behaviour. Five of these eighteen men felt that they had become more tolerant to other people, and more than half felt that they had become more socially skilled and thus more able to cope with a wider range of social situations. On the other hand, prisoners who could be categorized as vulnerable within the system appeared to be the group most resistant to any behavioural change. Only three of these eight men felt that their behaviour in prison had been in any way affected by their time at Grendon. It should, however, be pointed out that this finding could have been associated with the fact that these men tended to have spent shorter periods of time at Grendon. None of the men who fell into the category of 'vulnerable prisoner' had remained at Grendon for eighteen months or longer. Finally, among the men who had hitherto not presented any particular problems for prison management, there was a strongly held view that their period of therapy at Grendon had altered their perception of the world, but had left their institutional behaviour largely unaltered. This is perhaps only to be expected, given that these men tended already to have developed ways of coping with the restrictions of life in prison, and thus rarely found themselves in conflict with the prison authorities.

In many ways my behaviour in here is very similar to how it was before I went to Grendon. But inside there have been vast changes. The sorts of things I talk about with my family on visits, my attitude to my crime, and what I want to do in the future are vastly different. I'm also now able to see good in other people and, literally for the first time in my life, I've found some good in myself. All of that makes me a very different bloke in here. (Dave: eight years: local prison. At Grendon twenty-one months. Returned to system five months.)

There are two areas to which much effort and energy are devoted at Grendon and which could be expected to have some consequences for the management of prisoners back in the system. The first of these broadly concerns the dismantling of traditional prison culture and may be specifically examined in terms of how the men respond to Rule 43 prisoners, to illicit activities within the inmate community, and to the authority of prison staff. The second area of Grendon's activities which may be relevant to this discussion focuses upon the development of alternative strategies for dealing with stressful or potentially disruptive situations.

Attitudes to Rule 43 Prisoners

While they are at Grendon inmates typically report substantial changes in their attitudes and behaviour toward those men who would normally be segregated under Rule 43 for their own protection. But do these enlightened views persist once the men are transferred back into the system? And do those men who previously participated in aggressive and violent acts against the Rule 43s change their behaviour? As was mentioned in Chapter 5, the majority of men interviewed at Grendon expressed some doubt about their ability to maintain an egalitarian approach to these prisoners in the face of prison orthodoxy. But among those followed up in the system, it was clear that increased levels of tolerance which were initiated at Grendon were largely maintained after their transfer back into the system. Of the twelve inmates who claimed previously to have harassed and even physically assaulted Rule 43 prisoners, ten said that this had ceased, and that their change of behaviour was due entirely to the effects of their time at Grendon, attributing it to having gained some insight whilst at Grendon into the problems which these men faced and, through the empathetic processes of therapy, to having acquired an ability to reflect upon their reactions, rather than simply making a knee-jerk response. Only two men said that their attitudes and behaviour towards these prisoners continued to be hostile, but both of them had stayed at Grendon for only short periods of time, namely three months and six weeks respectively.

Attitudes towards Illicit Activities

When issues concerned with the control of illicit activities were considered, however, there appeared to be far less continuity between what the men did at Grendon and what they did back in the system. Only a quarter of the inmates said that in their present establishment they would take action to control the use of illegal drugs, including heroin. This compared with more than half who would have been prepared to take such action at Grendon. The men were generally more willing to intervene in order to inhibit the use of violence. But although three-quarters of them said they would have taken action at Grendon, fewer than a third would do so in their current prisons. Almost universally the men argued that these variations should not be read as indices of reversion to traditional prison culture, but as a means of survival within a system which is highly volatile and which tolerates little interference. The therapeutic programme at Grendon was said by the men to have provided them with a justification and reason for seeking to control illicit activities in that environment, but not anywhere else. For them the purpose of the Grendon regime was to help people to change; they spoke of a corporate responsibility for what happens within the communities and accepted that an atmosphere of safety is a prerequisite for any therapeutic activity to take place. The same imperatives were simply not seen to apply within the rest of the system. In their present establishments most men saw no overriding purpose or goal to the regime; they insisted that the ethos of the prison was highly individualistic; and they saw their personal safety as being dependent upon their not rocking the boat. Thus, unlike their attitudes and behaviour to prisoners protected under

Rule 43, their views about the control of illicit activities remained a highly pragmatic issue, largely detached from any moral imperative, and to be resolved by means which were fundamentally context-specific.

Attitudes to Officers

Earlier chapters have made clear that the breaking down of traditional barriers between inmates and prison officers is at the heart of much of what goes on at Grendon. But the issue to be considered here is whether these experiences have any consequence for the relationships which the men have with prison staff elsewhere in the system. The less authoritarian, more caring, and interested approach adopted by officers at Grendon was the factor most frequently cited by inmates as differentiating this establishment from other prisons. The kinds of relationships which the men enjoyed with officers in the therapeutic communities, however, were rarely rediscovered with staff elsewhere. But, notwithstanding this, half the men interviewed were able to identify ways in which their relationships with prison officers had improved since they had been to Grendon, and among this group were ten of the eighteen who had been categorized as previously presenting a disciplinary problem. It is also worth noting that, of the six men in this category who had been at Grendon for eighteen months or more, five claimed that their relationships with officers had become less hostile and that they were now able to relate to the individual rather than to the uniform.

All the men who claimed to have altered their behaviour tended to argue that two factors were responsible for the change. The first was that prison officers at Grendon had successfully broken down their prejudices and destroyed their stereotype of the 'prison screw'. The second was that changes in their own views towards themselves, and in their attitudes towards the resolution of difficult situations, had led to fewer inflammable incidents arising.

I learnt for the first time at Grendon that under that uniform they're human beings like everyone else. And now I seem to get on a lot better with staff. I take them as they come, and I'm much less ready to label people. I give them a trial first. (Michael: life: dispersal prison. At Grendon nine months. Returned to system two years, six months.)

I used to be a really hard-line militant prisoner, but now my whole attitude has changed due to Grendon. I'm much calmer now. I used to force arguments on to staff and work myself up until I hit them. It was almost like a sport. I just don't feel the need for that any more. (Philip: ten years: category B prison. At Grendon eighteen months. Returned to system nine months.)

Only two men with significant disciplinary records maintained that their attitudes to prison staff and their relationships with officers were unchanged, and both these inmates had spent very short periods of time at Grendon. The remaining six 'disciplinary' cases felt that, although their attitudes to prison officers in general had changed, the system in which they and the staff were currently operating did not facilitate a change in their relationship.

But it was not only those inmates who had previously offended against prison discipline who noted a change in their relationships with prison officers and who attributed this to their time at Grendon. Half those who had previously not presented any particular difficulties for management argued that their current relationships with officers had been influenced positively by their experiences with staff at Grendon.

I've never had any difficulties with authority, so I was never in any locked battle with them or anything like that. But I was secretive and I didn't talk to anyone: I stored things away and brooded. I don't think they ever had any idea as to what I was thinking. Now I'm much more open with them. I can talk to my reporting officer about personal issues without any hang-ups at all.' (Carl: life: category C prison. At Grendon two years, two months. Returned to system three months.)

Before I went to Grendon I saw the staff as objects of ridicule. Just there to herd you around and to be avoided. I feel much more in control now than I ever did before. I feel more able to negotiate with them and to retain some self-identity. It's a new way of working with them which I wouldn't have thought possible at one time. (Bob: life: open prison. At Grendon three years nine months. Returned to system five months.)

Relationships with staff appeared to have been least affected among those inmates who had previously presented a problem for management by reason of their vulnerability within the system. Only one in five thought that their time at Grendon had resulted in any improvements in their relationships with officers elsewhere. For the most part, these men spoke of feeling defenceless and without the props and supports they had grown accustomed to at Grendon. They expressed considerable hesitation in trusting officers within a system which they perceived as being, at best, uninterested in them as individuals and, at worst, openly hostile. It should be remembered, however, that these men had generally stayed at Grendon for shorter periods than those in the other categories.

Interactions with Other Prisoners

Some of the most common and potentially most threatening problems to prison management arise from inter-personal disputes, either between inmates or between inmates and staff. Almost half the men who were transferred from Grendon claimed that since their return to the system, they had either not had any arguments at all with other inmates, or had resolved them in their own time-honoured way, which had never presented any threat to prison discipline. However, there were some important differences between the three categories of prisoners. Those men who had previously presented problems for prison discipline were the group most likely to note a positive change in their behaviour. More than three-quarters of them reported that they had either successfully avoided arguments with other inmates or had resolved the arguments in ways which were less violent and aggressive. These men were, however, twice as likely as those in the other categories to have engaged in arguments with prison staff: almost three-quarters of them had been involved in at least one argument with a prison officer since returning from Grendon. Yet half these men maintained that they had resolved these arguments in new and socially acceptable ways.

I can now say my piece and walk away. Before Grendon I would just hammer my point home—quite literally—by thumping the bloke. Grendon taught me that I can be assertive without being aggressive. There's nothing that says I've got to be submissive, and God knows I saw enough blokes in Grendon who were there for being too submissive all through their lives. No, I'm never going to be a pussy cat, but I don't have to be a caged tiger either. (Jim: life: category B prison. At Grendon fifteen months. Returned to system four years.)

When the behaviour of the six men in this category who had been at Grendon for eighteen months or longer was considered, it was apparent that all of them had demonstrated positive changes. Two claimed to have successfully avoided all arguments, and the remaining four said that they had employed strategies they had learned at Grendon to avoid a confrontation and to resolve the dispute without resort to violence.

The Picture So Far

An attempt was made to synthesize some of the results in order to assess more clearly the consequences which Grendon's therapeutic programme appears to have for the management of previously difficult prisoners. Three specific adaptations to the conventional system were reviewed for each man: his relations with prison officers; his disputes and arguments with staff; and his disputes with fellow inmates.

It became apparent that those men who had previously not been a thorn in the side of prison management were the most likely to lay claim to changes which further increased their conformity to prison rules. Yet it was also found that half of all the men who had previously represented a threat to the discipline of the prison claimed to have made adaptations in all three areas which, from the point of view of prison management, could be regarded as positive and beneficial. Furthermore, almost three-quarters of these inmates alleged changes in at least two of the three areas under review. Only three men who had previously been disciplinary problems could be said to have made no positive adaptations at all, and each of these inmates had spent a very short period of time at Grendon. However, the vulnerable prisoners appeared to have made less startling adjustments. Only one of the nine men could be seen to have made the required changes in all three areas, and only half had adapted their behaviour in ways which prison management would find satisfying in at least two of these areas.

But again, it must be pointed out that time at Grendon appears to be a highly significant factor. When the whole sample is considered, all but one of the twelve men who had been at Grendon for eighteen months or more appeared to have made positive adjustments in all three areas.

Recorded Evidence of Re-Adjustment

It must be recognized, that all of the previous discussion has been based upon what the inmates say they have done. The question which must now be raised is whether there is any other evidence to support their somewhat optimistic reports. From the perspective of those who have to manage prisons, an important issue is whether there is any notable decrease in the level of disciplinary offending among those men who have in the past represented a problem for prison discipline.

All the eighteen men who could be described as a 'discipline problem' were serving long sentences: eleven of them were lifers and, apart from one man sentenced to four years, the remainder were serving eight years or more. Most of these men had been in prison for a considerable time: collectively they had notched up a total of 157 years, which meant that on average they had served nine years of their current sentence. During this time they had together amassed a total of 236 disciplinary offences, on average thirteen for each man. Even so, only five of these men could be described as presenting major difficulties for the good order and control of the prison. Representative of this group would be the man who had served seven years of a double life sentence for rape, and who, in the first two years of his sentence prior to Grendon, had been found guilty of twenty-six disciplinary offences, including possession of an imitation firearm, three cases of violence against an inmate, and two cases of violence against staff. The majority of the men, however, were not in this league and could perhaps be best described as presenting a major nuisance, rather than a major threat. One example would be the case of the man sentenced to thirteen years for armed robbery who, prior to Grendon, had accumulated eight offences over two years, mainly for making threatening remarks to officers and disobeying orders.

But the issue to be addressed is whether there is any evidence to suggest that since leaving Grendon these men have changed their behaviour so that either the number, or the seriousness, of their offences has reduced. The small numbers of men involved in this study inevitably place limits upon the extent to which it is possible to generalize from the findings. And there are also other limitations which should be borne in mind. First, there is an over-representation of lifers and long-sentenced prisoners in the sample which, as was explained earlier, is largely due to the fact that these men tend to stay in the system longer after leaving Grendon, and tend to be less transient and easier to locate. Secondly, in order to identify any change in each individual's rates of offending, it is obviously necessary to take into account, and control for, the amount of time they have spent back in the system. But, given that Grendon tends to receive inmates towards the end of their sentence, most men are transferred to other prisons with only relatively short periods left to serve. As a result, a significant proportion (39 per cent) of the sample had not been back in the system long enough for meaningful comparisons to be made between their previous and current disciplinary records. Finally, it has to be remembered that a man's disciplinary record is not necessarily an accurate reflection of his institutional behaviour. A prisoner may be committing or instigating offences of which he is never suspected or found guilty. Similarly, it is well known that there may be wide variations in the reporting practices of individual officers or in the degrees of tolerance of deviance exercised in different establishments.

Despite such qualifications, there was clear statistical evidence from disciplinary records that a third of the men who had previously represented a disciplinary problem had reduced their rates of offending. But, as mentioned earlier, it was not possible to compare the before and after offending rates for all men because of the relatively short periods of time they had been back in the system. For example, one man had seven offences listed against him over a period of eight years prior to going to Grendon, but had managed to keep a clean slate over the last twelve months since he had been back in the system. Clearly, cases of this kind make it very difficult to measure changes in institutional behaviour. But they also raise the question whether commitment to statistical analysis, which by definition must overlook these cases, is missing the point? While it is undoubtedly desirable to be able to calculate changes in offending rates, is it not also worth knowing whether those men who had substantial records of disciplinary offences had presented any kind of discipline problem since their transfer from Grendon?

When this issue was considered it was found that ten of the eighteen had a clean record. When only the five serious disciplinary offenders were considered, two of the men had demonstrated a clear reduction in their rates of offending. One of these men, in the two years prior to going to Grendon, had twenty-six offences listed against him, but during his five years back in the system had not been placed on report at all. The second man had previously collected thirty-three findings of guilt, but again had managed to keep a clean record since he had left Grendon twelve months previously. For another of the five men it was not possible to calculate a change in his rate of offending, since he had only been transferred for four months, but again, during this time he had not been charged with any infraction of prison discipline. The remaining two men demonstrated that they had not substantially changed their behaviour and were continuing to commit offences at roughly the same rate as before.

Clearly these findings are extremely tentative and provide only a rough indication of the consequences of the therapeutic programme at Grendon for the management of difficult prisoners. None the less, they do suggest that at least a third of the men had demonstrated a marked reduction in their rates of offending and that the institutional performance of over half the men had thus far been unproblematic, at least in terms of their recorded offending against prison discipline. A large-scale study would certainly be warranted, but it should be based upon back-records of men who have completed their sentences and should assess not only their rates of offending but also whether or not they have represented a disciplinary problem to management since their return from Grendon.

8
Current Dilemmas

One of the fundamental questions which this research set out to examine was whether a therapeutic prison is possible. The social organization of penal institutions is characteristically defined as being antithetical to rehabilitative efforts. Yet Grendon has survived for more than thirty years with the objective of providing psychological treatment for offenders. Earlier chapters have described how the prison accommodates the working practices of the therapeutic community and how the traditional prison roles of staff and inmates are modified to enable the communities to function. We have suggested that this co-operation between the prison and the therapeutic community is made possible by the fact that both institutions share the same personnel, and both are designed to exert control over a clearly defined and deviant population. In this final chapter we examine the nature of the control that operates at Grendon, the nature of the authority that underpins and legitimizes it, and how it differs from that which is exercised in conventional prisons. In addition, we explore the underlying forces which secure commitment to the institution on the part of both staff and inmates.

One of Grendon's defining characteristics is its enduring adherence to a rehabilitative ethos which has anachronistically survived the changing fashions in contemporary penal history. Such perseverance in the face of unpromising and inopportune circumstances requires some explanation. Indeed it would seem that Grendon has done more than survive: it appears to have flourished. A review of recent changes in the Prison Service reveals that much of the generic character of Grendon's regime has become increasingly assimilated into the prevailing orthodoxy of penal policy. We offer an interpretation of how and why this shift into mainstream penal politics has taken place, and what consequences it has for Grendon's future. We argue that a cruel irony has emerged, whereby Grendon's growing popularization has spawned the seeds of its own destruction. Changes in prison policy which, paradoxically, have been fostered by liberal reforms, are currently eroding the fundamental principles which enable Grendon to function as a therapeutic resource. Grendon is in danger of losing its unique identity and becoming one of a number of humane and well-managed prison establishments. We conclude by proposing a strategy which would halt this largely unintended process of attrition and establish a principled framework within which a therapeutic prison could function legitimately.

Control at Grendon

Grendon, like other prisons, is charged with producing obedience and discipline among both its inmate population and its staff. However, the extent to which it seeks to impose control ranges well beyond the bounds that are satisfied in other prison establishments. The therapeutic process ensures that the therapeutic communities are not simply concerned with the strict adherence to a catalogue of regulations which routinely govern institutional life, but are geared towards the corrective training of both the bodies and minds of their members. The system of control which operates at Grendon is thus more complete and more diffuse than at other prisons, in that it is designed to affect every moment and aspect of an individual's being. Yet Grendon is not generally perceived by those who live and work within its communities as operating an oppressive or coercive regime. Ironically, the intrusiveness and essentially coercive nature of its control appears to be far less visible than the more limited mechanisms operating elsewhere in the prison system. This shrouding of the repressive elements of penal power is largely produced by the interaction of three features of the regime. First, emphasis is placed upon achieving control through a series of rewards rather than punishments and, when punishment is resorted to, it is presented and understood as an enabling rather than a repressive strategy. Secondly, the aims and organizing principles of the therapeutic community distinguish its working practices from those of a conventional penal institution. And thirdly, there is a medical basis to authority within Grendon.

Punishment and Reward

In virtually all prisons, it is possible to differentiate between two ideal typical models of control: control by punishment and control by reward. The former traditionally employs strategies of denunciation and deterrence, which provide a series of disincentives that are intended to restrain or suppress certain forms of individual expression. From an ideal-typical perspective, control by punishment could be conceived as constituting a negative influence, in that its primary aim is to inhibit specific forms of conduct, rather than to promote distinct and alternative forms of behaviour. Because it relies on mechanisms of deterrence and denunciation to modify behaviour, the accompanying sanctions have to be clearly visible, either by way of direct observation or by means of a system of signs or representations. Its efficacy, however, is unaffected by whether individuals willingly subject themselves to its disciplinary methods or whether they are forced to comply.

In contrast to control by punishment, control by reward is designed to provide a set of incentives which foster conformity to agreed standards of conduct. While it serves to inhibit specific forms of deviance, it is more ambitious than control by punishment, in that it also aims to implant new and particular styles of behaviour which meet desired goals. The effectiveness of this type of control depends critically upon individuals wanting and valuing the rewards which conformity holds out to them and, thus, volunteering themselves as subjects. However, in order for the offer to be sufficiently tempting, individuals must believe that the advantages of conforming to the discipline outweigh those of struggling against it. The benefits for each person should, therefore, be made explicit and promoted, while the interests of those inducing the control are obscured or eclipsed. Motivation to conform can be triggered not only by the prospect of personal gain but also by more altruistic justifications which reinforce and enhance the rewards of compliance. Such methods of control are, however, difficult to maintain without the support of punitive mechanisms. Control by reward is powerless in the face of dissidence and must rely upon the support of punitive sanctions in order to protect its sphere of influence. The knowledge that punishment is lurking in the wings as an understudy, ever ready to replace the star performer, undoubtedly serves to enhance the attraction of the rewards of conformity.

At Grendon, the institutions of the prison and the therapeutic community do not separately accommodate and correspond to these ideal–typical models of control. Although the operations of the prison are more closely aligned to the imposition of punishments than to the distribution of rewards, they are not exclusively devoted to the achievement of control through punitive means. Incentives for good behaviour are central to effecting and maintaining control in all prisons. At Grendon, rewards for conformity to prison discipline include the usual range of inducements, such as eventual transfer to a lower security establishment, opportunities for home leave, and the prospect of a positive decision regarding parole. Within the institution of the therapeutic community, there is also a combination of punitive and reward strategies. However, an important difference is that the functioning of the therapeutic community relies more heavily upon a model of control by reward than the functioning of the prison.

As previously described in Chapter 5, routine control in Grendon is relegated by the prison to the therapeutic community. Hence, priority is given to achieving conformity by holding out a promise of reward. Indeed, it is the promise of reward in the form of a cure or relief that underpins and facilitates the continuation of the therapeutic regime. Inmates come to Grendon voluntarily and agree to submit themselves to the prescribed controls of therapy because they believe it is in their interests to do so. Throughout our fieldwork the men repeatedly testified to the insights they had gained into their own behaviour, to the improvements they had reaped in their interpersonal relationships, and to the positive consequences they anticipated all of this would have for their future readjustment to life outside the prison. However, inmates also justified and explained their continued commitment to therapy by reference to apparently altruistic rewards, such as protecting victims from further harm. In this way, they projected what Durkheim has described as a 'collective conscience', bestowing the benefits of inclusion and affiliation upon those who advocate and adhere to its values and beliefs.[1]

The continued compliance and obedience of Grendon's inmates to the discipline of the therapeutic communities cannot be assumed or taken for granted, but has perpetually to be reinforced. Efforts

[1] See Durkheim, E. (1933), *The Division of Labour in Society*, translated with an introduction by George Simpson, New York: Macmillan.

to this end are conspicuously directed to the promotion of rewards, yet they routinely function alongside the pervasive threat of punishment. The prison maintains a vigilant watch over the activities of the communities and is constantly poised to step in and impose disciplinary sanctions whenever it believes that the order of the establishment is under threat. It would, however, be wholly inaccurate to portray the therapeutic community as being devoid of its own punitive controls and completely reliant upon the prison for this type of back-up. Once admitted into the therapeutic community inmates are confronted with a battery of punitive sanctions designed to deter them from rejecting or abandoning the objectives of the institution.

The ultimate power of the community is the ability to expel recalcitrant members and to label them as 'failures'. Such men suffer denunciation by the community and risk the practical consequences of its reproduction within the domain of the prison in, for example, parole reports and other administrative evaluations of their worthiness for future rewards. More routinely, the risk of punishment is built into the every-day processes of therapy. Members of the therapeutic communities at Grendon who do not conform to the expectations of others may daily be exposed to criticisms and accusations. The perpetual appraisal of an inmate's commitment and progress, and the public expression of these assessments in the small groups and community meetings, facilitate numerous opportunities for ritual humiliation and denunciation. The effectiveness of these techniques at Grendon is verified by the infrequency with which the prison authorities find it necessary to intervene and impose their own methods of control.

From the inmates' perspective the sanctions that are employed by the therapeutic community can be just as painful and degrading as those imposed by the prison, and can lead to equally deleterious consequences. However, an important distinction may be drawn between the system of punitive control which operates within the therapeutic community, and that which is exercised by the prison, in relation to the meaning that is accorded to the sanctions and the ways in which they are presented to, and accepted by, inmates. Rather than perpetuating the contemporary view of penal punishment as essentially repressive, the therapeutic community promotes the belief that punitive sanctions serve an enabling and rehabilitative function. Thus, punishment is portrayed as a means by which

the perpetrators of undesirable conduct may be brought to understand the effects and consequences of their actions and encouraged
to learn alternative and socially acceptable forms of behaviour. For
example, a man who is sacked from his prison job because he is
shirking his responsibilities or abusing his position of trust by pil-
fering could find himself, like fellow perpetrators in other prisons,
unemployed or demoted to less attractive work. In Grendon, however, the process of censuring the individual is not a private matter
between the employer and employee, but is a highly public affair
involving the entire community. Criticism and disapproval of the
man's behaviour will be expressed in his small group and in the
community meetings, and the offender will be left in no doubt *why*
other members find his conduct reprehensible. This public process
of shaming can be as disagreeable and painful as the repercussions
of any disciplinary action. However, it is not a process which is
directed to stigmatizing the offender, but is geared to providing
him with opportunities for learning which facilitate his reintegration into the community. John Braithwaite has drawn a distinction
between two types of shaming: 'shaming that becomes stigmatization . . . [and] shaming that is followed by reintegration'.[2]
Stigmatization makes no effort to reconcile the offender with the
community, whereas reintegrative shaming incorporates ceremonies
and gestures which make it possible to 'decertify the offender as
deviant'.[3]

Much of the punishment which is meted out in the therapeutic
communities can be understood as social processes that are
intended to shame the offenders. The expression of disapproval is
geared to promote remorse in the individual and to invoke con-
demnation by the community. John Braithwaite's distinction
between shaming which stigmatizes and that which reintegrates is
clearly based on ideal–typical constructions. Within the therapeutic
communities at Grendon it is evident that both types of shaming
routinely occur and that the boundaries between them are not necessarily rigid or fixed. For example, the shaming of an offender
may begin with a reintegrative purpose but, in the event of this
individual failing to play his part in the bridge-building exercise,
will end in his stigmatization and exclusion. In other words, he

---

[2] Braithwaite, J. (1989), *Crime, Shame & Reintegration*, Cambridge: Cambridge
University Press, 102.
[3] Ibid. 101.

will be voted out of therapy and condemned to exile in another prison. On balance, however, the scales are tipped towards punishments which shame individuals in ways which permit their rehabilitation and reinstatement into the communities: 'It is shaming which labels the act as evil while striving to preserve the identity of the offender as essentially good'.[4] In this way punishment is viewed as an integral part of the therapeutic process and is, for the most part, accepted as such by inmates. In consequence the effectiveness of control at Grendon is enhanced and its essentially coercive nature is shrouded.

The Aims and Organizing Principles of the Therapeutic Community

The operation, influence and interaction of the aims and organizing principles of the therapeutic community constitute the second set of factors which combine to obscure the coercive quality of control at Grendon. In Chapter 5 we described the characteristic elements of a therapeutic community and identified five important features of its aims and principles that distinguish it from a prison. In summary they prescribe:

(a) that inmate attendance in a therapeutic community should be voluntary;
(b) that deviant behaviour should not be repressed but tolerated and actively fostered if its expression enables an individual to make therapeutic progress;
(c) that the development of an inmate's personal identity should not be inhibited but encouraged and its expression facilitated;
(d) that social divisions should be minimized in order for everyone to participate in democratic decision-making; and
(e) that social control should be based upon an acceptance of normative values rather than upon the imposition of a formal set of rules.

The ways in which these aims and principles are put into practice tend to produce two overriding and distinguishing features of control at Grendon. First, the combination of voluntary attendance, democratic decision-making, and normative codes of conduct ensures that control at Grendon is largely *self-imposed*. Secondly, the tolerance of deviant conduct and the encouragement of personal identity foster an ethos of *permissiveness*. It is these two

[4] Ibid. 101.

dominant characteristics which help to shroud the coercive nature of control at Grendon.

Self-Imposed Control

The powerful technology of control at Grendon is effectively concealed from those who live and work within the establishment because its architects and operators are identified and recognized not as the employees of the prison but as the collective membership of the therapeutic community. Everyone is reminded of the fact that inmates are not compelled to come to Grendon and that they are not forced to stay. They are free to accept or reject a place in therapy and they are free to leave the communities and abandon their therapeutic activities at any time. The rules by which the therapeutic communities operate, and the punitive controls which underpin them, are also self-imposed. The public spectacles of mortification that regularly occur in the small groups and community meetings are largely orchestrated by the inmates themselves, who also participate in the decision-making processes that lead either to the reintegration of deviant members or to their exclusion and rejection. It is the inmates too who herald the rewards of therapy to newly arrived members, advertising the benefits which they and others have accrued from their efforts. And it is the inmates who subvert the traditional prisoner hierarchy to identify and proclaim a new social order which awards status to those who submit to therapeutic intervention and demonstrate commitment and progress in therapy.

The task of controlling the Grendon population is presented, therefore, not as being assigned to a specially authorized body, but as being equally shared among all members. Protecting the therapeutic environment by policing the moral boundaries of the communities is depicted as the duty of each individual. This emphasis upon individual responsibility is supported by the 'no confidentiality' rule that prohibits inmates from keeping secret information, either about themselves or other members, which is relevant to the operation of the community. If an individual witnesses an act of violence then he is bound to report it. If he is confided in by another inmate and given information which this prisoner has failed to report to his group, he is again expected to ensure that full disclosure is made.

The utilization of a normative system of rules, together with the democratic process of decision-making, give the outward appearance that control is not only self-imposed but also self-determined. Yet there are clear limits to the extent that inmates within Grendon's communities can shape the content of the rules by which they live. We have already shown in Chapter 4 how certain common themes emerged across the different wings, in the content of therapy undertaken in the small groups and community meetings. An analogous pattern may also be discerned in the normative prescriptions which exist in each of the three communities. The reason the types of behaviour which attract censure are strikingly similar is largely that all the communities share a common interest in preserving their integrity and ensuring the continuance of the therapeutic regime, which is unable to function in a state of anarchy. At Grendon, therefore, the nature of the normative rules is governed by the need for the communities to meet their therapeutic objectives while, at the same time, meeting the requirements of prison discipline, order, and control. This is made possible by the imposition of the two paramount rules of 'no violence' and 'no confidentiality' upon the normative structure of the communities. The principle of 'no confidentiality', in particular, facilitates the effective policing of a wide range of behaviour and serves to distinguish the normative framework of control at Grendon from that which operates in other prisons. In a conventional prison there is a normative duty upon inmates to conceal information about deviant behaviour, whereas at Grendon there is a normative duty to disclose it. The intolerable disloyalty of 'grassing' on fellow prisoners is transcended and 'therapeutic feedback' is afforded a positive status, being portrayed as beneficial to the whole community and, sometimes, as serving the best interests of the individual.

Ironically, the self-imposed nature of much of the control at Grendon serves to strengthen, rather than weaken, its coercive and authoritarian nature. Many of the ameliorating influences which can curb the exercise of power in conventional prisons are undermined by the organizing principles of Grendon's therapeutic communities. The democratic basis of decision-making, for example, masks the identification of lines of accountability and precludes the apportioning of individual responsibility because all decisions are made collectively. In addition, because inmates enter the communities voluntarily and actively participate in the development and maintenance of the rules, their powers successfully to challenge unwelcome decisions are severely restricted. By coming to Grendon and by willingly participating in the democratic exercise of power they have agreed to abide by the rules and, by implication, the consequences which flow from them, irrespective of whether they are perceived as favourable or unfavourable, just or unjust.

Permissiveness

The encouragement given to inmates at Grendon to develop their own personal identity and to express their fears, insecurities, and deviance in the name of treatment inevitably means that the establishment must be prepared to extend tolerance to behaviour that would be unacceptable in a conventional prison. This results in an ethos of permissiveness which, far from being beneficent, feeds into, and indeed strengthens, the system of control. Together with the democratic power base and the normative system of control, the benign face of permissiveness serves to mask the contribution that inmates make to the system which controls them. The sense of security which is engendered by the avowed commitment to treatment objectives, and by the belief that the expression of deviant attitudes and behaviour will not automatically attract a formal disciplinary response, entices inmates to display conduct and divulge information that they would otherwise suppress in a conventional prison.

But while the expression of deviance at Grendon might escape the full weight of the disciplinary mechanism of the prison, it is not devoid of all consequences. The very enactment of symptomatic attitudes and behaviour provides crucial information on which decisions concerning an inmate's future are based. Such information may be recorded and referred to at any time, whenever the need arises. In consequence, its influence is not restricted to decisions concerning issues of treatment within the community, but reaches beyond the walls of Grendon to encompass decisions relating to an inmate's whole prison career. At its most extreme, it may be resurrected to justify the grant or withholding of parole, or of release on licence for those inmates sentenced to terms of life imprisonment.

The Medical Base of Authority

While all the professional groups at Grendon co-operate in the therapeutic endeavour, it is the doctors who have been granted ultimate authority over the treatment process and who hold dominion over the system of control by reward. The fact that this authority stems from medical knowledge operates to disguise still further the coercive nature of control within the communities. The discipline which is exerted over those deemed fortunate enough to have been selected for treatment is portrayed not as a coercive or repressive restriction of individual liberty, but as a rare and liberating opportunity. The knowledge base of medical science is presented as value free, and faith is placed in the ethics of the medical profession to use their expertise in the best interests of patients. Medical paternalism and the acclaimed altruism of medical practitioners thus serve to inspire the co-operation of the patient, who willingly surrenders to the benign authority of the healing profession.

The depiction of control at Grendon closely mirrors what Foucault has described as the modern technologies of discipline.[5] He argued that modern methods of state punishment have become increasingly privatized and sanitized, in that they are administered out of the sight of the general public, and in ways which recast or disguise their brutality and coercion. He emphasized that methods of discipline have become progressively less visible and yet more intrusive, engulfing a broader population and a wider range of social conduct. Foucault identified the rise of medical power as an example of the ways in which a social group can stake a claim to knowledge which empowers and legitimizes its dominion over numerous aspects of other people's lives. This observation has also been made by other writers, such as Ivan Illich in his discussion of medical authority. He describes, for example, how diagnostic imperialism has provided doctors with the authority to label individuals as sick or not sick, as deviant or not deviant, and has furnished them with the power to assign status based upon medical evaluation rather than civic opinion:

Medical bureaucrats sub-divide people into those who may drive a car, those who may stay away from work, those who must be locked up, those who may become soldiers, those who may cross borders, cook or practise prostitution, those who may or may not run for the vice presidency of the

[5] Foucault, M. (1979), *Discipline and Punish: The Birth of the Prison*, New York: Vintage Books, Random House.

US, those who are dead, those who are competent to commit a crime and those who are liable to commit one.[6]

Indeed, in pointing to the increasing social and cultural significance of medical science, Zola argues that it is becoming a major institution of social control, tantamount to the more traditional institutions of religion and law: it is becoming the new repository of truth, the place where absolute and final judgements are made by supposedly neutral and objective experts.[7]

The fact that the disciplinary methods at Grendon are not dominated by the infliction of physical restraint and brute force upon a resisting population does not extinguish or deny their coercive power. The extent to which dissidence is tolerated at Grendon has been shown to be limited and carefully circumscribed. At all times staff members of the communities retain full control over all decisions which affect discipline and control within the prison and under no circumstances do they ever relinquish that power.

Commitment to the Therapeutic Regime

The commitment of staff and inmates to the therapeutic regime at Grendon is significantly enhanced by the predominance of medical authority over the treatment process. However, within Grendon, the authority of the doctors has not gone unchallenged. Other professional groups engaged in the treatment process, most specifically the psychologists and probation officers, have questioned the relevance of medical psychiatry and have promoted their own special fields of expertise. Yet, ultimately these staff have not sought to abrogate the symbolic power of the doctors. In practice, they have condoned and supported the organizational structure which places the senior medical officer at the head of the therapeutic programme, awarding him the title of 'Director of Therapy'. However, this begs the question why medical hegemony exists at Grendon.

The professional dominance of the doctors has not derived from their actual activity in the day-to-day functioning of the therapeutic process, but has historically been accorded to them because of the elite status they possess in the wider society. This status emanates

---

[6] Illich, I. (1977), *Limits to Medicine. Medical Nemesis: The Expropriation of Health*, Harmondsworth: Penguin, 85.

[7] Zola, I. K. (1972), 'Medicine as an Institution of Social Control', *Sociological Review*, Vol. 20, No. 4, November 487–509.

from a grant of confidence, built upon a popular faith that the knowledge base of medical science is value free and that the technical enterprise of physicians conveys universal benefit. Prestmus[8] has argued that elitism is sustained where there is limited rank and file access and little or no opposition. Like other professional elites, the medical profession employs specific tactics to protect its autonomy. It lays claim to expert knowledge which is rooted within the discipline of science and accessible only to those who have undergone specialized and exclusive training. Doctors' use of specialized, technical language in the form of medical terminology constitutes one of the major bulwarks of professional privilege and militates against the development of a lay understanding of the medical enterprise. Furthermore, the process of accreditation within the profession, which encompasses training, examinations, promotion, and the handling of complaints, is conducted almost exclusively by other doctors. Thus, the historical predominance of medical authority at Grendon has effectively contributed to, and sustained, the sense of elitism which attaches to the establishment itself. This, in turn, has strengthened the propaganda which promotes the idea that is a privilege to be at Grendon.

The Inmate Perspective

The promise of salvation or cure, which constitutes an inherent characteristic of the treatment model, emanates from the medical base of authority within Grendon and plays a major role in securing the commitment of inmates to the therapeutic regime. But commitment can only be sustained as long as inmates believe that realization of the promise is within their reach. The therapeutic paradigm at Grendon may be distinguished from a pure medical model (as described in Chapter 1), in that the individual is not wholly disempowered but is granted some degree of autonomy over his own destiny. Continued faith in the curative potential of the institution is thus facilitated by the fact that therapy is presented as a matter of individual responsibility. Failure to achieve therapeutic targets can consequently be attributed to a defect in the individual rather than to a defect in the institution. Those who challenge this conceptualization are defined as therapeutic failures, unsuitable for treatment, and are transferred out of the communities.

[8] Prestmus, R. (1964) *Men at the Top*, Oxford: Oxford University Press.

Like sacrificial lambs, these men serve important symbolic functions. First, they act to remind inmates of the considerable personal effort and commitment required of them to participate actively in the therapeutic process. Secondly, they serve to mark out the bounds of acceptable and unacceptable behaviour. And thirdly, they signify the immense power of the institution to exclude those who challenge the values and precepts of the therapeutic regime and this, in turn, serves to enhance the sense of privilege that derives from community membership. This sense of privilege is communicated and reinforced both by the *ad hoc* rituals of denunciation that take place in the small groups and community meetings, and the formal procedures of initial selection, continuous assessment, and review, which are designed to determine an inmate's worthiness of a place in therapy. Finally, however, the continued compliance and commitment of inmates to the therapeutic regime are undoubtedly assisted by the fact that the coercive element of control at Grendon is disguised: shrouded by the benign cloak of medical authority and countermanded by the apparent empowerment of prisoners.

The Staff Perspective

The symbolic function of the doctors' role can be seen to serve the interests of all who work within Grendon, by contributing to the credibility of the therapeutic programme among those outside the institution. Our research has shown that prison officers regarded their work at Grendon as being significantly different from that undertaken by colleagues in other establishments. Their role within the therapeutic communities was generally perceived by them as enhancing their professional duties and expertise. Their engagement in the therapeutic process enabled them to see an end-product of their work and allowed them to develop methods of control and discipline which were based upon their personal status and interactive skills within the community, rather than upon the ascribed status and authority of their uniform. The flattening of the prison hierarchy, which enabled all members of staff to contribute to the therapeutic process, also helped to magnify and enhance the officers' professional status by defining their working relationship as a collaborative partnership with the medical profession.

Other professional groups also benefit from the elitist reputation of the establishment. Although psychologists and, to a lesser extent, probation officers challenged the primacy of psychiatric knowledge in the therapeutic process, they recognized that, in practice, they had considerably more freedom to extend their professional influence within the institution of the therapeutic community, albeit one defined by a medical authority, than they would within an institution circumscribed exclusively by a penal authority. The management team of prison governors, however, did not lay claim to expertise in the treatment process and had little to gain from the dominion of the medical profession. Their prestige stemmed from the reputation of the establishment as a prison. To the extent that the therapeutic regime enhanced Grendon's ability to contain a difficult population and to achieve the Prison Service Statement of Purpose, they facilitated its operation and did not challenge or inquire into the validity of its knowledge base. Their task was to provide and determine the space within which the therapeutic communities could function and, to that extent, they worked as allies with the doctors while simultaneously being their overlords.

Persistence of the Therapeutic Regime

One of the most curious facts about Grendon is that it has survived for as long as it has. Although the regime has evolved over the thirty years of its operation its fundamental commitment to the principles and effectiveness of the therapeutic community has remained firmly intact, despite the convergence of a series of inauspicious circumstances. For example, during the 1970s and 1980s Grendon was clearly out of step with contemporary penal practice which challenged, both empirically and theoretically, the feasibility and justification of the rehabilitative ideal. In 1990–1 it survived the physical disruption of separation and relocation to temporary accommodation while emergency maintenance was carried out on its buildings. Such perpetuity is especially curious given that Grendon is not a small therapeutic unit and that during the mid-1980s, when the prison population reached unprecedented levels and industrial relations were severely strained throughout the Prison Service, there were clear organizational imperatives which could severely have eroded Grendon's relatively costly regime. Furthermore, Grendon persisted throughout this period in the face

of unfavourable research evidence, which showed that the therapeutic programme was no more successful in reducing levels of
recidivism than conventional prison regimes.[9]

In our view Grendon's durability is largely explained by the con-
tiguity of three important factors. First, and most significantly,
Grendon has not manifestly failed as a prison. Breaches of security
have been rare, there have been no major disturbances by prisoners, and industrial relations have been relatively unproblematic.
Indeed, as mentioned earlier, prison officers have perceived their
professional status as being enhanced by their involvement in therapy, and inmates have widely accepted the view that it is a privilege to be at Grendon. Thus, although Grendon may have been
seen as unconventional, anomalous and even expensive, it could
not be accused of overtly failing in its primary custodial duties and
it could not, therefore, be charged with presenting immediate managerial problems to a service largely preoccupied by crisis management.

The second factor which has contributed to Grendon's continuity has been its identity and role as a 'jewel in the crown' of the
Prison Service. So long as Grendon persists, a claim can be made
that a political commitment to rehabilitation does exist. Sinking
this flagship, on the other hand, would signal not only an acceptance of defeat but also a renunciation of the principle. The liberal
lobby concerned with penal affairs has been adept at playing this
political card whenever Grendon's future has looked uncertain.
During the course of our fieldwork, when Grendon was perceived
to be under threat, a debate was orchestrated in the House of
Lords, journalists were mobilized both in the press and on radio,
and a flurry of correspondence was published in *The Times* and
The Guardian. The clear message behind all this publicity was that
the closure of the therapeutic communities at Grendon would mark
the Government's abandonment of hope and abrogation of responsibility for the social reintegration of serious offenders. In terms of
public relations, therefore, it could be argued that the damage
which would have been caused by closing Grendon, or seriously

---

[9] Newton, M. (1971), 'Reconviction after Treatment at Grendon', *Chief
Psychologist's Report*, Series B, no. 1, London: Office of the Chief Psychologist,
Prison Department, Home Office; Gunn, J. and Robertson, G. (1987), 'A Ten Year
Follow-Up of Men Discharged from Grendon Prison', *British Journal of Psychiatry*
151, 674–8.

eroding its regime, would vastly have outweighed any marginal alleviation of the operational difficulties being experienced elsewhere in the system.

The third factor which has contributed to the endurance of the institution has been the predominance of medical authority over the treatment process. The fact that the Prison Medical Service has always had a unique and direct responsibility for the therapeutic communities has meant that other divisions within the Prison Department have largely been excluded from any review or evaluation of the therapeutic process. Therapy has been defined as a form of treatment which is under the direct authority and regulation of prison doctors. By definition, therefore, it can only be scrutinized by those with relevant expertise, namely other members of the medical profession. In consequence, the competence of non-medical groups within the Prison Service to comment upon the Grendon regime has effectively been undermined and limited to those areas in which therapeutic activities raise questions for security and control. Any amendment of the therapeutic programme has thus been defined as a matter for prison doctors: the rest of the Service must confine itself to judging the establishment's performance as a prison.

Moving into the Mainstream

Although Grendon's identity as a 'unique psychiatric facility' has undoubtedly helped to preserve the treatment ethos of the establishment, it has also contributed to a widely held and longstanding perception of Grendon as a highly specialized institution, having little in common with other establishments and being of relevance to only a small minority of prisoners. In 1987, when this research began, there was a pervasive concern among both the civilian and uniformed staff at Grendon that the Prison Department did not value their work, and that the entire establishment was at risk of being closed down and reopened as a conventional prison. In recent years, however, there has been a discernible shift, which has propelled Grendon from the backwaters of the Prison Service into the mainstream of penal policy. Members of its professional and uniformed staff, together with selected inmates, have been invited to run training seminars at the Prison Service College; and the development of a national programme for the treatment of sex offenders has explicitly taken account of the work carried out at Grendon, both in the main therapeutic communities and in the more recently established sex offender treatment wing. Thus, although Grendon is still regarded as offering a special therapeutic regime, it has been increasingly recognized as a facility which can offer valuable expertise and experience in the development of inmate programmes across a wide range of establishments.

This shift of position is important because it raises fundamental questions about the future development of therapy at Grendon. It is the product of significant changes, both within Grendon itself and within the Prison Service as a whole, which have largely been precipitated by the rise of a managerial elite and the broad acceptance of the recommendations and proposals contained in the Woolf Report.

The Rise of a Managerial Elite

The 1980s marked the emergence of a new elite group, a cadre of public service managers, which promised the application of a new expertise to solve the longstanding problems of public sector organizations. Within the Prison Service this 'managerial revolution' heralded a new significance and appreciation of management techniques, and initiated a fundamental reappraisal of the ways in which the Prison Service was organized and managed. The 'Big Bang' of management reorganization in individual establishments occurred under a scheme called Fresh Start, introduced in 1987 after advice from a firm of management consultants. The publicity which this attracted largely focused on the 'buy-out' of prison officers' overtime and the consequent curtailment of union power. However, Fresh Start incorporated a number of diverse objectives, virtually all of which were directed towards a rationalization and regulation of staffing arrangements in individual establishments.

Following in the wake of these reforms some restructuring of the bureaucracy above establishment level was also initiated. The four large administrative regions, each under the operational control of a regional director, were replaced by a network of Prison Service areas, each with its own Area Manager; and within headquarters the administration was streamlined initially into four directorates and subsequently into only two. In 1991, a report by Admiral Sir Raymond Lygo on the management of the Prison Service recommended that the Service should become an Executive Agency under the government's Next Steps Initiative.[10] This was approved by the Home Secretary, and on 1 April 1993 the Prison Service assumed Agency status and the new position of Chief Executive was created, replacing the old post of Director General. The structural effect of these developments has been that Home Office ministers, while remaining ultimately accountable to Parliament for the Prison Service's operations, are now less involved in the day-to-day running of the organization. This falls to the Chief Executive, who has been assigned greater managerial autonomy than his Director General predecessors and who, in turn, delegates responsibility to the governors of individual establishments through their area managers. This process of delegation is achieved through a system of contracts which specify operational objectives and responsibility at every layer in the hierarchy. Officials in the prison bureaucracy are thus encouraged to perceive their role in relation to their contractual duties and to recognize that their performance will be judged according to how far these are fulfilled.

A transformation has thus occurred in the role of the prison governor, changing from that of a feudal baron-cum-house-parent to that of a corporate manager. Parallels have been drawn between the tasks faced by those involved in running prisons and the activities of those engaged in commercial enterprise. Prison staff, it was recognized, are required to provide a multitude of services to a range of different 'customers'. They must, for example, ensure that prisoners receive adequate and regular meals; that laundry facilities are in operation; that medical care is delivered; and that appropriate leisure facilities are available. The extensive prison estate must be cleaned and structurally maintained, and the range of prison industries and farms must be administered. The Prison Service is, above all, a labour-intensive organization and therefore a major employer, not only of uniformed and civilian prison staff but also of inmate labour. The need for business experience and expertise to permeate the prison walls was duly recognized and company directors, management consultants, and academics in business schools were recruited to run training seminars. Moving in the other direction, governors and prison administrators were despatched to both private and public sector organizations to identify and translate examples of 'good practice'.

[10] Home Office (1991), *Management of the Prison Service: Report by Admiral Sir Raymond Lygo KCB*, London: Home Office.

A new body of expert knowledge, which claims to provide universally relevant principles to regulate operational transactions, has burgeoned in credibility and status. Much, although not all, of this accumulated theory is rooted within a philosophy of free-market economics which can be traced back to the work of Adam Smith in the eighteenth century. When applied to penal institutions, however, it requires some modification. Within the Prison Service operational transactions, at least those involving prisoners, are uniquely structured in terms of the distribution of legitimate power. The degree of domination which characterizes the relationship between the service-providers and its consumers is unequalled in any other context, except perhaps that of a secure mental hospital. Although it is frequently asserted that it is the fact of imprisonment which constitutes the punishment and not what happens to the prisoner once in custody, the growth of managerialism has not, at least so far, produced libertarian prisons run entirely on free-market principles. Managerialism has, however, been instrumental in restructuring, at least to some degree, the *nature* of the authority which the Prison Service exercises over the inmate population.

Max Weber argued that 'a certain minimum of consent on the part of the ruled . . . is a precondition of every . . . domination'[11] and that, in consequence, those who hold power must inevitably seek to legitimize their dominant positions. Weber maintained that such claims to legitimacy can be distilled into three broad types: *traditional*, *charismatic* and *legal-rational*. Traditional domination rests upon an appeal to the dignity and sanctity of custom: the claim made is that this is how it has always been done. Typified by systems of patriarchy, it vests authority in the grace and favour of individual post-holders, granting them a wide discretion to facilitate continued obedience by extending and withholding a series of privileges. Charismatic domination, on the other hand, hinges upon the personal magnetism of a heroic individual. Legal-rational domination, however, does not vest authority in individuals at all, but appeals to the validity and propriety of a formal system of rules, which are applied dispassionately by an impartial bureaucracy that owes allegiance not to itself but to a higher political authority.

The Prison Service has increasingly moved away from Weber's traditional model to his legal-rational system of domination. The

---

[11] Weber, M. (1968), *Economy and Society*, Roth, G. and Wittich, C. (eds.), Berkeley, University of California Press (orig. pub. 1920), 1407–8.

patriarchal authority of the state over its prisoner populations, traditionally delegated to the discretion of individual prison governors and their staffs, has gradually been circumscribed by the increasing bureaucratization of prison management and the development of a system of dispassionate legal rules. This trend has been particularly evident since the demise of the rehabilitative ideal in the late 1960s. The flurry of prisoners' litigation during the 1970s and 1980s established a number of important legal rules and principles, which, although limited in scope, have defined and curbed the power of the state in specific areas of prison life.[12] But it is the impact of managerialism which has had the most significant influence on transforming the staffing structure of the Prison Service and on determining the ways in which prison personnel have been encouraged to redefine their relationship with prisoners.

Managerialism in Grendon

Grendon has not been immune from the managerial changes that have swept through the Prison Service. Its bureaucracy is now directly comparable with those existing in other establishments, and this has helped to authenticate its newly established position in the mainstream of the Service. However, the growth of managerialism at Grendon has had other important consequences which have further eroded its distinctive identity. Most significantly, it has had a profound effect upon the dominance of medical authority within the establishment, in terms both of its internal management structure and its relationship with the Directorate of Prison Health Care, now renamed the Prison Health Care Service.

Within the establishment the old system of dual accountability—to the senior medical officer, in relation to the functioning of the therapeutic communities, and to the governor, in relation to the running of the prison—has been redesigned to comply with the chains of command existing elsewhere. The senior medical officer must now occupy a subordinate position to the governor who, like his colleagues in other prisons, unambiguously assumes authority over all activities within the establishment. To some extent these changes have simply formalized a process of attrition which began in the mid-1980s when the original post of Medical Superintendent

---

[12] For discussion of these changes see Richardson, G. (1994), 'From Rights to Expectations', in E. Player and M. Jenkins (eds.), *Prisons After Woolf: Reform Through Riot*, London: Routledge, 78–96.

in charge of Grendon was replaced by a Governor-grade appointment. It has also been pointed out throughout this study that the institution of the therapeutic community is in a dependent and subordinate position, allowed to operate only by kind permission of the prison. However, it would be misleading to pretend that recent managerial changes are significant only at a symbolic level, and that the day-to-day reality in the communities can necessarily continue as before.

The senior medical officer, while awarded the title 'Director of Therapy', has had his operational power structurally curtailed within Grendon's bureaucracy. For example, under the old system the senior medical officer was responsible for overseeing and countersigning the annual staff reports in respect of all uniformed officers engaged in therapy. This is now undertaken by one of the governors without any reference to the opinion of the Director of Therapy. A similar process has occurred above establishment level, whereby the special responsibility and authority exerted over Grendon by the Prison Medical Service has been significantly diluted. The Prison Health Care Service is now designated to play an essentially advisory role in relation to the functioning of Grendon. Since 1 April 1994 senior doctors in the Health Care Service have been relieved of the responsibility of writing the annual staff appraisal on the senior medical officer: this has become the responsibility of the governor. Although the doctors working in the therapeutic communities remain answerable to the Prison Health Care Service for their professional conduct, they are accountable to the governor for their day-to-day work in the communities and he has no line of accountability to the Health Care Service.

The potential significance of these changes should not be overlooked or minimized. The elite reputation of Grendon has hinged critically upon the confidence and respect granted to medical knowledge and expertise. The commitment to the therapeutic regime by staff and inmates has also been closely related to the elite status of the establishment and the consequent sense of privilege that has been associated with living and working in the therapeutic communities.

As might be expected, the incursions of the new managerial elite have not been welcomed either by the doctors in Grendon or the medical bureaucrats in the Health Care Service. Yet their resistance has consisted of little more than a whimpering complaint and a gypsy's warning. The handicap which the doctors are under is that they have been conscripted into a battle which is being fought on foreign territory and refereed according to an alien set of rules. Doctors at Grendon are more used to operating within a traditional or even charismàtic framework of authority, than a legal-rational one. Although physicians rely heavily upon the legal-rational basis of medical science to validate their diagnosis and treatment of physical disability and disease, the scientific validity of psychiatry has largely focused on the clinical treatment of specific and limited areas of mental illness. The medical care of patients suffering from psychological disorders which have, as yet, no clear biological cause is less amenable to rigorous scientific method. Psychotherapy as a discipline has been particularly criticized for eschewing any legal-rational basis for its authority and for claiming legitimacy on the basis of highly subjective and frequently untestable assertions by individual therapists.[13] Although there has been a growing body of legal and ethical rules governing medical practice, considerable discretion continues to be accorded to individual practitioners in the treatment of their patients. Medical officers at Grendon are thus unfamiliar with legal-rational arguments to validate and legitimize their working practices in therapy and, in consequence, when challenged at Grendon by the new managerial elite, they have been powerless to resist the erosion of their authority within the therapeutic communities.

Grendon in Context

The changes that have taken place in the Prison Service have incorporated Grendon into the mainstream structure of the organization and have enabled some of the working practices of the therapeutic communities to be identified as expedient and beneficial methods of developing Woolf's prospectus in a wide range of establishments. By focusing upon this process of assimilation, however, there is an inherent risk of missing the wood for the trees. While Grendon's position has certainly shifted, it continues to retain particular features which not only distinguish it from other prisons, but which place it in an ambiguous and even contradictory

---

[13] Masson, J. (1990), *Against Therapy*, London: Fontana.

relationship to the rest of the Service. We will argue that, while Grendon's therapeutic communities function primarily according to communitarian principles, the rest of the Prison Service has shifted increasingly towards a libertarian model of social organization. While both can be seen to share a number of liberal ideals, there are fundamental and irreconcilable divisions in their philosophical foundations which, when translated into practice, have profound implications for Grendon's continued role as a therapeutic resource.

Individual Liberty and the Community

It is critically important to recognize that the changes which have occurred in the Prison Service are not isolated events within an idiosyncratic social institution but reflect broader changes in the political governance of British society as a whole. Although *liberal individualism* has tended to dominate political philosophy throughout the twentieth century, the victory of the Conservative Party in the General Election of 1979 marked the ascendancy of a new *libertarian* ideology which has fundamentally redefined the relationship between the individual and the state at the expense of communitarian principles of social order.

The dominant political rhetoric which has consistently underpinned the development of public policy throughout the 1980s and into the 1990s has repeatedly emphasized and promoted the rights and responsibilities of individual citizens, while claiming to curb the dictatorial incursions of state bureaucracies into the lives of 'ordinary people'. The 'nanny state' has been accused of stifling individual initiative and of encouraging an indolent dependence and parasitical attitude towards social institutions. Increasing the possibilities for self-determination by minimizing state 'interference' in social life has thus been held out as providing a universally liberating opportunity. It has been argued, for example, that consumers have been empowered by the competition of a free market; that workers have been rescued from the autocracy of trade union legislation; and that council tenants have been freed to buy their own homes. Within this framework social relations have been defined in terms of economic exchange: citizens are alternately 'consumers' and 'providers', pursuing their own interests according to the discipline of a free market. Thus, from this perspective, the social order is primarily conceived in terms of the regulation of a series of exchange transactions between individuals.

The supervision and control of social relations has, in some respects, become more visible, to the extent that there has been a substantial growth in the number of watchdog bodies overseeing transactions between the consumer and the provider. The regulatory role of the state, however, has become *less* visible as managerial strata intervene to create a buffer between the individual and the state. A number of examples, drawn from a wide spectrum of social life, illustrate this trend. There has been a notable increase in methods of alternative dispute resolution, whereby traditional adjudication in court has been replaced by private mechanisms of mediation, conciliation and arbitration. The Citizen's Charter provides one of the clearest illustrations of modern systems of regulation. It has provided a catalogue of 'normal expectations' for consumers of a wide range of services and has specified complaints procedures which may be pursued against providers who fail to achieve the required standards. The role of the state, however, is marginalized, in that the contractual relationship is depicted as being between the individual consumer and the increasingly self-governing provider organizations.

A similar pattern is discernible within the criminal justice process. The responsibility of the state for the control of crime has been counterposed by a growing political emphasis upon the role of the individual citizen in crime prevention. The responsibility of parents for the offending of their children has been placed on a statutory footing in the Criminal Justice Act 1991.[14] Owners of property have been pressed to invest in appropriate security devices to protect their property: public censure descends upon those who 'ask' to have their possessions stolen by leaving their cars unlocked, their domestic appliances unmarked, and the doors and windows to their homes inadequately secured. Neighbourhood Watch schemes rest upon an acknowledgement of responsibility by residents for the surveillance of their area, while national advertising campaigns promise that 'together' we can crack crime. The role of the state in the process of crime control has been further distanced by the rising use of private companies to undertake tasks traditionally associated with public authorities. The presence of private police is commonplace in shopping centres and industrial estates across the country.[15] Private security firms provide a

---

[14] Sections 56–8.
[15] Shearing, C D. and Stenning, P. C. (eds.) (1986), *Private Policing*, Beverly

uniformed force, equipped with various forms of sophisticated technology, to undertake routine observation, surveillance, and arrest within the boundaries of privately owned yet publicly accessible environments.

The most remarkable examples of private enterprise in criminal justice, however, have occurred in the Prison Service. Initially contracts were tendered for isolated functions, such as catering and the transportation of remand prisoners, but subsequently two entire establishments have been contracted out and are currently operating under private management. On 2 September 1993 the Home Secretary announced that twelve prisons are to be run by the private sector, seven of which are expected to be existing establishments. The adoption of agency status by the 'public sector' has already been discussed, but its underlying ideology and practical effect upon ministers' terms of reference are clearly consistent with current trends.

The Woolf Inquiry avoided being drawn into the privatization debate. However, many of the changes recommended in the Woolf Report reinforce the libertarian perspective on the relationship between the individual and the state. Woolf recognized that in prison society the concentration of legitimate power in the hands of the prison staff inevitably accentuates the existence of a centralized state authority. None the less, his prospectus for change may be interpreted as an attempt to modernize systems of penal control in ways which synchronize with the maintenance of order in contemporary society.

Many of the recommendations and proposals contained in the report are intended to import libertarian concepts of order into prison society by clarifying and redefining the relationship between the individual prisoner and the prison authorities. Woolf proposed that prisoners should 'take as full a responsibility as is possible for the conduct of their sentences' and that efforts should be made 'to prevent a creeping and all-pervading dependency by prisoners on the prison authorities'.[16] He emphasized the need to build 'incentives' into prison life to encourage inmates to conform to the discipline:

Hills: Sage; Johnston, L. (1991), *The Rebirth of Private Policing*, London: Routledge; South, N. (1988), *Policing for Profit: The Private Security Sector*, London: Sage.

[16] Woolf, Lord Justice H., and Tumim, Judge S. (1991), *Prison Disturbances April 1990*, London: HMSO, para. 14.13.

It seems to us incontrovertible that prisoners are likely to behave more responsibly, and to make the best use of their time in prison, if they feel that their responsibility and effort will be in some way rewarded. Those who have a high investment in the system are not likely to seek to destroy it.[17]

The report also recommended that the relationship between inmates and the institutions in which they are held should be regulated by a system of 'contracts'. Each prisoner would be offered the opportunity of entering into a 'compact' or 'contract' which would state 'in as precise terms as possible what it would provide for the prisoner. In return the prisoner would agree to comply with the responsibilities which the "contract" placed upon him'.[18] Woolf made clear that a prisoner would not be obliged to enter into the 'contract' but that 'it would be very much in his interests to do so'.[19] Opportunities (or rewards) would be extended to those 'prepared to take on the responsibilities laid down by the "contract" [and that by] refusing to enter into a "contract", the prisoner could lose the advantage of being able to rely on the "contract" to show that he had a grievance'.[20]

The regularity of prison disturbances during the 1980s, culminating in the devastating riots of 1990, can therefore be construed as a failure on the part of the Prison Service to keep pace with modern libertarian strategies of control in the wider society. Unlike the disturbances of the 1970s, which were concentrated in the dispersal system, the recent spate of disorder has been spread across a spectrum of different establishments and has involved a cross-section of prisoners, whose motivation to protest does not appear to have been associated with a single and specific issue, but with a more diffuse sense of dissatisfaction about their treatment by the prison authorities.[21]

Prisoners should, therefore, be given opportunities to make choices and should be held accountable for the choices they make. The social order of the prison is thus construed as a series of transactions which build upon and channel the self-interest of each individual prisoner. Although traditional coercive mechanisms designed to enforce social control are never far from the surface,

---

[17] Ibid., para. 14.23.
[18] Ibid., para. 12.120.
[19] Ibid., para. 12.127.
[20] Ibid., para. 12.127.
[21] For further discussion about the 1990 prison disturbances see Player, E. and Jenkins, M. (eds.) (1994), *Prisons After Woolf*.

there is a discernible trend to promote a neo-libertarian conception of individualism which affects an image of free choice, self-determination, and the rational pursuit of self-interest.

Within Grendon it is possible to discern similar traits of individualism. The freedom of individual choice is emphasized by the voluntary nature of inmate participation, and the development of individual responsibility is a central element in defining and assessing therapeutic progress. Within the therapeutic communities the maintenance of control has traditionally rested upon the promotion of incentives to 'good' behaviour. Contractual agreements, of varying degrees of formality, have routinely regulated the relationship between the inmate and the therapeutic community. Although the content of these 'contracts' has tended to refer to duties and responsibilities relating to the therapeutic programme, its emphasis on individual responsibility, voluntarism, and the prospect of reward, clearly reflects the regulatory principles advocated by Woolf.

Similarly, the ways in which Grendon advertises the benefits which accrue to those who devote themselves to therapy are deliberately directed to appeal to each inmate's personal desire for self-fulfilment. However, within the therapeutic communities the egoistic impulses of individual members are constrained by the promotion of a collective purpose. Thus, individualism within this context does not correspond to the *libertarian* perspective advanced within the prison system generally, but draws upon communitarian principles which conceive of individual action in relation to the 'authoritative horizons' of communal values.[22] Within Grendon there are well-developed and vociferously promoted moral codes which regulate behaviour within the communities and demand obedience to their discipline. Adherence to this discipline is portrayed not as a constraint upon individual freedom but as a fundamental condition for its existence within a societal context. The presence of a moral framework is, therefore, perceived as fundamental to human autonomy; its absence opens the door to anarchy and, from a Durkheimian perspective, represents a state of anomie.

This is not to argue that Grendon has a monopoly of moral principles and that the current movement to develop a libertarian social order in prisons is devoid of moral foundations. Within the

[22] Taylor, C. (1979), *Hegel and Modern Society*, Cambridge: Cambridge University Press, 157–9.

prison system as a whole it is possible to discern the existence of two fundamentally different and competing moral philosophies: moral utilitarianism, encapsulated in the work of Jeremy Bentham; and a rights-based theory of ethics, rooted in the work of Immanuel Kant. Both schools of thought provide a set of moral principles which coexist in all prisons. However, the degree and nature of their influence at any one time will vary. Contemporary penal reforms have predominantly been informed by Kantian ethics, whereas the social organization of the therapeutic communities, and the development of rehabilitative strategies generally during the 1960s, rest primarily upon the authority of moral utilitarianism. The ways in which these two ideologies function and interrelate within the prison system provide an important insight into the distinctive nature of the Grendon regime and its relationship with the wider Service.

According to Jeremy Bentham and other classical utilitarians of the nineteenth century, moral actions are those which promote the greatest degree of happiness to the largest number of people. Within Grendon, moral value is attached to behaviour which is deemed to have certain beneficial consequences for society. It is the social utility of such behaviour, rather than any intrinsic quality of the behaviour itself, which determines its morality. Engaging in therapy is thus deemed to be morally 'good' because it increases the potential for happiness in the individual, by improving his prospects for personal and social fulfilment, and reduces the risk of harm to other members of society by diminishing the individual's propensity to commit further offences. By definition, however, utilitarian conceptions of morality subordinate self-interest to the 'greater good' of the community. In all prisons it is possible to discern the employment of utilitarian principles to further a communitarian social order. However, this is considerably more marked in Grendon than elsewhere.

What constitutes a 'socially beneficial consequence', however, is subject to variable interpretation: how should the criterion 'the greatest happiness for the greatest numbers' be interpreted? Two components to this principle are immediately apparent. First, the requirement to *produce as much happiness as possible*: a principle of aggregation or utility. And secondly, the need to *distribute it as widely as possible*: a principle of justice. Some of the most difficult moral conflicts in social life are those between utility and justice.

How should happiness or social benefits be distributed: according to need or according to merit? The answer to this question hinges critically upon the nature of the social order one wishes to create or promote. Utilitarianism may therefore provide a moral framework for the development of a libertarian programme, or it may be used to justify a very different set of policies to underpin and rationalize a social system based upon principles of communitarianism.

The liberal reforms recommended by Lord Justice Woolf, which are consistent with broader changes in criminal justice,[23] resurrect the Kantian principles that moral rules apply to everyone without partiality, and are 'good' in and of themselves and not because they are useful in achieving other ends. The essence of Kantian theory is that human beings should always be treated as 'ends' and never merely as 'means'. To treat a person 'as an end' is to recognize that he or she has desires and choices which must be respected and taken into account. Ignoring or overriding such interests, in order to secure the purposes of oneself or of others, is to treat that person purely as a means, and this, according to Kant, is morally wrong. Slavery is an extreme example of such conduct, but a system of repressive control in prison which routinely undermines individual autonomy would also be defined as a moral violation.

The Kantian emphasis on individual rights and autonomy is clearly compatible with a libertarian concept of social order. It is, however, less accommodating to the development of communitarian principles of social organization. By definition, communitarianism demands the subjugation of individual liberties to communal interests, at least to some degree. However, it may be argued that the conception of individual liberty only has meaning within a communal context.[24] But Kantian ethics also permit a recognition of this contextual analysis. A central tenet of Kant's philosophy is that, while an individual has the right to be treated as an end in himself, he has a correlative duty to treat others also as moral beings. This implies that each citizen should have regard to the desires and liberties of others when deciding on his own course of action. Inevitably this conjoins the concepts of individual liberty and equality with that of fraternity. Hence it acknowledges the potential for individuals to act altruistically as well as in their own

---

[23] Ashworth, A. (1992), *Sentencing and Criminal Justice*, London: Weidenfeld & Nicolson.

[24] Raz, J. (1986), *The Morality of Freedom*, Oxford: Oxford University Press.

self-interest. But this, of itself, does not facilitate the development of a communitarian social order so much as the advancement of libertarianism. What is absent from this perspective, and central to communitarianism, is a metaphysical conception of community which enables it to be identified and valued as an entity in its own right, extending beyond the sum of its constituent elements. Kantian ethics do not embody this conception of community, recognizing only collectivities of individuals and, for this reason, they cannot further communitarian goals unless they work in conjunction with utilitarian principles.

Implications for Grendon

The two distinct moral frameworks embodied in the liberal philosophies of Kant and Bentham are both concerned to promote human welfare and to ensure fairness, justice and equality. The ways in which these issues are conceptualized, however, produce fundamentally divergent approaches to punishment. From the utilitarian perspective the purpose of punishment is defined in relation to the beneficial consequences it has for social control. Achieving the goals of deterrence, rehabilitation, and incapacitation may require individuals to be treated differently according to their needs and the needs of the wider community. The nature and distribution of sanctions are thus exclusively instrumental in the pursuit of social utility. Without this intention punishment would not be morally valid because it would fail to contribute to human happiness; indeed, it would constitute an act of immorality because it would only serve to increase the sum of human suffering. Kantian notions of justice, however, are premised upon the universal protection of individual rights against the demands of social utility. Punishment can only be justified on grounds of desert, when an individual has knowingly and deliberately committed a wrongful act, and equality of treatment demands that the degree of censure is commensurate with the seriousness of the offence, and not tailored to the supposed needs of individual offenders. Retributive punishment is thus morally justified on the ground that it recognizes the freedom of individuals to make their own decisions and their duty to be held responsible for them. Indeed, retributive punishment demands that sanctions are inflicted irrespective of the social consequences.

Within a libertarian social order the retributive theory of just deserts is comfortably accommodated because it upholds individual autonomy and recognizes the need to constrain collective power in order to protect individual interests. A utilitarian model of punishment, however, has inherent problems for the realization and protection of libertarian principles. In the event of a conflict of interests between the individual and the social group of which he is a part, the principle of social utility may demand that the interests of the individual are subjugated to those of the wider community. Conversely, within a communitarian social order punishments may be justified on utilitarian grounds if they protect community interests, whereas a retributive model of deserved punishments may violate communitarian principles if the interests of the individual and the community do not coincide.

These fundamental conflicts raise important questions concerning the future relationship between Grendon and the rest of the prison system. A major criticism advanced against the therapeutic regime at Grendon is that, in common with all rehabilitative programmes, it violates certain libertarian conceptions of justice, in that the nature and degree of punishment are determined not upon an evaluation of desert in relation to an individual's conduct but upon an assessment of need and utility. The distribution of punishments may, therefore, be uneven, resulting in differential treatment and claims of unfairness. Within the rest of the prison system the conception of just deserts and the regulation of state power to protect prisoners' rights has dominated the demand for penal reform over the last decade. The development of rights-based penal policy has been applauded for introducing important safeguards for individual prisoners against the draconian powers of the authorities.[25] However, unless this reliance on Kantian ethics to shape strategies for reform is balanced by a renewed emphasis upon social utility the decline of communitarian principles in prisons is inevitable. For Grendon this raises an apocalyptic spectre. The operating principles of the therapeutic communities are defined exclusively in relation to a communitarian social order and are eroded by the encroachments of libertarian policies.

[25] Livingstone, S. (1994), 'The Changing Face of Prison Discipline', in Player, E. and Jenkins, M. (eds.), *Prisons After Woolf: Reform Through Riot*, London: Routledge; Richardson, G. (1994), 'From Rights to Expectations' in ibid.; Casale, S. (1994), 'Conditions and Standards' in ibid.; Owen, T. and Livingstone, S. (1993), *Prison Law*, Oxford: Oxford University Press.

In Grendon the dilemmas which have to be resolved in deciding between the competing claims for justice extend beyond the boundaries of prison disciplinary procedures and strategies of penal control. The functioning of a therapeutic community within the context of a prison inevitably raises fundamental questions about the limits of the powers which can be exercised by the community over the individual members. Three examples illustrate the breadth and intrinsic nature of the conflict. A recurrent problem in Grendon concerns the claims made by category C inmates to be allowed periods of home leave in line with the 'normal expectation' contractually specified for inmates in category C establishments. In Grendon the allocation of home leave would normally be considered by the community and a recommendation would be made to the governor on grounds of therapeutic utility. Libertarian notions of justice, however, effectively remove the community's discretion and invoke a system of decision-making based on the dispassionate application of impartial rules. Obviously, no conflict emerges when the decision of the community corresponds with the official compact, but where there is disagreement a choice has to be made between these two models of justice.

The doctors in Grendon have recently expressed their concern about proposed changes to the provision of primary health care to prisoners in their establishment. The Prison Health Care Service has been urged to establish contracts with local GPs to provide a service equivalent to that available in the outside community.[26] It is intended that such an arrangement would safeguard prisoners' interests by ensuring that they gain equivalent primary care to other citizens and by protecting the confidentiality of their medical records. The doctors at Grendon, however, argue that each of them should provide primary medical care to the inmates resident on their wings. This, they claim, facilitates a holistic approach to the individual's therapy, permitting the evaluation of his physical health, and the prescription of any treatment, to be viewed in relation to his therapy in the community and, where appropriate, to be taken into account and examined in the therapeutic process.

The final example has emerged from the recent installation of personal television sets in inmates' cells. This innovation was

[26] Home Office (1990), *Report on an Efficiency Scrutiny of the Prison Medical Service*, and (1991), *Contracting for Prison Health Services: A Consultation Paper*, both London: Home Office.

proposed by Lord Justice Woolf,[27] and the White Paper announced that 'carefully monitored experiments in a small number of prisons' would be undertaken.[28] A consequence of this libertarian measure in Grendon, however, has been the reduction of social interaction among inmates, and between inmates and staff, during the evening. Personal TVs have provided all parties with an opportunity to withdraw from the demanding involvement of community activity.

It would be misleading and unrealistic, however, to conceive of the moral conflict in Grendon as a stark choice between two competing philosophical schools. In all prisons a balance is continually being struck between the rights and interests of individuals and those of the collective. However, when Grendon was opened in 1963 the balance which had to be maintained between libertarian and communitarian principles was far less acute than it is now, more than thirty years later. The Prison Service during the 1960s adhered to the rhetoric, if nothing else, of the rehabilitative ideal and, like the wider society, it fostered important communitarian principles. Today the libertarian reforms of the 1980s and 1990s must constantly be negotiated and accommodated within Grendon's therapeutic communities. For the most part resolutions are made on a case-by-case basis and in the absence of any clear guiding principles to achieve consistency. It is patently ironic that, at a time when Grendon appears to have achieved some credibility within the Service, its intrinsic identity is being insidiously weakened.

Guidelines for the Future

In earlier chapters we discussed Grendon's social utility from the inmates' point of view, from the perspective of prison staff working in the communities, and from the political and pragmatic prospect of the wider Prison Service. We take it as given, therefore, that a case has been made for Grendon's continuance within the existing framework of criminal justice and that we are justified on these grounds to seek to develop some guiding principles to protect Grendon's functioning as a therapeutic institution.

The fundamental question is how the communitarian social

[27] *Prison Disturbances*, para. 14.31.
[28] Home Office (1991), *Custody, Care and Justice: The Way Ahead for the Prison Service in England and Wales*, London: HMSO Cm 1647, para. 7.34.

order of Grendon's therapeutic communities can be protected against the encroachments of libertarian reforms without granting absolute and unfettered powers to the communities and risking the development of totalitarian regimes. Conversely, the question could be phrased in terms of how, within a communitarian society, it might be possible to protect the interests of individual members against the interests of the collective. Building upon some of the ideas developed by Nicola Lacey in her efforts to construct a communitarian theory of punishment, we have identified four guiding principles which provide a framework within which the decision-making processes of the communities could operate.[29] Stated briefly, these are the principles of equality, democracy, autonomy, and welfare.

Equality

Our proposals are premised upon the liberal belief that Grendon's purpose requires each inmate to be given an equal opportunity to benefit from the therapeutic process and for each inmate's progress to be accorded equal value. This starting point may be disputed by those who would argue that the rehabilitation of someone with a history of sexual violence is of greater social value, and thus has a prior claim to resources, than that of someone whose interpersonal problems are manifested in their social isolation and petty thieving. This argument is indisputable if it is accepted that therapeutic value is to be measured in relation to the prevention of specifically-ranked social harms. While this may be a justification for orienting the selection of inmates for Grendon in favour of the more serious offender, it does not, in our view, justify their differential treatment within the communities. If this were to be the case, the community would be stratified by a hierarchy of therapeutic 'worthiness', whereby the therapy of certain individuals would be more highly valued than others and afforded greater protection and promotion. In consequence, the therapy of some inmates could justifiably be sacrificed, used, or manipulated to benefit the progress of the 'worthy' cases. Thus, it must be recognized that, unless equal opportunity and value are accorded to each and every inmate admitted into the therapeutic communities, the rights of the

[29] See Lacey, N. (1988), *State Punishment: Politics, Principles and Community Values*, London: Routledge.

individual will be left unprotected and at risk from the tyranny of a variously defined social utility.

Democracy

The ethos of the therapeutic community is one of participatory citizenship, whereby the individual's concept of himself is developed from his relationships with others and his notion of self-interest is dependent upon the continuance of the community. The perpetual motion of social life demands that the balance between the competing interests of the individual and the community has repeatedly to be negotiated. Precisely where the balance is struck is a political decision. Within Grendon the effective functioning of the therapeutic communities demands that such decision-making is accomplished democratically. In this context, however, the principle of democracy cannot be satisfied by the delegation of power to representative bodies (although this may form part of the process), but requires the direct participation of all members on an equal footing. It is only by means of direct involvement in the decision-making process that individual members can recognize their interdependence and develop an active sense of responsibility and commitment to the goals and values of the community. At Grendon this ideal model of participatory democracy is desired and pursued, yet its achievement in practice is inevitably threatened by the overarching penal context within which the therapeutic communities must operate. In Chapter 5 we described the institutional conflicts which exist between the therapeutic community and the prison. In a conventional prison power relations among prisoners, and between prisoners and the prison authorities, repudiate the principle of democracy in decision-making. It is hardly surprising, therefore, that when prisoners and prison staff at Grendon seek to promote their own interests against those of the community, they are inevitably tempted to circumvent the democratic process and exert pressure through their penal power. Prison officers may resort to prison disciplinary procedures to justify the expulsion of an inmate whom they find awkward and difficult to work with in a therapeutic context. Similarly, prisoners may seek to gain certain advantages within the communities by manipulating and intimidating weaker and more vulnerable members.

Participatory democracy in Grendon can therefore be seen as being in a perpetual state of vulnerability. Although evidence of its existence can be pointed to in relation to the management of routine and non-controversial issues, its preservation at times of crisis is far less predictable. This is because Grendon has no means of protecting the democratic process against the incursions of penal power. No single group is explicitly charged with safeguarding democratic participation; indeed, certain powerful interests of staff and inmates may best be served by its temporary suspension. If the principle of democracy is to play a part in regulating the exercise of power in Grendon, it will have to be forcefully promoted and defended by a group vested with the necessary authority to enforce the principle against the pressure for alternative resolutions.

Autonomy

The preservation of personal autonomy is the third principle that should guide the working practices at Grendon in balancing the interests of the individual and those of the community. The notion of autonomy implies an ability or freedom to think or act independently and without compulsion. Yet this is an essentially relative concept:

As Joseph Raz has argued the fulfilment of the condition of autonomy is a matter of degree, having to do not only with the degree to which a person is free from subjection to the will of others, but also with the existence of an adequate range of options and . . . the lack of necessity to spend most of one's time struggling to attain the minimum standards necessary to a worthwhile life.[30]

In Grendon there are in-built safeguards which, to some degree, contribute to the protection of individual autonomy. The first is that all inmates are voluntarily referred to Grendon and may leave at any time. Yet, as we have argued in Chapter 3, the extent of such voluntarism is inevitably circumscribed by an inmate's perception of the likely consequences his decision will have for future parole applications. The second safeguard is that an inmate's sentence cannot be extended beyond the maximum period of custody set by the court, because of his failure to respond positively to therapy. However, the length of time an inmate actually serves may be shortened by favourable reports of his therapeutic progress. Life-sentenced prisoners are clearly in a particularly vulnerable situation, even though there is now a legal requirement to state the

---

[30] Lacey, N. (1988), *State Punishment*, 179.

tariff period of every life sentence and, for those serving discretionary life sentences, an independent panel has been established to review and decide upon issues of dangerousness in those cases where prisoners are being detained beyond their tariff.

Within Grendon the functioning of the therapeutic communities places a high value upon the principle of autonomy. The definition of personal autonomy is specifically related to the individual's participation in communal life and is not presented as a countervailing force of anarchy pitted against the restrictions of the community. The therapeutic lore at Grendon insists that the development of self-knowledge and personal identity reinvest the individual with a sense of his own worth, and enable him to make his own decisions and trust his own judgement. Submissive dependence upon the community or upon individual members is deemed to be antithetical to therapy, stunting the growth of the individual and weakening the vitality of the community.

Yet we have shown in Chapter 4 that, in practice, the range of permissible attitudes and behaviour at Grendon is often circumscribed by the prevailing organization and culture of the establishment. The lack of training for prison officers in group psychotherapy severely inhibits the creation of a non-judgmental milieu within which deviant motivations and vindicatory defences can be explored. In the community meetings and small groups an atmosphere of censure prevails which clearly identifies for an individual the approved therapeutic route which should be followed, and tolerates little divergence from the recommended itinerary. The range of options open to inmates is thus severely limited and individual autonomy is eroded by the imposition of predetermined community edicts. Clearly a therapeutic community must propound and prohibit certain forms of behaviour if it is to identify its moral and normative boundaries. But if this is to happen in conditions which respect personal autonomy it must allow members to choose freely the values of the community, and to recognize voluntarily the desirability of changing their behaviour, rather than manipulate them into positions which afford little option but to comply with the established orthodoxy.

Welfare

The final principle that should guide the decision-making processes at Grendon, and thus balance the interests of the individual with those of the collective, is encapsulated in the concept of welfare. This is defined in relation to both the community as a whole and individual members. Lacey depicts welfare as the fulfilment of 'certain fundamental needs and interests; acknowledged to be such within the community'.[31] She argues that, beyond the basic material conditions for human survival, what constitute fundamental needs and interests will be a 'function of social and political decision'. In Grendon an individual's welfare will be defined in terms of his therapeutic needs and interests, and consequently determined in relation to his specific configuration of problems and approved programme of treatment. Decision-making within the community must, therefore, be guided by the need to foster and support each individual's achievement of therapeutic goals and to avoid the creation of obstacles which retard, interrupt, or disable his progress. But the welfare of each inmate is substantially dependent upon the welfare of the community, which again is defined in relation to its ability to function therapeutically. The question arises how decision-making should be guided when the welfare of an individual stands in conflict with the welfare of the community. During our time at Grendon numerous inmates were voted out of the institution because they were felt to be too disruptive to the community, even though there was widespread agreement that they were in need of therapy, and that their intolerable behaviour was precisely what had prompted their referral for therapy in the first place. Inevitably a balance must be struck, but it should be a balance which is guided by certain principles rather than *ad hoc* pragmatism. Recourse to utilitarian arguments which routinely resolve the problem in favour of the 'greater good' constitutes too blunt an instrument for the fine-tuning which has to be achieved. In our view the principles of equality, democracy, and personal autonomy should inform and structure this process of resolution. In other words, deciding upon competing claims of welfare should be a democratic process involving all members of the community, which is guided by considerations of equal treatment and respect for individual autonomy.

In practice, however, conflicts are bound to arise *between* these core values or principles which will inevitably call into question their importance and relative priority. It is not difficult, for

<hr />

[31] Lacey, N. (1988), *State Punishment*, 180.

example, to conceive of a potential conflict between the promotion of individual welfare and the protection of personal autonomy. The welfare of an inmate who has problems in controlling his temper and managing aggression could arguably be served by requiring him to take a job which involves a lot of inter-personal contact and demands the exercise of considerable tolerance. If the prisoner resists this suggestion, however, a decision must be made how far he should be prevailed upon to change his mind. The threat of punitive sanctions could coerce the individual into compliance. His welfare might thus be served but his autonomy would have been undermined. But, as was pointed out in the previous section, personal autonomy is an essentially relative concept and precisely where the boundaries are drawn is a political decision which may change over time. We have suggested that at Grendon it is currently possible to discern the minimum conditions of personal autonomy as being the freedom of inmates to choose to come to Grendon and to opt out at any time, together with the fact that sentence lengths cannot be extended by reference to therapeutic need. Within these limits individual autonomy may be balanced by the pursuit of equality and welfare and by democratic decision-making. From this perspective, it may be entirely legitimate for pressure to be exerted upon an individual to take a particular job if the democratic view of the community is that this would best serve his welfare. However, if the inmate refuses to accept the community's view of his own interests, a collective response must be made which takes account of the effect of his decision upon the welfare of the community and balances this against his future welfare, the protection of his personal autonomy, and the requirement to treat all prisoners with equal value and respect.

Conclusion

It is obvious that by merely stating the desirability and necessity of these principles for Grendon's continued functioning there is no guarantee that they either will or can automatically and easily be followed in practice. Prisoners and prison staff working within the therapeutic communities may approve and accept the need for equality of treatment, democratic decision-making, respect for personal autonomy, and the promotion of individual welfare, but their working customs may inhibit the routine maintenance and delivery of these ideals. Our research shows that when there is conflict these communitarian principles become pragmatically redefined as problematic, unworkable, or irrelevant to the immediate situation. This process of reinterpretation need not be motivated by devious opportunism but by a genuine need to expedite a pressing problem. What is needed is a commitment to defend these core principles and to establish a means of protection which is built into and incorporates the power structure of the establishment.

Given all that has been said about the structural relationship between the prison and the therapeutic community, it is demonstrably clear that prison officers and governors, because of their primary allegiance to the penal institution, are impossibly situated to secure and protect the necessary safeguards—irrespective of whether individual members of staff are motivated to do so. In our view it is the doctors who must be charged with this responsibility. Structurally they are the only group within the establishment which has both the authority and the interest to guard and promote Grendon's communitarian society. This is not to argue that professional interests of medical practitioners are invariably aligned with communitarian ideals. But in Grendon, where the concept of treatment is dependent upon the effective functioning of the communities, the doctors' interests are inextricably bound up with the development of conditions which facilitate therapeutic activity. Undeniably there are other professional groups within the institution that also have an interest in protecting therapeutic activity. However, for reasons discussed earlier in this chapter, these groups are, both inside and outside Grendon, less powerful than the psychiatrists and possess less authority over concepts of treatment. The current impetus to erode medical authority in the therapeutic communities at Grendon may be motivated by an ideological commitment to emphasizing the multi-disciplinary nature of therapy and to removing any suggestion that the inmates who are admitted into the institution are in some way 'sick' or mentally abnormal. Many would argue that this is a laudable and defensible aim, particularly given the embryonic development of forensic psychiatry. There can be no doubt too that such an ambition fits comfortably within the Prison Service's managerial revolution, with its emphasis upon the rationalization of organizational structures and the efficient and economical use of resources. Grendon embodies much of Lord Justice Woolf's vision of a humane prison regime, and provides examples of good working practice which may be emulated in other establishments. But to focus upon these issues is to risk losing sight of what it is that has historically distinguished Grendon from other benign prisons. More than anything else, Grendon has aspired to be a *therapeutic prison*. It has not pretended to be a hospital, but neither has its prevailing culture matched that of the ideal-typical penal establishment. Throughout this book we have attempted to describe what it is that Grendon does, how it functions, and the purposes that it serves. We have concluded that it is possible to have a therapeutic prison which provides inmates with rehabilitative opportunities, without sliding inevitably and relentlessly into a state of tyranny which systematically denies any consideration of individual rights. Merely protecting against the excesses of social utility, however, cannot, in and of itself, safeguard an environment which is capable of delivering *therapy*. Such actions may secure the minimal conditions for a humane custodial regime, but the conditions for a *therapeutic prison* can only be met if a balance is struck between individual and community interests in ways which foster communitarian principles of social organization.

Appendix 1
Data Sets

Records (based on treatment wings only)

Population Census I	2 February 1987	138 inmates
Population Census II	2 February 1989	88 inmates
Transfer Census	1 March 1988–28 February 1989	82 inmates
Reception Census	1 April 1985–31 March 1986	Unused
Referral Census	1 June 1987–31 December 1988	332 inmates from 46 prisons
F1150 files	Used for follow-up sample: disciplinary records, P.24 information of special significance.	

Interviews

Reception Sample	71 inmates within first two months of reception into Grendon. July 1987–October 1988.
Main Sample	102 inmates on the three treatment wings who had been at Grendon for various lengths of time.
Transfer Sample	69 inmates on the three treatment wings awaiting transfer or release from Grendon.
Follow-up Sample	40 inmates transferred from Grendon to a wide range of other prisons (see Appendix III for list of prisons).
Prison Officer Sample	39 officers representing virtually all the uniformed staff attached to the three therapy wings and assessment unit.
Referring Medical Officer Sample	30 prison doctors and visiting consultants who were in a position to refer inmates to Grendon from a wide range of prison establishments.

Self-Completion Questionnaires

Representing all civilian staff working on the treatment wings:

5 Governor grades
5 Psychiatrists
3 Psychologists

3 Probation officers
3 Education officers
1 Psychodramatist

Observation

Small Group	Two groups were regularly attended for a minimum of six months, on each of the three treatment wings.
Wing Meetings	Regular attendance, at least one of each per week, for a minimum of six months on each of the three treatment wings
Staff Meetings	
Routine Activities	Including free periods of association. Evening 'Socials'.
Institutional Committees	Regimes Committee Policy Committee Race Relations Committee Therapists' Meeting

Appendix 2
Adult Male Prisons Not Referring to Grendon

Local prisons

Brixton   South East Region
Dorchester   South West Region
Risley   North Region
Shrewsbury   Midland Region
Swansea   South West Region

Dispersal Prisons

Full Sutton   North Region

Category B Training Prisons

Coldingley   South East Region

Category C Training Prisons

Ashwell   Midland Region
Haverigg   North Region
Littlehey   Midland Region
Northeye   South East Region
Preston   North Region
Ranby   Midland Region
Send   South East Region
The Mount   South East Region
Wymott   North Region

Open Prisons

Ford   South East Region
Kirkham   North Region
Leyhill   South West Region
Morton Hall   Midland Region
Rudgate   North Region
Stanford Hill   South East Region
Sudbury   Midland Region

Appendix 3

Prisons Visited for the Purpose of Follow-Up Interviews

Blundeston   Stocken
Channings Wood   Sudbury
Dartmoor   Wakefield
Featherstone   Wandsworth
Norwich   Wayland
Shepton Mallet   Wormwood Scrubs

Bibliography

ADAMS, R. (1992), *Prison Riots in Britain and the USA*, London: Macmillan.

ADLER, A. (1927), *Practice and Theory of Individual Psychology*, New York: Harcourt, Brace, Jovanovich.

ANGLIKER, C. C. J., CORMIER, B. M., BOULANGER, P. and MALAMUD, B. (1973), 'A Therapeutic Community for Persistent Offenders: An Evaluation and Follow-Up Study on the First Fifty Cases', *Canadian Psychiatric Association Journal*, 18 4: 289–95.

ASHWORTH, A. (1992), *Sentencing and Criminal Justice*, London: Weidenfeld & Nicolson.

BERGER, P. L. and LUCKMAN, T. (1967), *The Social Construction of Reality*, New York: Anchor Books.

BERNHEIM, J. and MONTMOLLIN, M. J. de (1990), 'A Special Unit in Geneva' in R. Bluglass and P. Bowden (eds.), *Principles and Practice of Forensic Psychiatry*, London: Churchill Livingstone.

BEYAERT, F. (1990), 'Dutch Forensic Psychiatry and the Pieter Baan Centre, Utrecht' in R. Bluglass and P. Bowden (eds.), *Principles and Practice of Forensic Psychiatry*, London: Churchill Livingstone.

BION, W. R. (1961), *Experiences in Groups*, London: Tavistock.

BLOCH, S. (1982), *What is Psychotherapy?* Oxford: Oxford University Press.

BLUGLASS, R. (1990), 'Prisons and the Prison Medical Service' in R. Bluglass and P. Bowden (eds.), *Principles and Practice of Forensic Psychiatry*, London: Churchill Livingstone.

BLUGLASS, R. (1990), 'The Mental Health Act 1983' in R. Bluglass and P. Bowden (eds.), *Principles and Practice of Forensic Psychiatry*, London: Churchill Livingstone.

BLUGLASS, R. and BOWDEN, P. (eds.) (1990), *Principles and Practice of Forensic Psychiatry*, London: Churchill Livingstone.

BOTTOMLEY, A. K. (1994), 'Long-Term Prisoners' in E. Player and M. Jenkins (eds.), *Prisons After Woolf: Reform Through Riot*, London: Routledge.

BOTTOMLEY, A. K. and HAY, W. (1991), *Special Units for Difficult Prisoners*, Hull: Centre for Criminology and Criminal Justice, University of Hull.

BOTTOMORE, T. B. (1966), *Elites and Society*, Harmondsworth: Penguin.

BOTTOMS, A. E. (1980), 'An Introduction to the Coming Penal Crisis' in A. E. Bottoms and R. H. Preston (eds), *The Coming Penal Crisis*, Edinburgh: Scottish Academic Press.

BRAITHWAITE, J. (1989) *Crime, Shame & Reintegration*, Cambridge: Cambridge University Press.

BROWN, D. and PEDDER, J. (1979), *Introduction to Psychotherapy: An Outline of Psychodynamic Principles and Practice*, London: Tavistock.

CASALE, S. (1994), 'Conditions and Standards' in E. Player and M. Jenkins (eds.), *Prisons After Woolf: Reform Through Riot*, London: Routledge.

COMMISSIONERS OF PRISONS (1963), *Report for 1962*, London: HMSO.

COOPER, D. (1990), 'Parkhurst Prison: C Wing' in R. Bluglass and P. Bowden (eds.), *Principles and Practice of Forensic Psychiatry*, London: Churchill Livingstone.

CORMIER, B. M. (1975), *The Watcher and the Watched*, Montreal: Tundra Books.

CULLEN, E. (1993), 'The Grendon Reconviction Study Part 1', *Prison Service Journal*, Issue 90, 35–7.

DEPARTMENTAL COMMITTEE (1895), *Report from the Departmental Committee* (Gladstone Report), C 7702, Parliamentary Papers, vol. 56.

DUNBAR, I. (1989), *Report to the Secretary of State on the Inquiries into a Major Disturbance at HM Remand Centre Risley 30 April to 3 May 1989 and the Circumstances Surrounding the Disturbance—Summary*, London: Prison Department.

DURKHEIM, E. (1933), *The Division of Labour in Society*, translated with an introduction by George Simpson, New York: Macmillan.

EAST, W. N. and HUBERT, W. H. de B. (1939), *The Psychological Treatment of Crime*, London: HMSO.

FAULK, M. (1990), 'Her Majesty's Prison Grendon Underwood' in R. Bluglass and P. Bowden (eds.), *Principles and Practice of Forensic Psychiatry*, London: Churchill Livingstone.

FELDBRUGGE, J. (1990), 'The Van der Hoeven Clinic, Utrecht' in R. Bluglass and P. Bowden (eds.), *Principles and Practice of Forensic Psychiatry*, London: Churchill Livingstone.

FOUCAULT, M. (1973), *The Birth of the Clinic*, London: Tavistock.

FOUCAULT, M. (1979), *Discipline and Punish: The Birth of the Prison*, New York: Vintage Books, Random House.

FOULKES, S. N. and ANTHONY, E. J. (1965), *Group Psychotherapy. The Psychoanalytic Approach*, Harmondsworth: Penguin.

GARFIELD, S. L. and BERGIN, A. E. (eds.) (1978), *Handbook of Psychotherapy and Behaviour Change*, New York: Wiley.

GLATT, M. M. (1985), 'Reflections on the Working and Functioning of an Addicts' Therapeutic Community Within a Prison: The Wormwood Scrubs Annexe' in Prison Reform Trust (ed.), *Prison Medicine: Ideas on Health Care in Penal Establishments*, London: Prison Reform Trust.

GRAY, W. J. (1974), 'Grendon Prison', *British Journal of Hospital Medicine* September, 299–308.

GUNN, J., MADAN, A. and SWINTON, M. (1991), 'Treatment Needs of

Prisoners with Psychiatric Disorders', *British Medical Journal*, 303, 10 August, 338–41.

GUNN, J., ROBERTSON, G., DELL, S. and WAY, C. (1978), *Psychiatric Aspects of Imprisonment*, London: Academic Press.

GUNN, J. and ROBERTSON, G. (1987), 'A Ten Year Follow-Up of Men Discharged from Grendon Prison', *British Journal of Psychiatry*, 151, 674–8.

HART, H. L. A. (1982), *Essays on Bentham*, Oxford: Oxford University Press.

HOME OFFICE (1964), *The Prison Rules*, London: Home Office.

HOME OFFICE (1984), *Managing the Long-Term Prison System: The Report of the Control Review Committee*, London: HMSO.

HOME OFFICE (1985), *First Report of the Advisory Committee on the Therapeutic Regime at Grendon*, London: Prison Department.

HOME OFFICE (1987a), *Report of an Inquiry by Her Majesty's Chief Inspector of Prisons for England and Wales into the Disturbances in Prison Service Establishments in England between 29 April and 2 May 1986*, London: HMSO.

HOME OFFICE (1987b), *Circular Instruction 21/1987*, London: Prison Department.

HOME OFFICE (1989), *Report of the Prison Department Working Group on the Management of Vulnerable Prisoners*, London: Prison Department Internal Document.

HOME OFFICE (1990), *Report on an Efficiency Scrutiny of the Prison Medical Service*, London: Home Office.

HOME OFFICE (1991a), *Custody, Care and Justice: The Way Ahead for the Prison Service in England and Wales*, London: HMSO, Cm 1647.

HOME OFFICE (1991b), *Contracting for Prison Health Services: A Consultation Paper*, London: Directorate of Prison Medical Services.

HOME OFFICE (1991c), *Management of the Prison Service: Report by Admiral Sir Raymond Lygo KCB*, London: Home Office.

HOWARTH, I. (1989), 'Psychotherapy: Who Benefits?' *The Psychologist*, 20 4, April, 150–2.

ILLICH, I. (1973), *Tools for Conviviality*, London: Calder and Boyers.

ILLICH, I. (1977), *Limits to Medicine. Medical Nemesis: The Expropriation of Health*, Harmondsworth: Penguin.

JOHNSTON, L. (1991), *The Rebirth of Private Policing*, London: Routledge.

JONES, M. (1952), *Social Psychiatry: A Study of Therapeutic Communities*, London: Tavistock.

JONES, M. (1968), *Social Psychiatry in Practice: The Idea of a Therapeutic Community*, Harmondsworth: Penguin.

KANT, I. (1909), 'Foundations of the Metaphysic of Morals' in *Kant's Critique of Practical Reason and Other Works on the Theory of Ethics*, translated by T. K. Abbot (6th ed.), London: Longman, 46–64.

KING, R. D. (1994), 'Order, Disorder and Regimes in the Prison Services of Scotland and England and Wales' in E. Player and M. Jenkins (eds.), *Prisons After Woolf: Reform Through Riot*, London: Routledge.

KOVEL, J. (1978), *A Complete Guide to Therapy: From Psychoanalysis to Behaviour Modification*, Harmondsworth: Penguin.

KRAMP, P. (1990), 'Danish Forensic Psychiatry' in R. Bluglass and P. Bowden (eds.), *Principles and Practice of Forensic Psychiatry*, London: Churchill Livingstone.

KYMLICKA, W. (1992), *Liberalism, Community and Culture*, Oxford: Clarendon Press.

LACEY, N. (1988), *State Punishment: Politics, Principles and Community Values*, London: Routledge.

LIVINGSTONE, S. (1994), 'The Changing Face of Prison Discipline' in E. Player and M. Jenkins (eds.), *Prisons After Woolf: Reform Through Riot*, London: Routledge.

MASSON, J. (1990), *Against Therapy*, London: Fontana.

MATHIESEN, T. (1965), *The Defences of the Weak: A Sociological Study of a Norwegian Correctional Institution*, London: Tavistock.

MCKEGANEY, N. P. (1983), 'The Cocktail Party Syndrome', *Sociology of Health and Illness*, 5 1, March, 95–103.

MCMAHON, M. W. (1992), *The Persistent Prison?: Rethinking Decarceration and Penal Reform*, Toronto: University of Toronto Press.

MORRIS, N. (1977), 'The Future of Imprisonment' in L. Radzinowicz and M. Wolfgang (eds.), *The Criminal Under Restraint: Crime and Justice Vol III*, New York: Basic Books.

NEWTON, M. (1971), 'Reconviction After Treatment at Grendon', *Chief Psychologist's Report* Series B, no. 1, London: Office of the Chief Psychologist, Prison Department, Home Office.

OWEN, T. and LIVINGSTONE, S. (1993), *Prison Law*, Oxford: Oxford University Press.

PARKER, T. (1970), *The Frying Pan: A Prison and its Prisoners*, London: Hutchinson.

PLAYER, E. and JENKINS, M. (eds.) (1994), *Prisons After Woolf: Reform Through Riot*, London: Routledge.

POLSKY, N. (1971), *Hustlers, Beats and Others*, Harmondsworth: Penguin.

PRESTMUS, R. (1964), *Men at the Top*, Oxford: Oxford University Press.

PRISON REFORM TRUST (1985), *Prison Medicine: Ideas on Health Care in Penal Establishments*, London: Prison Reform Trust.

PRISON REFORM TRUST (1990), *Sex Offenders in Prison*, London: Prison Reform Trust.

RAZ, J. (1986), *The Morality of Freedom*, Oxford: Oxford University Press.

RICHARDSON, G. (1994), 'From Rights to Expectations' in E. Player and M. Jenkins (eds.) (1994), *Prisons After Woolf: Reform Through Riot*, London: Routledge.

ROTHMAN, D. J. (1971), *The Discovery of the Asylum: Social Order and Disorder in the New Republic*, Boston: Little, Brown and Co.

SCHILDER, P. (1939), 'Results and Problems of Group Psychotherapy in Severe Neurosis', *Mental Hygiene*, 23, 87–98.

SCRATON, P. (ed.) (1987), *Law, Order and the Authoritarian State*, Milton Keynes: Open University Press.

SCRATON, P., SIM, J. and SKIDMORE, P. (1991), *Prisons Under Protest*, Milton Keynes: Open University Press.

SHAPIRO, D. (1989), 'A Process of Discovery', *The Psychologist*, 2 4, April, 153–4.

SHEARING, C. D. and STENNING, P. C. (eds.) (1986), *Private Policing*, Beverly Hills, Calif.: Sage.

SMART, J. J. C. (1973), 'An Outline of a System of Utilitarian Ethics' in J. J. C. Smart and B. Williams (eds.), *Utilitarianism: For and Against*, Cambridge: Cambridge University Press.

SMART, J. J. C. and Williams, B. (eds.) (1973), *Utilitarianism: For and Against*, Cambridge: Cambridge University Press.

SMITH, M. L., GLASS, G. V. and MILLER, T I. (1980), *The Benefits of Psychotherapy*, Baltimore: Johns Hopkins Press.

SNOWDEN, P. (1990), 'Regional Secure Units and Forensic Services in England and Wales' in R. Bluglass and P. Bowden (eds.), *Principles and Practice of Forensic Psychiatry*, London: Churchill Livingstone.

SOUTH, N. (1988), *Policing for Profit: The Private Security Sector*, London: Sage.

STORR, A. (1979), *The Art of Psychotherapy*, London: Secker and Warburg and Heinemann Medical Books.

STURUP, G. K. (1968), *Treating the 'Untreatable': Chronic Criminals at Herstedvester*, Baltimore: Johns Hopkins Press.

SULLIVAN, H. S. (1953), *Conceptions of Modern Psychiatry*, New York: Norton.

SZASZ, T. (1979), *The Myth of Psychotherapy*, Oxford: Oxford University Press.

TAYLOR, C. (1979), *Hegel and Modern Society*, Cambridge: Cambridge University Press.

TOWNSEND, P. (1993), 'The Repressive Nature and Extent of Poverty in the UK: Predisposing Causes of Crime', extracts from a speech given at the Howard League Conference, 8 September 1993, *Criminal Justice*, 11 4, October, 4–6.

WALKER, N. (1976), 'Treatment and Justice in Penology and Psychiatry', *The Sandoz Lecture 1976*, Edinburgh: Edinburgh University Press.

WALKER, R. (1978), *Kant*, London: Routledge and Kegan Paul.

WEBER, M. (1949), *The Methodology of the Social Sciences*, New York: Free Press.

WEBER, M. (1968), *Economy and Society*, Guenther Roth and Claus Wittich (eds.), Berkeley: University of California Press (orig. pub. 1920).

WHATMORE, P. (1990), 'The Special Unit at Barlinnie Prison, Glasgow' in R. Bluglass and P. Bowden (eds.), *Principles and Practice of Forensic Psychiatry*, London: Churchill Livingstone.

WOOLF, LORD JUSTICE H. and TUMIM, JUDGE S. (1991), *Prison Disturbances April 1990: Report of an Inquiry by the Rt. Hon. Lord Justice Woolf (Parts I and II) and His Honour Judge Stephen Tumim (Part II)*, London: HMSO, Cm 1456.

WHYTE, W. F. (1955), *Street Corner Society*, (2nd edn.) Chicago: University of Chicago Press.

YALLOM, I. D. (1975), *The Theory and Practice of Group Psychotherapy*, New York: Basic Books.

ZOLA, I. K. (1972), 'Medicine as an Institution of Social Control', *Sociological Review*, 20 4, November, 487–509.

Index